Praise for *Taxi to America*

In her memoir, *Taxi to America*, Stella Nahatis has delivered a compelling portrait of a girl who refused to be defined by a series of tragedies that would have defeated a person less brave—and less stubborn.

—John Christie, author of *The Prince of Wentworth Street – An American Boyhood in the Shadow of a Genocide*, and Co-founder and consulting editor, *Pine Tree Watch*

Taxi to America is a well-crafted and beautifully written story about loss and the importance of family and the personal core values of courage and resiliency in meeting life's challenges.

—Christine L. McGrath, Director of Operations, Massachusetts Association of School Superintendents

Taxi to America is a must read for anyone who wants to understand the immigrant experience on an individual level. From the age of eleven, Stella goes through the immigrant struggles of becoming part of the United States to providing her gifts to this country as a parent, worker, and community member.

—Diane Portnoy, Founder and CEO, The Immigrant Learning Center, Inc.

A primary loving, unconditional relationship is crucial to a child's development and, though orphaned at age ten and separated from her younger sister, Stella goes forth and gets "situated." She perseveres with her strength, belief in herself, and the blanket of memories of her loving parents and yiayia. *Taxi to America* is an inspiring memoir of resiliency and the right to be loved and happy.

—Patricia Burke, LICSW, Trauma Therapist

Beginning in the 70's, students arriving in America without command of the English language were often placed in special needs programs. Authorities confused a language barrier as a learning disability. *Taxi to America* is the first personal account I've read showing how the English as a Second Language program aided a child in acclimating to our country. Stella flourished. A great read!

—Janice Ambrose, Special Educator

Taxi to America offers readers an amazing and profoundly powerful journey of the deeply emotional experiences of adoption, immigration, and assimilation, seen through the eyes of a young child and into adulthood. From a small village in northern Greece to the bustle of Boston, MA, *Taxi to America* is the vivid story of resilience, embrace of a new culture and its emotional challenges and rewards—one of deep love for family, acceptance and rewards of different cultural norms, and the curiosity and resilience of a young girl to be accepted and thrive in her new country—while always carrying her love for her family and homeland. A must read.

—Marlene Seltzer, Retired CEO, Jobs for the Future, Inc. (JFF)
Professional expertise in Education, Workforce Training,
and Economic Development

Stella Nahatis takes us on the tumultuous journey of how multiple losses impacted her life. In *Taxi to America*, we find ourselves immersed in her experiences and emotions which she recounts with honesty and compassion. Loss became deeply personal with a tragic event in 1958 for Nahatis (aged 10) and her younger sister (7). The losses they endured would ultimately shape who they would become as adults. In this deeply felt story of resilience and determination we see Nahatis flourish despite all the adversities—a testament of her strength.

—Maureen Burge, MS, CLS, Pediatric Palliative Care Child Life Specialist

Taxi to America

Taxi to America
A Greek Orphan's Adoption Journey

A Memoir

Stella Nahatis

Author's Note: This book is a work of nonfiction. However, I have changed some names and assigned names to people whose real names I cannot recall.

Published by Stella Nahatis
https://stellanahatis.com/

Edited by Kate Victory Hannisian
Cover and text design by Judy Davison
All photos are the property of Stella Nahatis except where noted.

Library of Congress Control Number: 2022922079

Publisher's Cataloging-in-Publication data
Nahatis, Stella, author.
Taxi to America : a Greek orphan's adoption journey , a memoir / Stella Nahatis.
Includes bibliographical references. | Manchester-by-the-Sea, MA:
Stella Nahatis, 2022.
LCCN: 2022922079 | ISBN: 979-8-9867511-0-8 (hardcover) |
979-8-9867511-1-5 (paperback) | 979-8-9867511-2-2 (ebook)
LCSH Nahatis, Stella. | Adoption. | Greek Americans--Biography. |
Immigrants--United States--Biography. | Sisters. | Family. | BISAC
BIOGRAPHY & AUTOBIOGRAPHY / Personal Memoirs
Classification: LCC CT275 .N34 2022 | DDC 949.507/4/.092--dc23

ISBN 979-8-9867511-1-5 (paperback)
ISBN 979-8-9867511-0-8 (hard cover)
ISBN 979-8-9867511-2-2 (ebook)

First Edition. First Printing

Printed in the United States of America

Dedicated to my family: my husband Charles, my sister Lena, my son Paul Richard, and my grandson Trey.

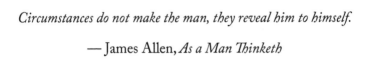

Circumstances do not make the man, they reveal him to himself.

— James Allen, *As a Man Thinketh*

Contents

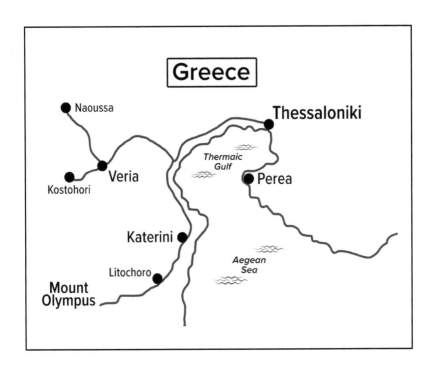

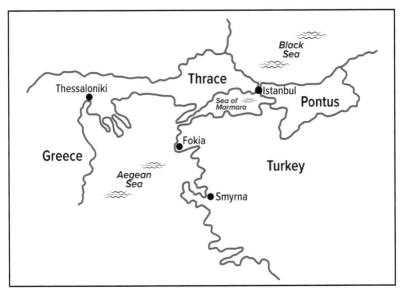

1
Our First Taxi Ride

"How did they get us into the taxi without an explanation?"

Every time we reflect on that grievous February morning in 1958, my sister and I repeat this question.

Mrs. Azat, our landlady back then, had come into the room our family rented from her, in what seemed like the middle of the night. Her voice was soft and gentle, but it sounded urgent. "Stella, Nitsa, wake up, you must get up and dress fast. Your uncle is coming to take you to the village." I felt the light tapping of her fingers on my shoulder.

If I had heard those words in the morning after a normal night's sleep, I would have jumped up and down on the bed. I loved our only uncle, Theo (Uncle) Pavlos. I enjoyed spending time with him, whether he was making a brief visit to our home in Thessaloniki, or we were making an extended visit to his village, Kostohori.

Mrs. Azat's message of "do as you are told" put us on autopilot. For our theo to be fetching us in the middle of the night—the antennas in my head broadcast "danger." At seven and ten years old, my little sister and I moved like robots, following the instructions to hurry and get dressed. A flutter in my heart signaled that something important was happening.

Growing up in Greece in the 1950s, we often heard these phrases: "Do as you are told." "Be a good girl." "Don't answer back to an adult." "Wait until your father gets home." They were used to shape our behavior into what our parents believed was appropriate for children.

Unlike my sister, I complied with the cultural rules. Whenever I pointed out her insubordination, my parents would say, "She's younger than you are. Don't concern yourself with that."

I could not understand why Nitsa blatantly misbehaved and got away with it. She was my shadow, following me around whenever and wherever she could. Why couldn't she follow the rules? I expected her to behave as I did. I was too young to realize we are all different and our reactions to the same situation are expressed in our own unique way. And so, because of her age, I accepted her whining and outbursts being forgiven. "You are older," I heard. "Be a good girl so she can emulate you." It never occurred to me to be anything else. I must have been born with something inside of me that guided me and steered me away from conflict.

After Mrs. Azat's orders, I got up first and waited for Nitsa to slide over. We slept head to toe on the single bed we shared. She, being younger, slept on the inside against the wall.

"Here, you pee first." I guided her across the room to use the chamber pot. We stepped down into the kitchen. With the room rental, we had access to the common areas of Mrs. Azat's house. We lived as one family.

Nitsa and I splashed the sleep from our faces at the kitchen sink. When we returned to the bedroom, we took off our nightgowns and presented our shivering naked bodies to Mrs. Azat.

The oil lamp shed enough light for me to notice our landlady's gray hair was disheveled. It touched her shoulders. She always had her hair slicked back into a uniform round bun at the nape of her neck. She wore her oversized black sweater over her long flannel nightgown, which made her slender figure look rotund. Perhaps because I wasn't totally awake, she looked scary.

She nudged me toward our parents' empty bed. Our beds were separated by my mother's cedar trunk. Neatly folded, my clothes waited for me on the double bed. She prodded Nitsa to our bed.

Something in my stomach didn't feel right. *Just do as you're told. Just get dressed. Please don't throw up.* Whatever was going on in my stomach moved to my head. It felt bigger and squirmy. *Hurry and get dressed.* I wondered if Nitsa was feeling the same way. In the past I would have reassured her with a "Bravo, Nitsa, you're doing a good job." If I reassured her that night, it would have been more to ease my anxiety than to comfort her.

I noticed our landlady's gentle movements as she helped my sister. My hands shook as I hurried to dress. I think back and wonder, which dress did I wear? The everyday one or my best dress that I wore on Sundays and on special occasions? I loved the white daisies embroidered around the neckline of the pale-yellow Sunday dress. In the limited light I could see Nitsa. Her attachment to me came in handy, as she followed my example and dressed without complaint.

Is Mrs. Azat caressing Nitsa's back to comfort her? Or just straightening the dress? She smoothed Nitsa's bangs and handed me the comb. I noticed the sweater she wore over her nightgown; it hung longer on one side. "You are a big girl now, comb your hair," she said. "You can do it."

My mother always untangled my hair before braiding it or pulling it into a sleek ponytail. I realized this was not a time to ask for help. The snarled ponytail went unnoticed by Mrs. Azat. My mother would not have been happy with my going out like that.

Our landlady appeared normal as she darted between us and the wardrobe where she had our coats ready to go. In the dim light, I detected nothing peculiar in her expression. We didn't dare ask the obvious questions. "Where are our parents? Why are we going with Theo Pavlos? Why are we going to the village? When are Mamá and Babá coming? Will they come to get us from the village?"

As we finished dressing, Theo Pavlos arrived. He and Mrs. Azat conversed in muted tones.

To my sister and me, he said, "Good morning, all ready?"

I thought, *that's all he's going to say to us?*

The somber expressions on the adults' faces brought back the squirmy tingle in my head. I told myself they were being quiet because it was the middle of the night. I was afraid to ask, "Why are we leaving with Theo Pavlos in the middle of the night?" My gut insisted I be a good girl; do as you are told. Whether we were afraid to hear the truth or just behaved the way they taught us to behave, neither my sister nor I dared to ask these questions. Mrs. Azat and Theo Pavlos ushered us out in our custom-made gabardine coats, the ones we wore only on Sundays or on special occasions.

Our neighbor, Mrs. Ismini, crossed the street and met us by the taxi. I noticed her white nightgown trailing under her black coat, just like I had seen in night scenes at the movies. We stood by the taxi. Mrs. Ismini's somber expression mirrored those of Theo Pavlos and Mrs. Azat. The squirmy feeling filled my head with a million ants. The two women bowed their heads. To Theo Pavlos, my sister and me, they whispered, "God be with you" and made the sign of the cross.

I noticed the black armbands on our coat sleeves. I wondered who slipped them on and why.

When I eased my bottom all the way back into the taxi seat, the strangeness of the moment disappeared. *Wow, I'm riding in a taxi. Too bad it's not daylight so the neighborhood kids could see us riding in a taxi.*

I helped Nitsa settle in the back seat with me. We had never been in a taxi. She smoothed her coat and looked around with a grin on her face. The seats were cushiony like the chairs in the living room. Nitsa poked the side of my thigh and slid away from me to the other side. There was enough light from the corner streetlight to follow Nitsa's finger as she drew an imaginary line down the center of the seat.

"This is my side. You stay on your side."

The heaviness of the previous hour lifted. Both of us had recovered from the morning's harsh awakening and hasty dressing experience.

"Too bad it is so early. I wish our friends were outside to see us in the taxi." Nitsa stood up and put her face against the window.

"Nitsa, don't touch any handles. Oh, look, they are coming in, sit back down."

Theo Pavlos, my adoring uncle, sat in the front passenger seat next to the driver. The two men whispered during the slow and gentle ride down the street. I did not try to eavesdrop on their conversation I wanted to feel the joy of being in a taxi.

Why did it have to be so dark? No one could see us in the milky gray pre-dawn light just before full daylight brightens the landscape. The light in which as an adult I find solace and appreciation, but that night it unnerved the ten-year-old me.

A few blocks from our house, the taxi made a stop in front of the iron gates of Saint Paraskevi Cemetery. Nitsa and I, engrossed in the euphoria of our first taxi ride, weren't concerned about this unannounced stop. I saw the silhouette of a man open the gates. The driver and Theo Pavlos got out of the taxi. Stooped shoulders replaced the usual erect posture of my uncle's slim, towering figure.

The two men approached the gate. In the eerie silence Nitsa and I looked at each other. I reached for her hand and squeezed it.

"Stella, why did we stop?" she murmured.

"Shish, I don't know."

The cemetery was a familiar place for Nitsa and me, but we sensed that something strange was going on.

On our way to and from school, we would walk across the street from the cemetery. It ran the entire length of our walk to our house. When the mood struck us, we and our group of friends walked through the cemetery, hoping to see a memorial service over a grave-stone.

In the Greek Orthodox tradition, a memorial service is held on a specific timeline following a death and on Saturdays of Souls.

When we walked, we would spread out, but within viewing dis-tance of each other. It was easy to spot a priest. They all wore long black robes and high black hats with a veil draped halfway down their back. On a Saturday of Souls, there were as many as six to ten priests in the cemetery.

When one of us spotted a priest, she signaled the others to follow him to the gravestone where relatives of the deceased had gathered. We would stand close enough to be noticed, but not so close as to be annoying. While I watched the service, my mouth would salivate at the prospect of eating the memorial wheat berry, the *koliva*, the traditional sweetened offering commemorating the dead. The wheat symbolizes life and regeneration. As with wheat seeds, we bury the body to have a new life. The combination of granulated sugar, confec-tioners' sugar, toasted sesame seeds, walnuts, and raisins mixed with the wheat is still a favorite of mine.

Although we were used to being in the cemetery without fear, something felt different that early morning.

We waited in silence. As we always did whenever we were fright-ened, my sister and I reached across the invisible line and held hands. We squeezed our fingers so hard into our palms that our nails dug into the flesh.

"Where are they? It's almost morning."

I didn't want her to be frightened. "Let's just be quiet, they'll be back soon."

I was pulling her over to my side when something heavy plopped into the trunk of the taxi. We had not noticed any movement. The sound startled us, and its movement jolted us up against the back of the seat and out of our morning stupor. The memory of those few minutes still gives me goosebumps. We said nothing to each other about the weirdness of it. I put an arm around Nitsa and held her close, like I had done in the past when she was frightened. Were we that well behaved? I had just turned ten and my sister was six months short of her eighth birthday. Why were we reluctant to question what was happening? It was especially unusual for Nitsa not to pester me with a million questions.

She would normally have demanded, "Where are we going?" and expected an answer and comfort from her older sister. She would have badgered me: "Ask Theo Pavlos, he will tell you." But why were two little girls being so well behaved, frightened, and frozen in place? I imagined Nitsa's insides were churning like mine. Were we too scared to know the truth? What truth could we even have imagined? Why didn't we ask the obvious question: "Why are we at the cemetery?"?

We sensed that something significant was happening. In our world, the use of a taxi was a luxury reserved for adults. We were envious whenever we saw a family with children in a taxi. After a taxi drove by us, we kids discussed how we would behave when we grew up and had money to hire a taxi. "I am going to take all the kids in the neighborhood to the park and buy them ice cream." "I am going to take all my cousins to the biggest toy store and buy them whatever they want." "I am going to ride in one all day long." On and on we dreamed. That early morning, we had felt excited, happy, and special to be in the back seat of one.

But we contained our excitement because of our startling awakening and the somber look on our theo's face, so unlike him. Even the taxi driver had a solemn and empathetic expression. By the time we reached the old national road, a two-lane divided highway connecting all the major cities from Athens in the south to Thessaloniki in the north, buildings and other vehicles became visible in the early morning sunshine. Soon we were driving through familiar towns on our way to Veria and on to Kostohori. But this time we sat in the back seat of a taxi, not on a bus like the other times, and it was heavenly.

The route reminded me of the times I went to visit Yiayia at Kostohori. Always on a bus with the nauseating smell of diesel fumes, which made me dizzy and brought the contents of my stomach up. That thought was enough to return me to the moment and sit back and savor the taxi ride. Nitsa and I had not exchanged any words from the moment we left the cemetery.

The passengers in buses and cars traveling in the opposite direction looked at us in a peculiar way. *They must be envious of us because we are in a taxi*, I thought. Nitsa had moved back to her side. Another peculiar thing was that pedestrians out on their morning routines came to a halt as our taxi passed through the villages. I noticed two grandmother types make the sign of the cross. Sometime Greeks did that when they couldn't believe what they saw or when they wished for someone to be in God's keeping. Several men sitting at a cafe stood up. I locked eyes with one of them. I believed they, too, were envious of us. But my imagination did not come close to what had happened. How could I have known their behavior was out of respect to the partially exposed cargo in the taxi's trunk? Their respectful demeanor was the customary way to show reverence to a passing funeral procession. Unbeknown to us, the cargo in the taxi's trunk was a coffin.

2

An Evening at the Bouzoukia

ME, NITSA AND MARY IN COSTUMES FOR CARNAVALI

The evening before that taxi ride, Nitsa and I had been excited about our parents going out to celebrate. We always looked forward to the rare nights when our parents went out, and they trusted us to put ourselves to bed. We had nothing to worry about. Either our landlady, Mrs. Azat, or her sixteen-year-old daughter, Mary, were a mere two steps and two rooms away.

Being on our own meant we could sneak our mother's red lipstick and play *koumbares* (godmothers), a favorite game among little girls. We used what we believed to be adult voices and replicated conversations we had heard during adult visits.

One of us would start with, "Good morning, Koumbara."

"Oh, welcome, Koumbara. Come in," the other would respond.

"How are you? Where are the children?" and so on.

"Here is your coffee, Koumbara," one of us would say while handing the other a coffee cup.

The game did not require props, although dolls, dishes, and demitasse cups added dimension to it. Our version generally involved the use of props.

When we played koumbares outside, finding props was a cinch. We collected stones, pieces of wood, pieces of a cardboard box, or anything we deemed utilitarian. Our guide was our limitless imagination. For the coveted lipstick prop, we improvised by picking red berries.

The Saturday night before our unexpected taxi ride, watching our parents getting ready for their night out supercharged us and put us in a giddy mood. As they dressed in their Sunday best, we anticipated an opportunity to play koumbares.

They had invited Mrs. Azat and the neighbors across the street for an evening at the *bouzoukia*. In Greek, the word bouzoukia (the plural for the stringed instrument bouzouki) means a restaurant or nightclub that offers food, music, and dancing. Going to the bouzoukia, in our family, was an extravagance reserved only for special occasions, as in celebrating a name day or a significant accomplishment.

That evening they did not tell us what they were celebrating, but whatever it was, it had to be something outstanding. Such an evening was an expensive night out, and that did not occur often in the lives of Sofia and Nikos Spentzouras.

Nitsa and I pranced around the room, stopping intermittently, puckering our lips.

"You missed a spot. Put some more on," I implored my mother. Putting a hand on my shoulder, she tilted my head slightly and pretended to apply more lipstick.

"I need more as well," Nitsa whined in her usual way.

"Of course, come here you," our mother replied with a patient and sweet voice as she pretended to apply lipstick.

We happily smacked and licked our lips and pretended to like the cosmetic's waxy texture. We knew the texture because we had snuck the tube out many times when we were home alone. My responsibility was to replace it in its original position to avoid detection and punishment. It never occurred to me that our mother would figure it out and choose to ignore the use of her coveted tube of ruby-red lipstick. How could she not have figured it out? Two little girls applying lipstick and leaving it the same way they found it is an unlikely feat. I suppose it was her way of indulging us with a treat for our not resisting their leaving us alone.

Applying the deep ruby lipstick was the ultimate treat for us. The creamy white tube with ridges all around was a prized possession of my mother's, which earned it a place of safekeeping in her trunk along with other valuable family possessions. The lipstick came out only for festive occasions such as weddings, christenings, and the bouzoukia. Mesmerized, we watched our mother carefully trace her lips with the tube, paying particular attention to form the two points in the middle of her upper lip. We thought she looked like a movie star.

Attempting to mimic her elegance and to replicate her full lips threw my sister and me into a fit of laughter. Our mother's radiant face filled the room with joy that evening. Our father wore one of his own creations. A brown thin-striped suit from his tailor shop showed off his streamlined stature. I watched him rub his palms together before he patted down his thick, wavy hair. In our eyes, they looked like the popular movie star couple, Aliki Vougiouklaki and Dimitris Papamichael. They exuded glamor, excitement, and anticipation.

Nitsa and I followed our parents out of the room. We snickered at each other when our father placed an arm around our mother's waist and gave her a warm embrace. We pushed each other to be closest to them as they entered the living room. Mrs. Azat fumbled with her black purse as Mary draped the elegant black lace wrap on her mother's shoulders. She ceremoniously smoothed the wrap with a flair I had seen in movies. We dashed to the balcony and watched them walk down the steps.

Mrs. Ismini and her two sons crossed the street. The bounce in their steps and excitement in their voices signaled a fun evening ahead. My mother got in the motorcycle's sidecar, while Petros, Mrs. Ismini's younger son, sat behind our father. The kickstand went up, and the trio took off for a festive evening. From the balcony, Mary, Nitsa, and I watched until they were out of sight.

Mrs. Azat, Mrs. Ismini, and her other son, Christos, walked to the corner of the street, and turned right toward Vardari Square in Thessaloniki, to find a taxi.

After an evening of merriment at the bouzoukia, everyone returned home, except our mother and father.

With help from the authorities, Mrs. Azat and Mrs. Ismini summoned Theo Pavlos from his village, Kostohori, eighty-six kilometers away. In those days, the only telephone servicing the entire village was at the taverna, owned and operated by the Katarahias couple. The taverna was a restaurant, coffee shop, convenience store, gathering place for a game of backgammon, and the venue for celebrations. Its location at the center of the village made it equally accessible for all the households. I suppose the couple was accustomed to the inconvenience of emergency calls at inopportune times with requests to convey messages to the villagers. It is my understanding that Mrs. Azat implored such an action that night to reach my mother's brother, my theo Pavlos.

When I visited Theo Pavlos, I had seen this process in action during the daytime. Either Mr. or Mrs. Katarahias would shout to whomever was close by "Run, go over to so-and-so, tell them to come right away for a phone call."

Another way to reach someone in an emergency was to contact the police in Veria, in which case they would drive the fourteen kilometers on the mountainous dirt road to deliver the news.

Late that night, I imagine one of the taverna owners roused Theo Pavlos, my mother's younger brother and the closest next of kin.

Nitsa and I had never met any of my father's relatives. As far as we knew he did not have any living relatives in Greece. My father's family had fled Smyrna (or Izmir), Anatolia (Asian Turkey) after the Great Fire of Smyrna in 1922. The fire was the culmination of the Ottoman Empire's effort to obliterate not only the Ottoman Christians but also other ethnicities in Asia Minor. The genocidal practice of the empire included the elimination of Greeks, Assyrians, and Armenians to achieve a homogeneous nation. It began during World War I (1914) and ended in 1922. In its quest to reach its goal, the Ottoman Empire forced about one million to migrate from Turkey. It is estimated that anywhere from hundreds of thousands to 1.5 million died by massacre or by some other form of brutality. On September 13, 1922, fires were set by the Turks to destroy the waterfront district of Smyrna and lasted two weeks. The fire demolished the entire Greek and Armenian quarters, and an estimated 10,000 to 15,000 people perished. After the fire, the remaining Greeks in Turkey had no choice but to abandon what remained of their homes, their businesses, and their belongings to migrate to Greece. My father's family settled in Kaminia, near the port of Piraeus, along with other survivors from that area of Turkey.

My mother's side of the family was all we knew. My mother's older sister, Thea Anna, had moved from Veria to Athens when the Greek Civil War ended. Theo Prodromos, her husband, had a falling-out with the family due to their political differences. Therefore, Mrs. Azat had just one person available to call, Theo Pavlos. My mother's twenty-six-year-old brother was the only relative available to deal with the aftermath of our family's most tragic event.

When the taxi reached Veria, the uneasiness I had felt earlier in the morning returned. My heart pounded and my mind wandered. I didn't know what to expect. *Why did Theo Pavlos have to get us in the middle of the night? Why didn't he tell us the reason? Did our parents go away?* Not liking the direction my thoughts had taken, I turned my attention to the interior of the taxi. I patted the smooth leather seat and retreated to my enjoyment of the ride.

3

A Black Cloud Over Kostohori

After hours of basking in what we believed to be opulence, we could see that our taxi ride was about to terminate. The final bend on the road into Kostohori loomed ahead. The imposing *platanos* (plane tree) appeared like a protector of revered ground. Its massive branches formed a canopy that reached out and over a fountain and the dirt road. Spring water gushed out of a pipe into a large stone basin the size of an extra-large bathtub.

Every time I caught sight of this scene, butterflies in my stomach signaled the sweet sensation of my yiayia's embrace. Even after Yiayia's death, I continued to think of my grandmother whenever I saw the platanos and the fountain. I had always prepared myself for the final bend. If I was on the bus, I secured a seat on the left side. When I was in the back of a horse-driven farm wagon, I craned my neck to catch a glimpse of the plane tree.

For weary travelers returning on foot after the long climb up the mountain, the fountain and the platanos had a practical purpose. People stopped and refreshed themselves before going home. They quenched their thirst, letting the spring water trickle down their chins. They splashed water on their faces and allowed it to dribble down their necks. The donkeys and horses kept their muzzles in the water, snorting and blowing until their owners tugged at their reins.

Travelers on their way out of the village also made a convenient stop at the spring. They gave their animals a final drink before their descent to the city or to their fields. They filled their aluminum *pagouri* (canteen) with spring water for personal use and filled a larger vessel for their animal.

Finally, we will find out the purpose of this taxi ride. The taxi made the final turn. The platanos and the fountain were in view. *Why is the taxi slowing down?*

Usually at this point of the trip, my heart raced with excitement as the first and only house on the street became visible. Many times, my mother had to pull me back to sit on her lap and remind me that we were almost at Yiayia's house. However, on that morning, the sun's rays revealed a scene I had never experienced.

Nitsa and I turned to each other. Nitsa's eyes pleaded for an explanation. All I could do was to reach over and pull her close to me and hold her trembling hand in mine. We continued to convey our curiosity without words, just as we had been doing from the beginning of the ride. We had been exchanging glances, pinching each other's arms, poking our elbows, holding hands, and rolling our eyes.

What is going on? Why are all these people gathered? We shut our lips tight, but our eyes could not have opened any wider as we observed the incomprehensible scene. A crowd waited beyond the fountain. Women dressed in black resembled a field of crows. Among them, men with bowed heads appeared to be searching for something on the ground. The older children went about their normal curious way, pushing through the adults so they could get a glimpse at whatever the fuss was about. Adults tugged at the little ones as they attempted to play. Roaming dogs and chickens disturbed by the unusual commotion created their own distraction with their barking and clucking.

When the taxi reached the crowd, the women in mourning attire were crying, clutching their clothing on their chests, shrieking "No, no," and making the sign of the cross. They were close enough to touch the taxi, which moved in pace with the crowd. These were people we knew. They pressed their wet faces against the windows. Streams of tears were wiped away by white handkerchiefs, edges trimmed with black crochet. The faces outside the window changed but the expressions were the same. Their red noses and swollen eyes revealed unabashed sympathy.

By the time the taxi and its entourage reached the house, Nitsa and I were crying just because everyone we could see was crying. Nitsa nuzzled up to my side with such force I thought my shoulder would push the door open. Our hands' tight grip did not stop our trembling nor our crying. Both of us had become overwhelmed with curiosity over all the wailing, screaming, and thrashing surrounding the taxi.

When finally, someone let us out, we realized we had a good reason to cry.

"No, NO, Sofia!"

"Oh, Sofia. NO, Sofia!"

Like crows flying from tree to tree, the black-clad women screamed out as the men removed a coffin from the trunk of the taxi.

"Oh God, how could you do this?"

"So young, oh so young." They wailed incessantly.

"Why did she go on the motorcycle with him? Why?"

"Why, God? Why?"

They went on and on, saying the same thing.

I had no doubt that our mother's body was in the coffin.

Nitsa and I were silent as the black-garbed women continued to wail and tug at their clothing. I drew my little sister away from them. Amidst the wild commotion, my sister and I had realized the obvious.

"Stella? That's what they did at the cemetery. Isn't it?" she cried.

I wrapped my arms around her. "Probably. The thump we heard. That must have been when they put the coffin in the trunk."

I wanted to block my ears, block out their screams. My head felt like ants crawled all over it. Why couldn't they cry quietly? Nitsa withdrew from my embrace and joined the other children away from the chaos. It appeared they were safe from all the commotion and could observe from afar.

It would be years later that we would learn about the tradition of moirologists (professional mourners) at a funeral. At our mother's funeral they were friends and neighbors, not paid professionals. These mourners lament the deceased and provide support for the family members during the wake and funeral. The custom traces back to the early Greek dance of tragedy.

Even today, my sister shudders every time we talk about the scene. She abhorred the mourners insisting on hugging us and crying over us. She recalls, "I struggled to withdraw from their suffocating embrace. I could not stand their tight hold on me and their lamenting."

No one said to us, "Your mother died." It was obvious once we heard them calling out her name. It was another one of those traditions of the 1950s in Greece. Protect the children; if you don't talk about it to them, they won't know the scary and sad stuff going on.

In our culture in those days, children were forbidden to look at the dead and to attend funerals. I wormed my way through the crowd toward the room where the loudest wailing was taking place. Before

I could reach the doorway one of the mourners shouted, "Take Stella away from here."

The woman next to me snatched me and steered me through the throng of wailers and deposited me with the group of children beyond the crowd. My insides churned, I could not join in the idle play with the others. *I want to see my mother. I'm going back in.*

No one interrupted my sneaking through the grieving crowd. They were absorbed in their grief. I was able to get into the large room that Yiayia always referred to as the *onta*, the Pontian word for a large room. The onta and the little kitchenette attached to it were my yiayia's entire house. This was the bedroom, living room, and dining room, a part of a larger gray stone structure. In addition to the onta and kitchenette, the structure contained a barn and a large storage area. The barn housed the horse, the donkey, and the cows. The storage area had the capacity to accommodate enough supplies for the winter months. Lined up against one of the walls the length of the oversized pantry were wooden beer barrels of *stipa* (pickled cabbage and green tomatoes).

In the middle of all the confusion and wailing, I thought of how waiting for the stipa to be ready for consumption was a test in patience. Not only did we have to wait for them to be pickled, but we were not allowed to go into the pantry unless an adult sent us to fetch something.

My friend Noula and I had often broken both rules. We would sneak into the dark room. Noula lifted the cover off the barrel while I gingerly removed another cover used to hold the veggies down, and then with our bare hands we had reached for our forbidden treats. A bite into the salty and sour green tomato would send a stream of garlicky juices dripping down our chins. Hastily we replaced the covers and got away from the building as fast as our skinny little legs could carry us.

On the opposite wall there were legumes and other dry goods in twenty-five- to thirty-five-kilo burlap bags. The home-churned butter and homemade feta cheese were kept in forty-kilo tin cans and stored in the coldest area next to the outside wall.

The onta, a fourteen-by-fourteen-meter area of the structure, was the large room where our mother's coffin was placed in the center in front of the two beds, across from the woodstove.

In Greece, the Greek Orthodox tradition dictates that someone stays with the dead until the burial. Typically, in addition to the immediate family, relatives and friends stay for the vigil from the moment the body is laid out. The family places thin plain beige candles at the entrance of the room next to an urn filled with sand. Sometimes the mourners bring their own candles.

Inside the onta, the wailing and lamenting that had greeted the taxi had become louder and scarier. As soon as I entered the room the acrid smell of candles reminded me of church. I saw the women take turns throwing themselves on the open coffin, obscuring my mother's face. I caught a glimpse of her brown Sunday dress. The one she had worn to the bouzoukia. Its small fabric-covered buttons down the front were perfectly lined up. *How did it not get ruined in the accident?* I wondered. *Did someone clean it up enough for her to be buried in it?*

I could hear their piercing cries. "Why, why God?" "She was so young." "Thank God Despina, my yiayia, is not alive to bear this blow."

Thea Chrissa, not a blood aunt, but everyone in the village, whether related by blood or not, was a Thea (Aunt) or a Theo (Uncle), said to her daughter, "Maritsa, take Stella and Nitsa to our house. They will sleep with you tonight." We stayed there the night and the next day until after our mother's funeral. A bunch of us gathered in my yiayia's yard waiting for the adults. We still referred to it as hers even though Theo Pavlos and his family continued to live there after Yiayia's passing.

The stream of mourners returning from the cemetery interrupted our tag play. They piled into the onta and out of curiosity, we followed them inside.

The well-meaning friends and relatives talked as if the children were not there. "At least the father is still alive, he can remarry so they'll have a mother to raise them." The sentence that reverberated in my head the most was: "Children are truly orphaned when the father dies, not when the mother dies. He can remarry." I was to learn later that in those days it was unacceptable for the widows to remarry. The men, on the other hand, were expected to marry again to have someone to raise the children.

The same comments echoed every time a new visitor entered the room. I was relieved to know my father was still alive. According to what I overheard, my sister and I would be safe. As comforted as that should have made me feel, I cried for my mother's death. *She is gone forever. What's going to happen to us? Will my father come to take us back to our house? When is he coming? No one is telling us anything.* My information was limited to the comments I overheard.

As if the horrifying shrieks and comments were not annoying enough, the mourners looked at Nitsa and me with pity. I recognized those looks from having seen and heard grown-ups discussing someone's misfortune in the past. I had seen the same expressions on their faces, a combination of sadness, melancholy, and suffering. I didn't want them to feel sorry for us. I tried to stop crying. I didn't want them to see my sadness and feel sorrier for me. I felt my face was on fire, and my fists were by my side, ready to lurch toward those annoying, but well-meaning creatures.

What does this mean? Just like with Yiayia, we won't see her again? Not touch her? She won't hold us? She won't kiss us? That's it? What's going to happen to us? Is our father dead too?

4

What Now?

NITSA AND ME WITH OUR MOTHER, SOFIA.

After the interment, tradition dictates specific offerings. Small liqueur glasses of Metaxa brandy were set on a tray along with a bowl of dark-chocolate-covered almonds. Designated neighbors and friends continually made Greek coffee and filled the demitasse cups with the bitter brew. Just before taking a sip of the brandy or the coffee, sniveling guests uttered the phrases, "May she rest in peace," "Good paradise," and "May we live long enough to remember her." The offerings were served by nonfamily members because the family was in mourning and too distraught to be hosts. At the age of ten, even though I knew my mother was dead and buried, my eyes fell on the bowl of chocolate almonds. I remembered the times my yiayia had taught me how to do the grown-up thing of serving friends.

"Hold the tray with two hands. Say 'here you are' and let them take the treat."

So, without hesitation, I seized the opportunity to play hostess. Like magic, the blanket of confusion and sadness I had felt up until then lifted. I dashed to the tray next to the coffees, picked up the bowl of chocolate almonds, and approached the first of the black-clad women. And just as Yiayia had taught me, I smiled and said, "Here you are."

A hand yanked the bowl from my hands. I heard Thea Kitsa's stern voice. "What are you doing? You are in mourning."

Thea Kitsa, Theo Pavlos's wife, looked older in her black dress. The black kerchief on her head let a few light-brown curls fall loosely on her forehead. In addition to her red nose and wet cheeks, she added to her face the familiar one raised eyebrow, like she did whenever she was cross with me.

My cheeks burned; tears streamed down my cheeks. I was embarrassed, angry, and sad. Instead of lashing out at Thea Kitsa, I darted to the yard and blended in with the children. I went from being excited to be old enough to serve treats, to being diminished to tears. I didn't know I was supposed to behave a certain way because I was in mourning. Obviously, I had violated the mourning code by doing something fun and festive. *My mother is dead, I don't know when my father will come to get us, and Thea Kitsa is mean.*

At that age I had not yet been taught the mourning traditions. And, should they apply to a ten-year-old? My mind went to a safe place as I thought of my yiayia and how she had allowed me the special privilege of serving her friends when they visited

I cherish my memories of my yiayia and her village.

My yiayia's village, Kostohori or Koustohori, is at an elevation of 700 meters in the Vermio Mountain region in northern Greece in the prefecture of Imathia. Veria, the capital of Imathia, is at the base of the mountain. A narrow unpaved thirteen and a half kilometers of zigzag and hairpin turns connect the two communities. Access to the city of Veria, during my childhood, required advance planning and endurance.

A one-lane dirt road for vehicles and horse-drawn wagons connected the village and the capital. For those who made their trip on foot or on a horse or donkey, a steep trail, or as they called it, a *monopati*, had been carved out to circumvent most of the zigzagging of the dirt road. The monopati had its perilous moments.

At some turns the trail was steep and slippery. I could feel my cheeks jiggle like vanilla pudding as my feet left the ground and my bottom coasted to the low point of the hill.

"You are fine. Just get up," Theo Pavlos would say.

However, there were times when skin met rocks or tree roots, and there was blood. In those instances, if there was a woman traveling with us, she tended to the cuts. If not, Theo Pavlos poured spring water from his pagouri, dried it with his handkerchief, and declared, "It's nothing, you are fine." That could have been the foundation my theo laid to encourage stoicism. Whether I got that from Theo Pavlos, or it was innate in me, it would serve me well throughout my life whenever I had to pull myself up and move on.

The trip between the capital and Kostohori was anywhere from two to three hours on the serpentine mountain road. When a vehicle (like a Mercedes taxi) or a horse-drawn wagon faced another coming from the opposite direction, the driver on the inside of the hairpin turn had to find a space and snuggle up to the side of the mountain, very close to the rock ledges and wild brush. As two vehicles or two carriages faced each other, for a minute neither driver would make a move. Instead, they flung their arms in the air as if swatting at flies.

"Aahh, don't you see where you're going?" A booming voice accompanied the arms pointing to the sky.

The response came, equally robust, "Who, me? You are the one who is blind."

I enjoyed the echo that reverberated and disturbed the serenity of the forest. I tried to count how many times their fiery words repeated across the mountainside. Once they resolved the conflict, they acted as if nothing had happened and drove off. I watched them lower their heads and wish each other well. On each occasion I wondered why one of them didn't move over from the outset. When their loud voices pierced my daydreaming, I wasn't afraid. I knew that's how they communicated. The expression *We are not fighting, we are Greek* applies to their discussions.

On that February day, I had no idea of how far away I would end up from the village of my grandmother. Although the memories of my yiayia's village are happy ones, I realize now that when I was a child, I was not aware of the hardships the villagers had endured.

The original settlers of Kostohori were the refugees from Pontos or Pontus, the region on the coast of the Black Sea and the Pontian Alps in Anatolia, today's Turkey. The Pontians were sent to Greece in 1922 under the compulsory exchange of population agreement between Anatolia and Greece. The agreement became official and was signed in 1923 in Lausanne. A systematic genocide of Christian Ottoman Greeks between 1914 to 1922 led to the population exchange.

Following the long and arduous journey from Turkey, the one hundred settlers of Kostohori built their homes on the land given to them by the Greek government. The new citizens were granted land according to their skills, talents, and expertise. My grandparents' group, who were farmers and sheep herders, were given the mountainous region of Kostohori, 513 kilometers north of Athens. The twenty-five families claimed their land and built their homes on the lower side of the mountain in the Vermio mountains. The herders had access to the hills, and the farmers claimed the fertile fields in the valley.

These industrious people who were forced to uproot and travel far did not speak of their ordeal. They uttered phrases which meant the same thing: they were ugly years, a lot of suffering, poverty. They did not share details. It was the common reaction among survivors of the genocide. They did not speak of their suffering during the massacres nor of their ordeal during the strenuous trip to Greece.

Between 1914 and 1922, during the Greek genocide, more than 200,000 Greek Orthodox natives of Asia Minor were killed and another million either fled or were part of the population exchange. Their native language Pontiaka (Pontian Greek), a dialect different from the Greek spoken in their new country, was also the first language for my mother's generation. The first generation became bilingual by the mere nature of immigration. When my generation came along, our grandparents talked to us in Pontiaka and our parents in Greek. At the time we were not aware of the negative nuance of the Pontian dialect. When I got older, I learned the Pontians are considered distant cousins of the Greeks in Greece. They are often the butt of humor and are considered inferior in intellect and uninformed compared to native Greeks. If that premise is true, then what these people lack in sophistication, they make up for it with their warmth, resilience, perseverance, and *filotimo*. Filotimo (or philotimo) is not easily translated. It is one word that encompasses several virtues: doing good, having gratitude, being above reproach, being kind and generous; hospitality, goodness, or a combination of all and loving unconditionally. From my observation of Pontians I have met beyond Kostohori, I have witnessed their indulging in life with joy and optimism. Of course, I attribute the resilience and determination I possess partly to my maternal heritage.

The citizens of Veria had not accepted the Kostohorians nor recognized them as equals. Their refugee status, the language barrier, and the reputation attached to them as inferior in intelligence had created a wedge between them and the natural citizens of Veria. It's unfortunate they were and are characterized as such because they exemplify many of the characteristics associated with Greeks. They are warm, hospitable, family oriented, and fun loving.

However, on that February day following my mother's funeral, no one was celebrating. Instead, a blanket of sadness hovered over Kostohori. The mourners lingered in and around Yiayia's house.

Night had finally cast its black veil over Kostohori. *When are these black-clad creatures going to leave?* I was grateful the crowd had dwindled down to a few relatives gathered around the woodstove in the onta. Over and over, they rehashed the day's event. Their wailing had de-escalated to a quiet lamentation as they grieved over a young mother taken away from her family too soon.

"It's a shame, so young." Shaking their heads.

"Poor Sofia, thank God at least Nikos survived." More tears.

"Why God, why?"

"God have mercy on the two girls." They made the sign of the cross. They went on and on.

Nitsa and I snuggled in the bed we shared next to the fire's warmth.

"Remember when we slept here with Yiayia?"

"I think I do. It was a long time ago."

"Look, look, Nitsa, up in the sky. Now Mamá is up there with Yiayia. Mamá had told us that is where Yiayia went when she died. Mamá had said, 'Way up high in the sky,' remember?"

We turned and faced out the window, staring at the millions of stars dotting the sky.

"Which ones do you think are Yiayia and Mamá?"

"The two biggest." I pointed to the right corner of the window. I felt the chill coming off the windowpane. There was no kilim hanging from the window like my yiayia used to hang during the winter months. She used the tightly woven rug on the window at night to keep the cold out.

Nitsa's arms fell limp and her quiet breathing assured me she had drifted to sleep. I escaped the background chatter with the memory of Yiayia's routine for putting me to sleep.

"Come under the covers." She would hold up the corner of the coarse blanket and patted a spot on the mattress.

"I don't want to go to sleep yet."

"Come, come, it's nice and warm and I will tell you a fairy tale and stay with you until you fall asleep."

"I'll come but you will tell me two fairy tales."

That night, there were no fairy tales, just sad phrases buzzing around the onta. That night I could not burrow my head in Yiayia's cushiony bosom. It had been a year since I felt Yiayia's willowy body under the covers. Her callused hands felt like sandpaper on my cheeks as she lovingly caressed me, stretching my skin down to my jaw. I felt safe and loved in her embrace. Lying in her bed that night and thinking of her, I floated between feeling comforted and feeling sad. I thought about my mamá and my yiayia, the two women in my life on whom I could count to make me feel safe and loved. *I will never again feel their heartfelt hugs, nor their caresses, and their kisses. I will not hear their soothing voices after a fall or a skinned knee.* I also recalled the sounds of their stern voices during the times they threatened punishment and, in my sadness, lying on Yiayia's bed, I decided I would miss those voices too. *Who will replace these two women?*

I pulled the blanket over Nitsa's scrunched-up little body. I envied her in her deep sleep. She didn't have to listen to them still talking as if we weren't present. *Why are those people still here? When will they leave?*

I hung on to the mourners' repeated comment, "Children are orphaned when the father dies." I figured out the fact that my father was alive was a good thing. My sister and I would be taken care of because he could remarry, and we would have a new mother. *But what about my mother, I want her, not someone else.* Amidst the sniveling, sobbing, and constant chatter, exhausted, I floated away into dreamland.

5

Sealed Room

DURING ONE OF OUR VISITS TO THE VILLAGE. OUR MOTHER SOFIA GIVING US A BATH.
THEA KITSA IN THE BACKGROUND.

Our two-year-old cousin's babbling woke us up in the morning. As tradition dictates, Theo Pavlos's and Thea Kitsa's first born was named Despina after our late yiayia. Little Despina hovered over our faces. As a mother and grandmother, I know that seeing the sweet and innocent face of a toddler staring down on your face first thing in the morning is heavenly. But as ten- and seven-year-olds, my sister and I found it most annoying.

"I want to sleep." Nitsa turned toward the wall and pulled the blanket over her head.

Despina tugged at my hand until I got out of bed and led me to the kitchen.

"Go get your sister," Thea Kitsa said as she spread butter and marmalade on thick slices of bread.

"Nitsa, Thea wants you to get up. She wants us to eat breakfast now."

I helped her get out from under the covers and then put on her dress that lay on the chair next to the bed. We wore our dresses under our blue robe-like school uniforms.

"Go, go wash your face before she comes in. I have to get dressed."

Neither one of us went to the outhouse. We must have used the chamber pot during the night. We sat on the floor pillows around the table. Our thea gave us our bread and homemade orange marmalade. The fire was crackling in the woodstove. I watched Thea as she tended to the pot of milk. I had watched my mother prepare our milk and remembered she stood over it the entire time so as not to let it boil over. That process was the method they used to pasteurize either cow, sheep, or goat's milk. Nitsa and I licked and bit our lips, waiting for the hot milk.

"Wait, it's too hot, and only one teaspoon of sugar," Thea said.

We watched the steam subside and when Thea Kitsa was not looking, I heaped a mountain of sugar in each cup. We waited until we could hold on to the metal cups without burning our hands. The froth was the best part, light and fluffy, and fun. We made mustaches and tiny beards just at the tip of our chins while Thea was busy with Despina. We continued to play, having drawn a curtain over the previous day's happenings. However, our revelry came to a quick halt when Theo Pavlos walked into the room.

"Send the little one to school today and I will take Stella to Thessaloniki with me," he said. "Take off your uniform. We will go to see your father today."

"I want to come with you. I want to see Babá too," Nitsa whined.

"Listen to me, Nitsa, you are too young. You be a good girl and go to school."

"Where is he now?" I asked.

"At the hospital in Thessaloniki. We are going to see him there."

The marmalade and milk swirled in my stomach as I watched Nitsa walk up the hill toward the center of the village on her way to school. Theo Pavlos hoisted me on Kanelos's saddle. His cinnamon-colored coat shimmered under the sunlight. His long mane and tail had been brushed to a glistening sheen. Despite all the beauty, strength, and calm he emanated, his size scared me. I felt I was as high off the ground as if I was on top of a house. *Don't try to get off by yourself. You'll fall again and cut your forehead.*

"Theo, I want to walk. Can I please? I'll walk fast."

"Stella, like I told you, if you don't try to get off you will be fine.

Nothing will happen to you."

At the fountain we made the customary stop to water the horse and fill the vessels with water. Kanelos knew where to turn and pick up the meandering trail.

After leaving Kanelos at the stable in Veria, we walked the remaining kilometer to the bus terminal. Once we boarded the bus the thought of seeing my father intensified my anxiety. I needed to know when he was taking us back home. I held on to the words I kept hearing the day before, "Thank God Nikos is alive, he can remarry."

Before we reached the national road, passengers seated on the left side of the bus made the sign of the cross and gasped. I scooted over my theo's lap for a look. I pressed my head against the window and got a glimpse of the spectacle. *Is that a coffin in the back of the taxi?* That explained the making of the cross and "rest in peace" and "good paradise" I heard the passengers muttering. I wondered if that's what happened two days earlier when Nitsa and I were enjoying our taxi ride. And just like that the diesel smell got to me, I stopped looking out the window and looked ahead to prevent throwing up. I wonder how Theo Pavlos felt. Did he experience a déjà vu moment? Later when he related the incident to friends and relatives, he expressed his astonishment, but I did not hear anything about how he felt.

The taxi disappeared, in the direction of Veria. Our bus continued in the opposite direction toward Thessaloniki.

A sense of comfort came over me when I jumped off the bus at the terminal. I could move away from the diesel smell and the fumes. I felt at home as we snaked through the lunch crowd at the familiar Vardari Square to catch the tram to the hospital. Good thing I had a dress on to keep my heart from leaping out. Such was my anguish in anticipation of seeing my father. I wondered if Theo appreciated that he didn't have to drag me to keep up with him. My feet glided on the pavement. And there it was, nothing extraordinary just a long white concrete building.

"Wait here and don't wander off," Theo Pavlos said as he disappeared beyond the glass doors.

The wooden slats dug into my bottom, but I stayed on the bench. I watched people on crutches struggle across the dirt walkway. Nurses in their starched white dresses and cute little white hats with a red cross right in the center above their foreheads moved with purpose in their step. After what seemed hours, Theo Pavlos emerged.

"Where is he? Is he coming out?"

"No, he can't come out."

"Take me in to see him."

"They don't let children in."

"I will be good, tell them. You can tell them to let me in."

He looked at the ground, his shoulders were drooped even after he looked up. He placed his hands on my shoulders. I looked into his glassy blue eyes, and he said, "You can't go in. We will go to Mrs. Azat's to pick up some of your things and go back to the village."

Theo held my hand and guided me away from the hospital. We boarded a tram to Vardari Square and walked to my home. Mary, Mrs. Azat's daughter, distracted me with a game of cards. Theo Pavlos and Mrs. Azat were whispering at the other end of the room. I had become accustomed to the secretive voices and expected a serious revelation at some point soon.

I overheard that our room, in essence our home, had been sealed off by the authorities. I stopped playing cards with Mary and eavesdropped on the adults.

Mrs. Azat and Theo passed by us in the direction of our room.

"You see? No one can enter. Filipas is assigned to the case." Mrs. Azat pointed toward our room.

Mr. Filipas was a court magistrate. He, his wife, and two daughters the same age as my sister and me had been family friends and neighbors. Mr. Filipas and my father were the same age and had the same physique. Even their mustaches were the same shape and length. *Why is he assigned to the case? What case? Why is he in charge of the girls' welfare? They're talking about me and Nitsa, but I don't know why.*

I felt Mrs. Azat's leather belt against my head as she held me close with one hand while caressing my cheek with a tender touch. The only other time I felt that kind of affection from her was the morning she sent us off with our theo following our mother's demise. Mrs. Ismini from across the street appeared, sniffling and wiping away tears with her handkerchief. The demeanor of all three reminded me of the mourners back at the village but without the wailing. A tearful goodbye followed their afternoon coffee. Theo Pavlos and I walked to

Vardari Square and boarded the bus to Veria as I continued to wonder why I hadn't been allowed to see Babá.

In Veria my feet did not move as fast as they did back in Thessaloniki.

"We have to hurry so we can get to the village before dark."

I stumbled and tripped as I tried to keep pace with my theo's gigantic strides. I was relieved to finally arrive at the stable. I thought for sure my arm was now longer because of Theo's tugging at it. The stable master led Kanelos out. Theo's demeanor had changed after we left the hospital. Our stop at Mrs. Azat's was enigmatic. The question *what is going on* was on my mind then and again as I observed the mild manner with which he spoke to the stable master.

After a short walk we were on the path to the village. I was happy to see familiar faces also returning to their homes. I wanted to see my theo engage with them in the customary gregarious manner I knew. I wanted things to be normal, not secretive and glum. Instead, I saw more of the same. His head hanging like he was carrying a tree on his shoulders. His voice so soft and somber it didn't even sound like his. And never mind about seeing any sparkle in his Aegean-blue eyes. I hadn't seen the spirited spark in his eyes since the day he collected my sister and me from Thessaloniki.

We did make it home before dark. And at the sight of what appeared like an invasion of jet-black birds, gathered in groups in the yard, I felt my face turn to an ember. *Why are those women all dressed in black still here? And why are the men scurrying to take the horse from Theo?*

"Pavlos, what is this that has befallen you?"

"What's going to happen to the girls?"

These new questions brought back the somersaults in my stomach.

"Where is Nitsa?" I wanted to find her. I wanted to make sure she was okay and to ask her if she knew anything.

"She is at Thea Chrissa's. Why don't you go there to be with her? And you can play with your friend, Maritsa."

"I am not going anywhere. Why do you want me to leave? Why is everyone here again and crying?"

"Go inside, it's too cold for you to be outside."

I complied and went inside where the old men and women were

holding their mourning ritual. Some were crying, others spoke of the horrifying event, or just moved their heads in disbelief. This crow-like crowd was a milder version of the one outside. Once again, they spoke as if I wasn't there. And again, their pitying glances annoyed me. I wanted to shout at them. *All of you leave. Go. Leave us alone.*

They whispered but I could hear them. Hours before my theo and I returned, they had buried my father.

This can't be right. They don't know what they are saying. Theo Pavlos would have told me if he knew.

I bolted out of the room, my face ablaze and my tears slithering down my cheeks.

"What are they saying? Those old people in there, they said my babá is dead too and they buried him today." I tugged on Theo Pavlos's jacket and implored him, "Tell them to leave and to stop saying that Babá is dead."

"Stop, stop come with me." He led me to the bench where Yiayia and I had sat countless times.

"Listen, they are not lying. Your babá died. That's why we could not see him at the hospital."

"You should have told me, why didn't you tell me?" I watched my tears fall on my clasped hands.

"I thought it would be best to get home and then tell you. When you can be with your sister and Thea Kitsa."

"Where is he now? Where did they take him?"

He pressed my quivering body against his bony body. At the same time a swarm of bees slowly and methodically penetrated my head. I got that feeling of fading away and at the same time I wanted to hear his answer.

"They buried him while we were in Thessaloniki."

In 1958 the dead were buried within twenty-four hours of the time of death. They did not embalm the bodies and the burial had to take place before 7 p.m. in the summer and before 5 p.m. in the winter. They still follow this ritual in the villages and in much of Greece today. If there are extenuating circumstances, funeral homes have the technology to preserve the body until it can be buried. Back then, even if we had returned in time for the funeral, I would not have been allowed to attend.

6

Theo Pavlos

MY THEO PAVLOS.

Theo Pavlos knew we would not make it in time for my father's funeral. He was informed at the hospital of my father's death. They released the body to be transported to Kostohori so he could be buried with our mother.

My eavesdropping rendered all the information I could manage, and it overwhelmed me. Every bit of it tugged at my heart. *I don't want to hear any more.* But I didn't listen to my inner voice, I didn't walk away, I heard more. *Why am I listening? It's making me want to cry even more.*

The Katarahias Taverna had received the call in the morning. A messenger relayed the news to Thea Kitsa.

"Nikos is dead. His body is on its way to the village. Mrs. Ismini's two sons are accompanying the coffin."

The funeral took place right after the coffin arrived.

I heard my theo relay, with certainty, that the taxi we saw on the highway on our way to Thessaloniki earlier that day was transporting the coffin that held our father's remains.

"I tell you, it was his coffin. If only I knew we could have gotten off at Makrohori and taken a bus back."

I watched him as he pursed his lips and reached for the bitter cup of coffee.

I had heard enough. I wandered into the onta. The morbid scene of women in black dresses and black kerchiefs filled the big room. Some made their way out and like blackbirds changing their perch, they took turns to greet Theo.

I dawdled at the threshold so I could hear them. Between their wailing and lamenting, they reassured Theo that everything for the funeral followed the traditions. Red eyes, barely visible below their kerchiefs, had sadness and disbelief written all over them. This time their comments did not anger me, they frightened me. "Poor orphan girls." "Pavlos, you can't take care of them." *Why not? He loves us and we love him.*

"At least the young one can be adopted."

"What's going to happen to the older one?"

"Who's going to take care of her?"

"What's going to happen to them now?"

None of that made sense to me. I did not comprehend why we couldn't stay with Theo Pavlos. At ten years old, staying with him made total sense to me. I did not understand why the villagers kept asking my uncle what he was going to do with us. Our parents had been dead for three days and their focus was on finding a place for us. If our yiayia was alive they wouldn't be talking like that. And since Thea Anna was estranged from the family, there was no one else to care for us.

But Theo Pavlos had been part of our lives from the beginning. He had been a frequent visitor in our home during his military service. We felt blessed to have him stationed near us, in Thessaloniki. His visits added a positive dimension to our lives. My mother enjoyed seeing her brother, whose presence reconnected her to the family she left behind in the village. I lingered around them while they sipped their coffee and caught up on what was happening in each other's lives and the lives of relatives and village friends. I pretended to be part of their conversation. I felt grown up.

During his visits Theo Pavlos appeared engrossed in every detail of the village news. I had not realized how precious these visits were to the two siblings. I hovered around them in anticipation of my alone time with Theo Pavlos. I looked forward to our walks, which always included stopping at the *periptero* (kiosk) a few blocks from the house where I could choose a treat. It seemed every corner had a periptero.

The kiosk offered a myriad of items, and it stayed open from early morning until late at night. How they fit all the merchandise in that little yellow structure is mind-boggling. My mother had sent me there on errands often.

"Stella, go to the periptero and ask for a white spool of thread. Make sure he gives you change." On other occasions it was to bring back matches, or a pencil.

One could find cookies, koulouria, and tiropites. A variety of cigarette packages filled the shelves behind the proprietor. People bought two or three cigarettes instead of a pack. There were lighters, school supplies and household necessities. The newspapers and magazines were either stacked up in front on the sidewalk or hanging on a string across the front of the kiosk, like laundry, held up with clothespins. I was in awe to see the faces of famous people, actors, queens, and kings hanging from a clothesline alongside the comic books. The public telephone had become an asset to the periptero.

Once Mamá and Theo caught up with their news, and Theo Pavlos stood up, I would spring off the chair. It was the moment I had been waiting for. With my hand engulfed in his palm, I strolled next to his imposing figure, proud as if I was saying "See this handsome man? He is my theo." I wonder why I felt pride reverberate throughout my insides as I strolled next to him. It wasn't as though I could take credit for his captivating appearance. To me he was as handsome as Andreas Barkoulis. I had seen the actor's picture on the magazines displayed at kiosks. My theo's official army photograph shows off an unequivocal sparkle in his crystal-blue eyes, which seem to penetrate through the black-and-white photograph. To this day whenever I hold that photograph, I can feel his warmth.

If Mamá deemed the day was warm enough for an ice cream, there was no thinking about it. I chose a chocolate-covered bar every time. The challenge to keep up with licking the ice cream off my hand fast enough to prevent its trickling down my arm was another thing. I had to keep it off my clothing at all costs so as not to lose the privilege of getting an ice cream next time. On cooler days the choices were a

Noisetta milk chocolate bar with hazelnuts, a bag of hard candy, or a *koulouri* (the crispy sesame-covered ring-shaped bread dough). On our way back to the house he promised to come back, and we would go to the periptero again.

We looked forward to our vacation in Kostohori. Yiayia and Theo Pavlos were the family we knew. My bond with Theo Pavlos developed during our visits to the village and during his leave as a soldier. Our relationship continued to flourish after he completed his military service. Even after his marriage and the arrival of his first child, we visited and stayed in the onta, with Yiayia and Theo's family. The bond my mother and Theo shared extended to me. The closeness I felt for him left no doubt in my heart that Nitsa and I should live with him in the village.

Despite the strong and loving relationship between us and Theo Pavlos, nothing could have prepared the twenty-six-year-old with a wife and a young family for what he encountered when he arrived at Mrs. Azat's house early that February morning in 1958 to pick up his two nieces.

For days after the funerals, mourners continued to stop by the house. I did not know that according to tradition, visitors are supposed to drop in to provide support to the grieving family during the forty days following a death.

Thank God Nitsa and I had a reprieve from their presence and their disparaging remarks. "What's going to happen to the girls?" "The orphanage won't take the older one." "Poor Sofia, she died so young."

We attended the one-room schoolhouse Monday through Saturday. Nitsa's fondest memory from attending the village school is the bright yellow American cheese they gave us at snack time.

"I liked the bright yellow. It was spongy, not firm like feta or our beige *kasseri*."

Two weeks after the funerals, I had a carefree feeling. The knots in my stomach had loosened. *Since we are still here, we must be staying with Theo and Thea.* Then one morning our routine was interrupted.

"Where's Nitsa? We are going to be late for school."

"Nitsa is not going today. You go on, don't be late," Thea Kitsa said as she opened the door for me to leave for school.

When I returned from school, Thea Kitsa informed me Theo Pavlos had taken Nitsa to Thessaloniki.

"Why? Why didn't he take me too?"

"Change from your school clothes and don't ask questions." Her usual sing-song voice sounded stern.

I couldn't hold back the tears. "Tell me now. Why didn't he take me?"

"Go change and when your theo comes home, ask him."

After I had changed, I sneaked out and climbed up on the barn roof where I used to hide and waited for Theo Pavlos.

"What are you doing up there? Come down here." His voice was soothing.

Blood gushed down my face. In my haste to come down, the edge of the tin roof had grazed my forehead as I slid off.

He took my hand.

"Come, come it's nothing."

We walked to the house. I saw red drops land on my shoe. It made me cry harder.

"Kitsa, get a towel and alcohol."

"It stings, stop it." I tried to get away but did not.

The stinging stopped.

"It's a small cut, the size of my thumbnail," Theo said.

He led me to the bench where Yiayia had pierced my ears.

"All better?"

I didn't answer. Sitting on the bench with my uncle was unusual. He never sat there with me. That's where Yiayia and I sat, where she wiped tears away, or where she gave me a treat.

"Where is Nitsa?"

"She will stay with Mr. Filipas's family for a few days."

I remembered Mrs. Azat had told Theo that Mr. Filipas had been assigned to the guardian committee overseeing the case of the two orphan girls.

"When is she coming back?"

"Listen to me. It's for her own good. She is going to live with a couple in Katerini. They will adopt her, and they will be her parents."

"Can I go with her?"

"No, my girl. Couples only adopt one child. We will try and find a couple to adopt you."

"I'm going to go play now." I sprung off the bench and scurried toward Maritsa's house.

There was the uneasy feeling again, in my heart, in my stomach, in my throat. *What am I supposed to do? I can't bring her back. He said it's for her own good. What about me? Shouldn't I be with her?* Confusion dominated my mind. At the same time a voice inside me was telling me I must accept my theo's decisions. *It's what is supposed to happen.*

Newspaper stories had reported the fatal accident which killed Sofia and Nikos Spentzouras, the young parents of two little girls. A Greek tragedy played out in the news. Strangers mourned the untimely death of the young couple.

"The newspapers published the accident. People talked about it for days," Mrs. Azat informed us years later. "Lawyers contacted eager childless clients to inform them of the availability of the two little girls."

7

For Her Own Good

After reading the story about the accident and the plight of the two girls, Mr. Apostolos Papaefthemiou, an attorney from Katerini, inquired about adopting one of the orphans. Mr. Apostolos and his wife had not been able to have children and had to wait until his wife, Mrs. Nitsa, was post-menopausal. According to the law at the time, women had to be post-menopausal prior to adopting a child. It protected the adopted child. It diminished the possibility of the couple's ability to subsequently have a biological child. The law's premise assumed that if the adoptive couple had a biological child, they might favor that child over the adopted one. Or even worse, the adoptive parents might mistreat or abandon the adopted child. My sister spent a few nights with our old neighbors until Mr. Filipas informed her of the nice couple who would become her parents.

Mr. Apostolos and Mrs. Nitsa Papaefthemiou had opted to adopt the younger orphan. Yup, my little sister and her potential mother had the same nickname, Nitsa, from the popular Greek name Eleni (Helen). A diminutive of Eleni is Elenitsa, which can be shortened to Nitsa. Since then, the nickname has lost its popularity and is currently considered provincial.

Mr. Filipas informed Nitsa the couple was coming to take her to Katerini, a city one hour away from Thessaloniki. That's where her new home would be with her new parents. Nitsa did not understand the meaning of it. "I assumed it was a temporary solution until you and I would reunite," she recalls. "No one had informed me nor prepared me for our separation. All Theo Pavlos told me when we left the village was that he was taking me to Thessaloniki, and I would stay with Mr. Filipas's family for a few days."

Our theo did not say anything about an adoption to either one of us. From today's perspective it sounds cruel. Today, when we explain and discuss everything in an age-appropriate manner with children, this approach of handling a child is unconscionable. It may have been the normal way of doing things in Greece in the 1950s. One could excuse the twenty-six-year-old uncle from the village. He didn't know any better. But we see the court magistrate an educated person in the big city, behaving in a similar manner. He didn't say anything to my sister until the day the couple was due to arrive to take her home.

My sister has told me a myriad of times her first thoughts when the couple entered Mr. Filipa's house. "The thing I noticed first was that the couple was old. They could be my grandparents but not my parents, I thought. I just sat there silently looking at them and thinking, this can't be. I am not leaving with them. I sat there not saying anything. I listened to the adults discussing legal details, but I did not think any of it had anything to do with me. But when the couple stood, looked at me and said, 'It's time to go,' I panicked. I was in utter disbelief." She shivered as if shaking the memory away.

She could not believe she was to leave with them. "Suddenly I found my voice, stopped crying and told them, I must tell Stella where I'm going. Where are we going?"

"You will be fine," Mr. Filipas attempted to reassure her.

"No, I have to tell her where I'm going," she insisted and cried, to no avail.

Mr. Apostolos kindly and firmly told her, "You are going with us to Katerini, you will be fine. You don't need to inform Stella."

"Yes, I do. I have to tell my sister where I am going."

"Go, my girl, you will be fine." Mr. Filipas added.

"I felt as though they whisked me away before the scene escalated. Just like that, they took me away from our old neighborhood. We walked down the familiar street along Agia Paraskevi Cemetery on the way to Vardari Square, but I felt apprehensive and angry."

She has told me how devastated she felt about our separation. Until then, we had been inseparable. Ever since we can remember, she was with me all the time. Even when she was old enough to play with her own friends, she wanted to be with me. So, either I joined her and her friends or I convinced my friends to let her tag along with us, which is what happened most of the time. When my friends and I turned nine years old, they balked at the sight of Nitsa next to me. They implored me to send her back home. "She's too young for us. Tell her to go find her friends." My mamá and I failed to convince the little one to play with her friends. Whenever I attempted to send her home, she pulled one of her famous tantrums. The tantrum was always the same. First, she whined, then she cried, and when that didn't work, she held her breath. After that, she unleashed her biggest weapon. She held her breath long enough for her tongue to recede down her throat, at which point someone had to pull out her tongue from her throat, enabling her to breathe again.

When I turned nine years old, my mamá informed me, "Stella you are now old enough to learn how to pull out her tongue." My body recoiled at the thought of having to do it.

"I'm afraid, I don't want to learn how to do it." The idea of failing to pull out her tongue scared me.

"This way you won't have to call me whenever she swallows her tongue. You will be able to do it."

I had watched the process countless times, and it scared me every time. Watching her body tense up like an ironing board, her lips resembled pale blueberries, and the deafening silence made me think she wouldn't ever take another breath. Evidently, my parents did not know the body automatically takes over and the child will breathe again.

Even though my mamá convinced me I could help Nitsa, I gave in to my sister's demands to avoid a tantrum unless an adult was nearby. I didn't want to have to test my ability to perform the new skill my mother was so confident I had mastered. Although by the age of three, most children outgrow tantrums, Nitsa held on to hers. She engaged in the power of her tactic anytime she was told she couldn't be with me.

When the two strangers urged her to leave with them, a tantrum was brewing. Although she panicked, she avoided having one. "I kept telling myself I must find Stella and tell her where I am. I could not imagine facing life without you, but I did not pull a tantrum." And that day her tantrums ended forever. Unfortunately, they were replaced with bed-wetting.

She left our old neighborhood with those thoughts whirling in her mind. Amid her anguish and anxiety about where she was going without her sister, she was informed of another change in her new life as they approached Vardari Square.

"From now on you will be called Lena," her new mother said.

Lena is a sophisticated nickname for Eleni. In the long run it turned out to be a good thing, rather than having the provincial nickname of Nitsa. But to a seven-and-a-half-year-old little girl, it represented another loss in her life.

Mrs. Nitsa inflicted yet another blow on Nitsa soon after they left our old neighborhood.

"With one sharp move, she yanked the black armband off my gabardine's sleeve. I was furious. I liked it because it made me feel grown up to wear one. I had only seen adults wearing one. It signified the loss of my parents, my mamá and my babá."

I had never seen a child with a mourning armband. It must have been a village tradition, not something the city folks practiced. But to my sister it was a loss and a second strike against her new mother.

At Vardari Square they engaged a taxi to Tsimiski Street, the upscale shopping street of Thessaloniki. She recovered from both changes her new parents had imposed on her as soon as she slid into the spacious seat of the taxi. She thought, *wow, another taxi ride.* The magic continued when they entered Thessaloniki's largest department store, Lampropoulos.

"I felt like Cinderella. We followed the saleswoman throughout the little girls' departments. They bought everything I could possibly need. I couldn't believe the quantities they were buying. One dozen each of white underpants and white tank tops. I don't remember how many nightgowns and pajamas. A coat, sweaters, shoes, slippers, dresses, everything in abundance. The intoxication of the shopping spree lifted my apprehension about being with strangers."

However, when they boarded a bus destined for Katerini, she wanted nothing to do with them. They put her between them in the two reserved seats.

"I didn't want her to touch me or have me sit on her lap. Instead, I sat on the edge of the seat between them and held on to the seat in front of me."

Lena's anger and fear prevented her from appreciating the single-family home with its decorative fence and iron gate. She was consumed by the thought that her big sister did not know her whereabouts. The mysterious separation from me terrified her.

Mrs. Nitsa struggled to bring some cheer to the little girl. She spread out their purchases in hopes of seeing the same awestruck look she had seen at the department store. Instead, she was rewarded with questions and demands: "Where is my sister? I want to see my sister."

After a night in her new home and in her own bedroom, Lena continued to be in a state of turmoil. She could not understand what was happening to her, to us, nor why. She kept wondering why the two of us could not be together.

"We are your parents now," they insisted.

"I know I have a sister and when I find her, I will leave here," she retorted to their attempts to coddle her. Lena admits she was relentless with her threats to leave them. In the beginning she hurled her threats with regularity and as time passed her threats became intermittent.

An array of surprises filled the first day of her new life. Aunts, uncles, and cousins streamed through the house. It was orchestrated in a way that was supposed to make her feel as though she had been in their lives all along. Not only did she know it wasn't so, but she also saw it in the puzzled expressions of her supposed cousins.

She recalls, "Some of them were my age. Some were older. But I knew we were thinking the same thing. That we did not know each other." She felt like a spectacle on display. "When we were older and friends, they confessed they had been instructed by my father not to say anything about the adoption and to not upset me."

It was a parade of adults and little people. The cousins exchanged clandestine looks. They nudged at each other's elbows. The adults appeared more natural and casual. They talked about the up-and-coming masquerade plans. *Carnavali* (Mardi Gras) was in February in 1958 and two weeks after our parents' death. Once the conversation turned to the costumes, Lena and the cousins, boys and girls, became animated.

"I'm going to be a pirate."

"Yesterday my mamá bought me a white ballerina costume."

"I only need to find a gun and then I'll be a perfect cowboy."

"Lena, what do you want to be?" her mother asked. "We can go shopping tomorrow."

"I want to be a princess."

The corners of Mrs. Nitsa's mouth curved, almost reaching her cheekbones, her crinkled eyes met Lena's green eyes. Mrs. Nitsa's sisters nodded their heads in unison as if to say, "See? She will come around."

Lena fluctuated between euphoria and despair. When her new parents doted over her, she felt like Cinderella. But when she was by herself doing her homework, she regressed to feelings of loss and separation. She liked her new environment. She was getting used to Mrs. Nitsa's full figure and conservative style. Her father's towering figure was reminiscent of our Theo Pavlos, but the slight stoop of his shoulders betrayed the decades that separated the two men. Eventually, Lena made amends with the fact that both were older than our parents and the parents of her cousins and accepted that she would be staying with them permanently. What she could not accept was not having me with her. Or to at least know where I was and how to be in contact with me. She has told me several times about how awful and embarrassed she feels regarding her threats to leave them if she found me. She regrets and feels ashamed for calling them "Aunt" and "Uncle" for two years before she would call them "Mamá" and "Babá." She grew to love and appreciate them as her parents who offered her everything she needed to succeed.

8

Help from Memories

ME AND MY GRANDSON TREY.

Both my sister and I were experiencing confusion in our separate ways. Both of us were wondering why we couldn't be together. She wanted to at least know where I was. I knew where she was but felt confusion as to what would happen with me. Anger had become my reaction to hearing the villagers say to my theo, "What will you do with the older one?" *Why don't they tell him to keep me here with him? Here, where Yiayia always took care of me when we visited.* My first two years of life, during the civil war, my family lived with Yiayia. The way our grandmother loved us, I know she would have kept me and Nitsa with her in the village.

I recall one of my first memories of her is her outstretched arms waiting until I got close enough for them to draw my head tightly against her bosom. Then she held me by the shoulders, moved me just far enough away from her to take a good look at me before she enveloped me in her big strong arms again and said, "*Na lelevo se*" (the literal translation is "to enjoy you"); it is akin to "I love you." Yiayia used that expression often and I longed to be in her arms and to hear her say, "Come here you, na lelevo se." Instead, I endured the unpleasant comments of her friends and relatives.

As the weeks put a distance between me and my sister (now called Lena), I focused more on adjusting to the village life and less on what happened to my sister. By all accounts she was in a better situation than I was. I overheard the adults saying things like: "The little one is lucky the lawyer adopted her." "She lives in the city; she will go far." "It's the older one Pavlos has to worry about."

I found comfort in daydreaming about my yiayia. Thoughts of being nestled in her tight embrace as I sniffed for the familiar aroma of garlic and onions on her apron or hands so that I would know I was in for a treat of crispy *keftedes* (fried meatballs) and fried potatoes. The image of her weathered face framed by the black kerchief tied on her head, ending in a point down her back and covering her long black-and-gray braid loomed clearly in my mind. The warmth and conspiratorial look in her eyes when she looked at me made me feel deep down in my gut that I was Yiayia's favorite. That thought elicits a physical sensation of the warm and joyous feeling I experienced whenever I thought of her, whether back at home in Thessaloniki or in her arms in the village.

To this day when I indulge in her memory, peace and tranquility wash over my entire physical and spiritual being. "I hope I live long enough for my grandson to remember me" was my mantra following Trey's birth. It is not so much that I want him to remember me, Stella the grandmother, but to remember the good feelings he experienced from our bond. For him to know he was created a perfect human being and that he can achieve whatever he desires. I believe I acquired a sense of security, confidence, love, worthiness, and acceptance from my yiayia and I hope I imparted those attributes to Trey. As of this writing, Trey is sixteen years old and I believe I have lived long enough to have given him a loving *Yiayia experience.*

And so, in the midst of confusion and uncertainty at the village, revisiting the fond memories of love, security, and childhood joy enabled me to endure the disparaging comments from the adults and the scornful treatment by the teacher.

The deep gray stone construction of the one-room schoolhouse conveyed strength and stability. I thought inside its walls I would feel the security that was missing in my life. Instead, my experience turned out to be humiliating and distasteful. My new, tall, young, and handsome teacher was the antithesis of the teachers I had in Thessaloniki. They had been caring, friendly, and encouraging. Mr. Gerasimos was condescending and especially so to me, the new girl in school. Something about the way he carried himself in and out of school disturbed me. He draped his suit jacket on his shoulders and strutted in a way I had heard adults describe as arrogant. I didn't know what it meant but they spoke of it as something undesirable. His cold and dispassionate manner mirrored the frigid temperature we encountered each morning upon entering the schoolhouse. It took a while for the warmth of the woodstove to reach the back of the room.

"He put me in the back of the room," I whined to Thea Kitsa.

"What can we do? It's a big stone building."

"But I bring in firewood just like the other kids, we should take turns sitting near the stove."

"He is the teacher. You must do what he says."

Perhaps a more experienced teacher would have been a better fit for the village kids. A teacher who could empathize, one who had a passion to help the peasant children to rise out of their subsistence lifestyle.

Despite Mr. Gerasimos's demeanor, the villagers were exceptionally kind to him. They were happy to have found a teacher for their kids after a two-year search.

I kept thinking Yiayia would have intervened and would have made things better for me. But she was no longer there. The only person who could make it better was Theo Pavlos. I had not realized it then, but to me he had become every person I had lost: Yiayia, Mother, Father, and Sister.

Neither the teacher's treatments nor the villagers' comments were enough for me to want to leave the security I felt in my yiayia's village. My nine-year bond with her had instilled in me incredible strength on which I relied when life presented me with adversity. Whenever anything worked out for me, I felt I deserved it, and it was the right thing to have happened. That kind of belief brings to mind the teachings of people like Louise Hay and other Hay House motivational authors. Louise reminds us we are born to be loved and to be happy. She emphasizes we were all born complete and good enough. Way before I read or heard of motivational speakers, I listened to my inner voice for guidance. The times I did not follow my inner guidance system and had an undesirable outcome confirmed my inner voice was correct and that I should have listened. In every wrong decision I was fortunate to be protected by a Divine intervention with no harm done. I attribute a lot of my perseverance, confidence, and belief in myself to the bond I shared with my yiayia. I believe the feelings I derived from that relationship reinforced my inborn strengths.

From the moment I found out I would become a grandmother; I had the desire to impart to my grandchild the tender sentiment residing within me and which I felt I learned from my yiayia. A sentiment that is different from our parental bond. A sentiment that hopefully my grandson, Trey, feels and can call upon for strength whenever he faces a challenge or a struggle. For him to think back on our bond and smile when things are going well for him. A feeling that warms his heart and brings peace to his being. I want to believe that the innate goodness with which all of us are born was not diluted in him by the imposed environmental rules that break down or lower a person's self-worth. I do believe having been an integral part of Trey's first six years of life and our continued connection offers him the opportunity to embody a loving yiayia experience.

Trey and I have created a plethora of memories. Our time together during his first six years was ideal for Trey's exposure to the Greek culture. Not only did we converse in Greek, but we cooked and baked Greek foods. He was totally immersed in the Greek thing. His embracing the Greek traditions caresses my soul. As I write this, I visualize my yiayia and me sitting on the bench in Kostohori. She is smiling and caressing me.

Throughout the years and to this day I believe the bond my yiayia and I developed gave me the confidence to take care of myself. Between the love my parents and my grandmother showered on me, something solid must have developed within me. How else can I explain the fortitude I had to stand up for myself at an early age? Of course, I also believe that we are all born with innate abilities to cope with and understand our circumstances. My heart used to race at the prospect of seeing Yiayia. I ran to her for protection when anyone threatened my well-being. I found safety wrapping my arms around her legs as I pressed my head behind her knees.

With those memories and feelings of my yiayia, I could not understand how Theo Pavlos and everyone else wanted to uproot me out of the village. I would need all the strength and resilience within me for what lay ahead.

9
Veria

Two months had passed since my parents' funerals. My sister had been gone almost the entire time. I lived in Kostohori with Theo Pavlos's family. At that point I wanted to believe I would be staying forever despite the chatter that circulated in the village.

I studied and did my schoolwork while I continued to endure Mr. Gerasimos's insults. In the back of my mind, I knew this arrangement wasn't forever. I knew I had to be "situated." That's the word I kept hearing, whenever adults came to visit.

"What's going to happen to the older one, where will she be situated?"

"It was good luck the young one got adopted."

I knew I was there temporarily, and everyone was hoping I would be lucky enough to get adopted.

One day, Theo Pavlos returned from Veria and announced, "Stella, there is a couple in Veria that wants to adopt you."

I folded my embroidery and looked up at Theo Pavlos's face. I am not sure if I read relief or concern in his sparkling blue eyes. I cried and pleaded to stay. I promised to be a good girl. "I will help Thea Kitsa with Despina and do more housework. Please let me stay with you."

Theo Pavlos's kind eyes focused on me as he lifted my trembling chin and explained. "It is for your own good to grow up in the city with a respected couple who can provide for you in the same way your parents had planned to do. We cannot give that to you in the village."

I wiped the tears and the saltiness running down my nose off my lips. Theo handed me a handkerchief. I dried my hands and face while the familiar words reverberated in my numb head, "What will you do with the older one?" Remembering the chatter, I knew there was no avoiding it, I had to go.

The next morning, we stopped at the fountain to fill our pagouri and the straw-encased bottle with water before we embarked on the two-hour trip to Veria. After watering Kanelos, my uncle lifted me up onto the saddle.

Yellow and blue crocuses had sprouted along the sides of the monopati. I tried to focus on the sound of water trickling down the mountainside to distract me from my fear of being on the horse. It hadn't been that long ago since I had fallen off the horse and ended up with a scar on my forehead.

I exhaled a sigh of relief at the first sight of civilization. The red tile rooftops of Veria sprouted up ahead. We reached the barn at the entrance of the city and left the horse to be fed and bedded down.

We continued our journey on foot. Our route along the main street leading to Elia Square showcased orange and olive trees on the wide paved street in a stark contrast to the dirt streets of Kostohori. They resembled the streets of Thessaloniki. When Theo Pavlos started to pay attention to house numbers, the uneasy feeling in my stomach intensified when we stopped in front of the black iron gate. I knew that was it. He would leave me here with two strangers.

After what seemed an eternity, the couple, older than I expected, came to the gate, and greeted us. They shook hands with Theo and led the way along a walkway edged with pansies all the way to their front steps. *Why am I here? They are so old! They are like a yiayia and a pappou.* The flowerpots on the balcony reminded me of Mrs. Azat's house. I wanted to go back to that house or back to the village with Theo Pavlos. I wondered if my little sister felt the same way when she went to Katerini with her new parents.

The tufted sofa and chairs in the living room were like Mrs. Azat's. The lady set the tray with traditional refreshments on the coffee table. Normally I would be salivating at the sight of the syrupy wild cherry *glyko*. Instead, I focused on the moving reflection on the surfaces of the wood coffee table that wasn't covered with the white embroidered table scarf. Theo Pavlos accepted the glyko. I opted for a bonbon. The flurry in my heart increased as the conversation waned. Neither treat could have toned down the squirmy feeling in my heart.

My father-to-be was tall, soft spoken, friendly, and gentle. I watched him remove his black rimmed glasses. He rubbed the sides of his nose where the glasses had been, before placing them on top of his head. My mother-to-be impressed me in a totally different way. Her large body was a departure from the trim and fit village women I was accustomed to seeing. Her graying hair, a symbol of old age to me, bothered me.

Why do I have to stay? She is not friendly. She is looking at me as if I am beneath her. I had heard adults talk about a certain type who looked down on peasants or village people. I imagined that she was the type of person they described. *He is nice and friendly. They are too old to be my parents. How can I be seen with them? They look like my grandparents. I will be so embarrassed.*

While I was having these thoughts, she reiterated how lucky I was. "Do you know you are a lucky girl? We are giving you the opportunity to leave the village life behind."

I wanted to shout out, "I don't want your opportunity."

Instead, Theo Pavlos agreed with her. "Of course, we know how lucky she is to be taken in by you."

I suppose he had to say it.

And then he stood up. I couldn't surrender to the fact that my uncle was abandoning me. The tears, again. I was getting used to them. It was happening often. I grabbed his hand, and I just wanted him to say thank you for the treats and for the two of us to walk away. Instead, he let go of my hand, and hugged me. I watched my tears hit the cement like a slow-dripping faucet. A ray of light entered my heart when they invited Theo to come visit me periodically. I held on to the gate as I watched Theo Pavlos turn around for one last look before he disappeared around the corner.

What happens now? I'm going to call them Mamá and Babá. They are so old. Settling into my new home offered a variety of challenges and opportunities. Sure, I had my own room in a single-family home on a beautiful street in Veria. The next-door neighbors provided a glimpse of light. They were a young family. Our first meeting gave me hope for some normalcy in my new environment. The two daughters and I exchanged shy glances. They stood close to each other and held hands. Since they were the same ages as my sister and me, I couldn't help but feel a pang of nostalgia. *Where is Nitsa? We could be holding hands.*

The mothers enumerated all the things we would be doing together, such as going to school, playing in each other's yards, and going for an ice cream. It all sounded good but not good enough to take my mind off Theo Pavlos. As it turned out, the girls and I became friends and did a lot together. School turned out to be a safe and enjoyable experience. It reminded me of my school in Thessaloniki. Every grade had its own classroom. My fourth-grade teacher welcomed me and showed interest and compassion toward me. Quite a contrast from Mr. Gerasimos.

At home, I learned how to carry out my chores. I was already good at some of my responsibilities such as folding my clothes and putting things where they belonged. Dusting furniture and washing dishes was somewhat daunting. On Saturdays, clean-the-house day, a tightness in my chest kept me company until my chores were done. *What if I break one of the knickknacks while I'm dusting the tables? What if I break a dish?* I wasn't afraid of my father, but my mother was another story. Deep in my heart I knew I should not cross her.

Funny thing about childhood memories. How do we decide what we remember? One of my early memories with my new parents is a dinner. My favorite meal was *fasolakia ladera*, a vegetarian green bean dish. Most of my friends preferred this dish with meat but not I. The first time she served the dish I asked for more. I could feel my cheeks burning as the tears rolled down after she refused me a second helping of the fasolakia.

"You had enough, we need to save some for another meal."

I knew they weren't poor. They owned a pharmacy; he was the pharmacist and she assisted him. They were well known and respected in the city. In my mind it didn't make sense to refuse me a second serving. It may have made more sense if it had meat in it. In those years families waited for Sundays to indulge in a meal that included meat. But on a weekday, refusing seconds of the beans? This dish is still my favorite meatless fare. The basic recipe without meat, without potatoes is simple. First, add onions to a pot (I can hear the onion sizzling in the olive oil). Next, we add beans and simmer without water for a few minutes until they wilt. We then add canned crushed or chopped fresh tomatoes, salt, and pepper. We let them simmer until tender and add herbs. And then you have a delicious lunch or dinner. Oh, the aroma of mint and parsley permeates the nostrils and spreads throughout the kitchen.

At ten years old, my taste went beyond food choices. I knew girls my age maintained long hair. One of the first actions my new mamá took was to cut my braid off into a short bob.

"It will be easier to wash your hair," she responded to my objections. It seemed every action she took toward my care elicited tears from me. She insisted that I wear my school uniform even when it wasn't required. Any school activity including field trips, I wore the uniform. I tried to ignore the need to somehow make myself invisible. I wanted to wear the stylish pedal pushers with the bib panel on my chest and the straps buttoning on the back. Just like the two sisters next door. But Mother said no. I wanted to wear a straw hat like most of my classmates, but again, no. Looking frumpy and being seen with the old-fashioned woman who was supposed to be my mother made me squirm. My hand always released hers when we passed people on the street. In my mind that proved I wasn't her child.

Before the end of fourth grade, I lost another father. *How can this be happening?* Of the two new parents, the father was the good one. I felt secure and protected when he was home. And he died. I couldn't imagine living with just her. In my mind, I played scenarios of her yelling at me and him not being there to rescue me. *I cannot be stuck with her, where is my theo to take me away? Where is my sister?*

I found solace in the family next door. Mr. and Mrs. Pantazi invited me to their Sunday afternoon outings to Elia Square. Dimitra and her younger sister, Fotini, became my saviors. Their ages and their family's similarity to what my family was before my parents' deaths brought them closer to my heart. Meanwhile, my new mamá became the epitome of what a widow is supposed to look like.

Every time she dragged me somewhere I wanted to magically disappear. What I wanted to do was to walk behind her and pretend I didn't know her. Every day I tolerated the black-clad witch-like figure hovering over me. As if wearing black from top to bottom wasn't enough, she also wore what was considered the ultimate mourning headgear for a widow, the *blereza*. The traditional formal headpiece became a fixture on the foyer coat rack. I cringed every time she reached for the pillbox hat with the veil. I endured the turmoil in my stomach until the forty-day memorial service for my adoptive father was over. Finally, the blereza was stored away from sight.

Another source of embarrassment on a weekly basis was our visit to the hammam, the Turkish bathhouse. Many former European and Balkan territories of the Ottoman Empire continued to operate the bathhouses long after the Turkish occupation ended. For Greece the occupation ended with the revolution of 1821. And although indoor plumbing was available in most homes during the twentieth century, in the 1950s the hammams continued to operate in Veria and other cities. The bathhouses offered a different element in the lives of those who could afford them. First, their elegant architecture possessed attributes for appreciation. Circular facades with towering marble columns beckoned the passerby to enter and soak up the anticipated luxury. They provided an abundance of hot water, palatial space, and social status. Inside, the floor-to-ceiling marble walls and columns amplified my discomfort.

Instead of enjoying the luxury of the majestic atmosphere, and the soothing earth tones of the marble, I tried to find ways to avert my eyes from the naked women. I traced the veins in the marble bench. It wasn't enough to keep my eyes from glancing up at the naked bodies. Other than my sister, I had never seen anyone naked until my first visit to the hammam. And at every visit I pretended not to be looking at the full breasts and especially at the hairy triangle between their legs. Somehow it had been ingrained in me that those were private parts, and I should not be looking at them. No one told me it was okay to look at naked bodies in a bathhouse. Was it okay for a child to look? Up until that point in my life I had not scrubbed anyone's back. Someone had been washing my back but not the other way around. But here not only was I the only child in the bathhouse but was also rubbing a sponge up and down and sideways on my mother's blubber. Hiding from anyone's view was not an option but keeping my visits to the hammam from my friends was, and I managed to do so. In my heart I knew I could not live with that woman the rest of my life.

10

It's Not Gonna Happen

ME, FOTINI, AND DIMITRA ON OUR WAY TO A SCHOOL FIELD TRIP.

In late fall, the day of reckoning came. When Theo Pavlos arrived at our house, I sensed apprehension in his greeting to me and my mamá. I ran to the door to greet him. After a hug and a kiss, I felt joy and unease. That morning had started off with my mother saying, "You are not going to school today. Put on your good dress."

"Where are we going?"

"Get dressed. Your theo is coming soon."

Is he coming to take me back? He will love my lavender dress with the tiny pink roses all over the sleeves.

We stood in the front hall while they exchanged pleasantries.

Theo pried his hand from mine. "Don't cry. Why are you crying?"

"Just because" was the only thing I could say. I asked, "Where are we going all dressed up?"

He dropped his gaze to the floor. "We are going to court for the official adoption. This is a legal and final step for you to be her daughter," Theo said.

I don't recall our walk through the city to the courthouse, but I have a vivid memory of the scene inside the imposing courthouse.

It is one of those moments we have in our lives that no matter how many times we recall it, its intensity, and all the emotions it conjures, it's as if we are experiencing it right now.

We mounted the wide white marble steps, with a black wrought iron railing, into the massive hall. Our attorney approached us at the top of the staircase and Theo Pavlos introduced Eleftheria to my mother. The lawyer was a friend of our family; I remembered her from Thessaloniki. I was so impressed to know a young woman could be a lawyer. I thought she looked beautiful, with dark brown waves that barely touched her shoulders.

People streamed in; they filled the massive hall and spilled over to the curved staircase. A flurry of activity ensued in the smoke-filled hall. The lively crowd waited for their cases to be called. I didn't mind the wait. I needed time to figure out how to get out of making this woman my legal and permanent mother. *There must be a way. I can't stay with her.* I looked around the room and realized I was the only child there.

The four of us stayed together next to the only window at one end of the hall. Men paced back and forth and tried to get a glimpse inside the courtroom every time the monstrous wooden door opened. Groups of threes and fours leaned against the peeling walls that screamed for a fresh coat of paint.

Clients were demanding their attorneys to have their case heard next. They argued they had to get back to work. They had not planned to be gone all day. Smokers stepped on their cigarette butts and swiped them aside with their shoes. Even as a ten-year-old, I was aware of the irreverence to the gray and burgundy mosaic floor. Whenever an official came out and called someone else's case, my spirits were lifted. I didn't want this legal thing to go through. I couldn't imagine living the rest of my life with that woman.

Lawyers took turns checking on the time of their cases. Like a thunderbolt, Eleftheria's voice struck my ears. "They called our case, let's go in."

It came out effortlessly, spontaneously. "I am not going in."

All three of the adults looked at each other. Theo Pavlos spoke. "What is this? Don't be afraid. We will go inside, and the judge will tell us to sign some papers."

"I am not going in."

"I'll ask for a delay," Eleftheria said.

Meanwhile Theo Pavlos appeared disheartened. He struggled to convince me to go in willingly the next time we were summoned. God knows what my mother was thinking. She said nothing. The crowd had thinned out when they called our case a second time. Eleftheria looked up to my theo and tilted her head toward the gigantic brown door. He put his hand on my shoulder but did not get the result he expected.

"I am not going in."

"Pavlos, we don't have time. It's our turn."

Theo Pavlos placed his hands on my shoulders and leaned over with pleading eyes. "We must go in so you can legally stay with your mother."

She's not my mother and I don't want to stay with her. "I am not going in." Under different conditions I would be tugging at the bottom of his suit jacket and begging him to take me away. But I knew it would not work. Instead, I planted my feet on the mosaic floor that had mesmerized me earlier and stood my ground. "I am not going in."

"I will ask for a delay." Eleftheria shrugged her shoulders.

For those few minutes I was oblivious to the bystanders. I didn't care who heard me or noticed my distress. All I knew was that I didn't want to live with this woman and that I must go home with my uncle. At the time I didn't think about what thoughts occupied her, but I did think about it when I got older. I don't have to wonder how Theo Pavlos was feeling. The corners of his mouth had been turned down most of the day and now his eyes were focused on the floor. Without lifting his gaze, he attempted to comfort my mother.

"It's probably all the people making her nervous and afraid."

"No, she is being stubborn. That's how she is."

Alas, we were the only ones left rooted by the window at the end of the hallway. My back against the wall and next to Theo Pavlos, we stood there during the entire session. I didn't know what I expected, I just knew I did not want this official thing, whatever it meant, to happen.

With deliberate steps and determination, Eleftheria announced, "We are the last case, and we must go in now."

"Come on, my girl, let's go. The judge is waiting." Theo placed his hands on my shoulders again and pleaded.

A loud and resolute "I AM NOT GOING IN" accompanied my tears.

All three hovered over me saying the same things.

"You have to come, we have to go in, the judge is waiting, we are the last ones, this is what we came for." On and on they went and like them I went on and on.

"I am not going in," over and over. The deluge of tears shattered the confidence I felt all day. I had convinced myself I would leave with my theo and never come back to this mother. My unwavering determination and the flood of tears convinced them I was not budging.

Eleftheria disappeared behind the big door for the last time, and I began to relax. I was certain they could not force me in.

Between sobs, I began expressing myself to my theo. "I want to go back to the village with you. I don't want her for my mother."

"You never said anything like this to me before. You didn't complain when I saw you last." I had seen him once when he came to my almost-father's funeral.

"I kept waiting for you to come back. I kept thinking one day you would just come and take me back. I kept waiting and hoping for that day."

He again tried to reason with me. "I will not be able to educate you and provide for you in the same manner."

I clung to his arm and through my tears I gave him the best answer that made the most sense to me. "I will become a seamstress like Thea Kitsa, she can teach me, I don't have to go to college."

At that point Eleftheria returned and announced she would file for another date.

"I am going back with you, Theo."

And in silence we proceeded down the deserted staircase just as the janitor arrived to clean up the cigarette butts.

Outside the courthouse Theo Pavlos and Eleftheria agreed to reschedule the date. With hunched shoulders and a wink, he shook her hand, a mixture of disappointment and embarrassment reflected on his face.

The saga continued on the front steps of the imposing building.

My mother reached out to my chest. "I will take back this cross and chain. And everything else I bought for you."

I suppose she tried to appeal to the little girl who wanted stylish clothes and hair. She didn't realize none of that was more important than having the security of my past. And at that juncture in my life, my security was to be with my theo. None of them realized how strong the power was that had come over me to say NO. This power was stronger than any jewelry or material things she could offer me. I wanted love and affection. I turned around so she could unhook the chain and take it.

"I don't want any stuff from you."

The entire time I was holding on to the hand of a bewildered Theo Pavlos. At this point I could see he realized I was not going to surrender.

We retraced the morning's steps to the house. Nothing could pry loose the grip I had on my theo's hand. I strained to hear their conversations. They held on to the premise that I was nervous and scared of the courthouse scene. Back at the house, Theo suggested he take me back.

"She will forget about today and I will bring her back. She was just nervous with all the people around."

"I am not coming back."

I knew they didn't believe me. She made me change into the clothes I wore when Theo had brought me to her and to her husband back in the spring. She stood with her arms crossed and watched me change. We didn't take any of my things since the assumption was that I would be back. At the gate Theo Pavlos lifted his head long enough to say goodbye to her and to promise, "I will bring her back."

I couldn't wait to leave the house. I felt like jumping over the gate and running. The gate's metallic clang behind us beckoned my heart to celebrate freedom and happiness. I wanted to skip along Theo's side, and I would have if I thought he was as happy as I was. Instead, he held my hand and asked, "Why didn't you say something before?".

"I kept waiting for you to come back for me."

In a way he did come back for me, even though he hadn't planned it. We left Veria together. The courtroom scene played over and over in my head. The more I thought about it the better I felt. *I am on my way back to my yiayia's village with my beloved uncle.* I was proud I had stood my ground.

Theo Pavlos and I walked the streets of Veria in the direction of the road to Kostohori. I imagine the courthouse scene evoked different thoughts and feelings in him.

I felt lighthearted and joyful after my liberation from that woman. My thoughts turned to my fond memories of Veria and to the time I lived there with my parents and sister until I was five years old and my sister two and a half years old. We had moved from Kostohori to Veria following the conclusion of the Greek Civil War.

My father, Nikos, had left his impoverished life in Kaminia outside Athens at age seventeen with a teenager's idealistic ideas about the future of his homeland. He joined the resistance movement in the war. His unit ended up in Kostohori where he met Sofia, my mother. She, along with other young women from the village, had joined the resistance and fought in the hills of Mount Vermio. Young in this case meant teenage boys and girls. They were only kids, fifteen, sixteen, seventeen years old, fighting along with the men. *O Emfylios Polemos* (The Civil War) between the Greek government army and the Democratic army of Greece began in March 1946 and ended in August 1949 with the Greek government army the winner. In addition to the estimated 100,000 to 150,000 lives lost, Greece's economy also suffered a catastrophic loss.

The pain and suffering of a war aside, love stories had emerged. As Sofia and Nikos fought for their beliefs on the mountainside of Vermio, they discovered their love for each other. It is a strange phenomenon that love, marriage, and childbearing defy the war's interference. When I reached adulthood and experienced the strength and fervor of romantic love, I fancied that I was conceived during the passionate time of my parents' love story before they even got married. Contentment flows through my heart whenever I think of that. The idea that I was a result of a young and passionate love story enchants me. In my mind the feasibility of being a child created during the war's turmoil and in the depths of love makes perfect sense. After all, I was born a year before the war ended.

Almost to the exact date of the one-year anniversary of the war's ending, my little sister was born.

As the memories of my earlier Veria days flashed before me, Theo Pavlos and I traversed the city's streets in the direction to Kostohori in silence. The memories of my young and loving parents and baby sister comforted me.

The courthouse scene kept popping into my head, interrupting my beautiful thoughts, and my mind shifted to Thea Kitsa. I speculated what her reaction would be when she saw me with Theo. *Why did I have to think of her?* I wiped my sweaty hands on the sides of my dress and reached for Theo's hand.

The kink in my stomach disappeared as soon as my feet pounded on the familiar rocky trail. Now I knew for sure we were on our way to the village. I could have run up the hill, I did not need to ride on Kanelos.

I got the feeling that Theo felt he was stuck with me. His gaze appeared empty as he conversed with fellow travelers who had merged with us on the trail. I wondered why he didn't look as tall. His vigorous voice was barely audible. And with slumped shoulders he looked desperate and of the same age as the older men in the group.

In my universe it seemed the most natural thing for us is to be together. I had assumed he and his wife would want me to be with them as much as I wanted it. Years later I realized how naïve my thinking was relative to their feelings toward me and my sister. As an adult, I realized what a relief and comfort it must have been for them when my sister got adopted and when they found a place for me in Veria. They were young with a child. When I returned from the failed adoption, I met their new baby boy. It was logical given their circumstances that two additional children would add dramatically to their hardship. But at the age of ten, all that was beyond my understanding. And at the same time, deep down I think I knew something had to happen with me. I heard it all the time. "She has to be situated elsewhere."

Thea Kitsa came out holding a baby swaddled in a blue blanket.

"What happened? How come you brought her?"

"She is going to stay with us a few days."

"Come on, let's go inside while your theo takes care of the horse."

Nothing had changed in the onta except for the addition of a wooden cradle at the foot of the double bed. Despina was on top of the double bed, playing with her rag doll.

"Despina, I came back." I ran and sat next to her.

Thea Kitsa placed the sleeping baby in the cradle and called me over.

"Come here, sit." She patted a spot next to her on the single bed across the room. Instead of the embrace I expected, she said, "How do you think you are going to end up, growing up in the village? We cannot educate you beyond grammar school. You cannot give up the opportunity this good woman is offering you."

Theo Pavlos must have told her what happened at the courthouse.

"I don't want to be educated. You can teach me to be a seamstress."

"And then you won't have a life beyond the village." She shook her head and got up abruptly. "Watch the kids, I'm going to find your uncle."

The next morning, she got me off to school. *Now, they are stuck with me.*

As soon as I walked out of the yard, I skipped up the hill. I left Thea, her comments, and my troubled heart behind. The surprised looks from the villagers did not interrupt my stride. And when I caught up to my friends, Maritsa and Noula, I announced, "I am back. I didn't stay in Veria; I am going to live here."

We held hands the rest of the way. I got a nugget lodged in my stomach when we reached the school yard. A surge of dread replaced my excitement of seeing my friends as I caught sight of Mr. Gerasimos. The horrible teacher with his jacket draped over his shoulders was looking out from behind the schoolhouse door.

"Look at who is back. Let's see what you learned in Veria." He pointed to the last desk.

I yearned for my fourth-grade teacher from Veria, Mr. Dimitris, who was encouraging and nurturing. The antithesis of the village teacher. I overheard my theo telling Thea that when he picked up my school records, Mr. Dimitris implored him to find a way to return me to his school. He had told him, "She is an excellent student, it's a shame for her to be in a one-room schoolhouse."

Something in me found a way to cope with Mr. Gerasimos's disparaging remarks. After a bout of tears, I would bounce back. Even at the age of ten, I knew he was wrong to do that. I knew my yiayia would have said, "Don't pay attention, *na lelevo se.*"

But what concerned me was the constant reminder I heard from relatives and friends who had not stopped their "What's going to happen to Stella?" *They can't send me away after all this time.*

11

"You Are Going to America"

Snow replaced the leaves on the ground, and I continued to believe I was staying with my beloved uncle and his family, forever, in spite of the chatter I kept hearing. February 1959, my parents had been dead for a year, and I had just turned eleven. It was six months after the failed adoption in Veria. To me it felt like I always lived in the village. There wasn't a lot of space in my mind to reflect about the loss of my parents and the separation from my sister. Was it selective childhood amnesia? Or was it my innate ability to block it out because it would have been too painful? Or was I too absorbed in adjusting and assimilating in what I believed would be my permanent home?

Whenever relatives and friends gathered around the woodstove in our large one-room home, the conversation, invariably, included speculation on what was best for me, and what Kitsa and Pavlos were going to do about my situation. "Kitsa, what's going to happen?" "You can't take care of her." "She'll be much better off living in the city with another family." "Can't you find someone to adopt her?" *Why are they talking like that in front of me?*

Over and over: "She has to be situated."

I didn't understand why I had to leave. I didn't even like the teacher and my chores were taking time away from being with my friends, and still I wanted to stay. I had become Thea Kitsa's lackey; in addition to helping her with my cousins, Despina and her baby brother, Kostas, I was responsible for several chores around the house. The chore I detested the most was to fetch and lug our drinking water.

On several occasions I overheard Mrs. Katarahias comment to her friends as I passed the taverna, "What is the matter with Kitsa, sending a small child to carry water?"

Regardless of my chores and my distaste for my teacher, I still wanted to stay with her and my theo. In the early spring, when the first crocuses broke ground, deep down in my gut I knew I had to go. I knew I wasn't going to be allowed to stay and become a seamstress. No, Thea Kitsa was not going to teach me her craft. It appeared the entire village espoused the phrase "she has to be situated" as if it was their mantra. I got to the point where hearing it didn't bother me. Instead, I enjoyed my life in the village with my theo, his family, and my friends. Even though deep down, I knew I had to go.

And then it happened. Along with the blooming of crocuses and daffodils, the expected cannonball exploded and shook me from my world.

The horse's snorting in the yard announced Theo's return from Veria. Thea Kitsa bolted out of the onta. I knew the routine. He handed the shopping to Thea, unloaded his farming supplies, and led Kanelos to the barn.

When Theo came in, little Despina handed me her rag doll and bolted toward her father. With one fast swoop he lifted her above his head and swiftly landed her on the floor.

Louder than Despina's landing, wham, with a jovial voice my theo announced, "Stella, you are going to America." There was no prologue.

My grip on the rag doll tightened as my body tensed, I gasped, and looked up from where I sat on the floor. I stared at Theo in amazement. My theo, whom I adored, loomed above me and looked excited. *He looks happy. This is probably going to happen. I am going away.* I leaped up, my head was spinning, I wanted to run outside. I didn't want it to be true. I wanted to question him about what he had said and to object. But suddenly my demeanor changed as I fiddled with the doll. My head stopped spinning and I came to the realization that I had to go. I felt my anxiety melt away and acceptance engulfed me. Theo sat on the bed where I had been sleeping for the last few months, he pulled me over next to him. He placed his hand on my shoulder and rested his head on top of mine.

Across from us on the other bed I was certain I saw joy, gratification and relief stamped on Thea's face.

"Imagine that, Stella? America," she said.

Thoughts like unwanted guests occupied my mind. *Is this for my benefit? Am I supposed to get all happy and excited? Like Theo Pavlos is?* I glanced at Thea Kitsa and from the glee I saw on her face, I felt she must have been thinking, "Finally, the older one will be situated."

In those days, to the Greeks, America meant the United States of America, the USA. I had overheard people talk with envy about anyone going to America. They daydreamed about going to the land of prosperity. They talked about America as being the ultimate in getting out of poverty. "There you can get a job doing just about anything." I had heard them during visits or at the taverna. Everything they talked about was about how marvelous America was.

Theo Pavlos turned my head to face him. His smile widened, and he fixed his blue eyes on me. "They are a very nice couple. They are from Naoussa but live in America now," he said.

I had heard of Naoussa. I had been there once with my godparents during Carnavali (Mardi Gras). The city is twenty-nine kilometers from Kostohori, situated on another mountainous area of the Vermio region. But I was not destined for nearby Naoussa. From what I imagined, America was as far away in the world as I could go.

"They want to adopt an older child," he said. I listened as the thoughts churned in my head.

"Stella, listen to me, this is a good opportunity. You are lucky they want you. You will be so much better off with them."

My silence was not the right answer. Thea Kitsa encouraged him to go on.

"Tell her, Pavlos."

I thought, *Tell her what?*

"They are good people; you will have everything you need and want. You will get a good education."

Thea Kitsa added, "Do you know how many kids would love this opportunity?"

I really didn't care how many kids wanted this opportunity. I knew I didn't want it. Six months had passed since the unsuccessful adoption in Veria. I realized, *this time I must go. And this time it has to work.* I felt it in my gut, I had to go. My heart was breaking. I blurted, "Okay, I'll go."

They both sat back, and I could sense they breathed easier.

Theo continued to share the information the lawyer had given him about my soon-to-be parents. "Marianthe and Steve (he had changed his Greek name Stergios to Steve) Pardalis married late in life and cannot have children."

Steve had been in America for years in pursuit of a better life for himself and to help his family in Naoussa. He and his sister,

Elisabeth, lived with their widowed mother. Being the only male in the family he became head of the family as per tradition. Also per tradition, a brother was not allowed to marry until his sister was married. After Elisabeth's marriage, Steve emigrated to America.

He persevered and attained the American Dream. He sent much of his earnings back home to his mother and his sister's family. That type of financial aid was understood by the immigrants and expected by their families back home. After his attaining a chef's position at the Somerset Club, a private men's club on Beacon Hill in Boston, he returned to Greece to find a wife. The matchmakers used his title and position at the Somerset Club to lure a wife for the sixty-six-year-old Americano.

At the age of forty-five, Marianthe was introduced to Steve. The two families agreed to the wedding and the dowry was negotiated. A few months later they were married in Boston. After three years of trying to have a child, they decided to adopt. It was a cultural belief in that era that a couple needed at least one child. I had heard adults say, "Every couple needs a child, especially a daughter. Who else would take care of you in old age?" At forty-eight, Marianthe was post-menopausal and by Greek law at the time, she was qualified to adopt a child.

My theo's words, "They want to adopt an older girl," replayed in my mind. Even though I had said yes, and in my heart, I knew I was going for good this time, I cried. I didn't think I wanted to cry but the tears kept coming.

I knew I had to go; I had accepted it, but my thoughts kept coming. *I just want to be with them, here in the village. They don't understand I know them and love them, and I know the people in the village. I don't care about the opportunities the new parents will offer me. I want to be near my sister even if we don't see each other.*

"Don't cry, you will have a good life." Theo and Thea took turns reassuring me. Meanwhile, my little cousin, Despina, entertained her baby brother, who had awakened, with her rag doll, oblivious to the drama I was in. I wiped my tears and nose and listened to Theo Pavlos's reassurance of how good my life would be with the nice parents in America.

12
The Handkerchief

ARCH OF GALERIUS (KAMARA), THESSALONIKI.

After the big announcement, the arrangements had been made for the nice couple from America to adopt me.

I find it difficult to explain my inner dialogue and the feelings I experienced while I waited to leave the village. I kept thinking, *I have to go.* That is what the chatter had been since the funerals, she has to be situated—that is the literal translation, which means "arrangements need to be made for her." I was also thinking, *I want to stay with Theo.* I could not understand why I couldn't stay. I didn't think I was in any way disturbing their household. *Why wasn't anyone telling my theo and thea to keep me?* I grappled between surrendering to the adoption and the desire to remain in the security of my theo.

Once again, Theo Pavlos and I set out on another adventure. Relatives and friends stopped by the night before to wish us a safe journey. I could sense that everyone hoped this time would be for good. Not like the failed adoption in Veria. The sun shed its bright rays on the platanos just as we approached the fountain, for us villagers the equivalent of today's "city limits" sign.

Yiayia Anastasia, one of my yiayia's friends, was waiting for us. She wanted someone to accompany her to Veria.

"I will return with my son in the afternoon," I had heard her tell Theo the night before.

After the morning greetings, they filled the canteens, and we began our trek down the monopati. I felt I was saying goodbye forever to the fountain and to the plane tree. *Will I ever be here again?* It seemed every tree, every boulder, prompted me to think, *will I be here again?* I even wondered if I would ever again smell the offensive stench of the sheep that passed us by.

We zigzagged the familiar footpath to Veria. From there a two-hour bus ride would transport us to Thessaloniki and to my new life. I was relieved the old lady had joined us. This way I could daydream and wouldn't have to listen to my theo telling me over and over about the wonderful life I was destined to have.

Two thoughts dominated my mind—like a seesaw, up and down. One was telling me I would go to the city, meet the new relatives, I would tell my theo I don't want to stay, and we would return to Kostohori. The other thought brought sadness. It penetrated deeper, filling my entire body. It was conclusive. It was as clear as the fountain's spring water. It told me my days with my theo, the man I loved so much and thought of as my protector, had reached the end. It told me I would stay with the new family, and I would go very far away. And somehow after a while, thinking about the finality of that did not feel so bad. I had to go.

"Pavlos, you are doing the right thing. What could you possibly give her? In the end, just a sack of meager belongings for her dowry," Yiayia's friend had said to him when we approached Veria. How could she approve of and encourage what was happening to me? I could not believe those words were coming out of her mouth. I wanted to take her walking stick and let her stumble all the way down the trail. I wish I hadn't heard her. I had been distracted by the wild purple and yellow crocuses poking up their perfect little heads between the rocks along the side of the trail. I was enjoying my daydreaming and then I heard her.

When we reached Veria, it felt good to be rid of her. On our way to the bus station, Theo prepped me for our meeting with my new family. His usual thundering voice was soft. "We will only meet your mother. Your father has returned to America."

It struck me as strange that he referred to the couple as my mother and father. *Already? How can that be? I haven't met them yet. Just like that I will call them Mamá and Babá?*

He explained that Marianthe, my new mamá, would stay long enough to handle the paperwork for the adoption and then return to the US.

I kept my eyes on my dusty beige leather shoes, avoiding Theo's eyes. *I will ask for something to clean them with when we are on the bus.*

"You will have a yiayia, again."

That was supposed to make me feel good, but I didn't want a new yiayia. I had the best yiayia and I loved her even though she was dead.

After the two-hour walk from the village, I sat on the bus and was ready to sleep. Not only because I was tired but also because I wanted to avoid getting motion sickness. As always, when the driver turned on the engine it was as though he turned on a sickness in my stomach. The pungent smell of diesel was already in my nostrils from just being at the bus station. The nauseating odor I remember is a mixture of burnt oil and kerosene. If I didn't sleep through the nauseating fumes I would vomit. Sad to say, I only remember a few vomitless bus rides.

Two hours later we arrived at Vardari Square in Thessaloniki. After a few minutes on the ground, I regained my equilibrium. I wanted to get away from the fumes fast. We traversed the square in the direction of Kamara, the Arch of Galerius. If we had taken a left turn, we would be going toward the Agia Paraskevi Cemetery and to Mrs. Azat's house. But not taking a left turn did not bother me. It had been over a year since we left that neighborhood. Instead, we headed straight on Egnatia Street. When I caught sight of Kamara, I felt light-hearted. For a reason I did not know, the familiar massive arches of Thessaloniki's famous monument eased my apprehension. Perhaps the familiarity of the city and my surrendering to Theo's decision soothed my mood into tranquility.

When we turned onto Arrianou Street, my mental state changed. We would reach our destination in a few city blocks. I did not know what to expect. *Is Theo going to just drop me off and leave?*

"We are here, number forty. It's a brand-new building."

Six floors high plus a penthouse. It was two floors higher than the other two high-rise apartment buildings. I would find out later that the neighborhood was under a major transformation. Developers were buying up small old houses and converting them into multiple-story condominiums.

This is it. I cannot believe I'm going to be with another family. What if they're not nice to me? I will be very far from Theo. I will be in a different country. I may never see my sister again. I was not alone in my anxiety. I noticed Theo Pavlos's pursed lips and frown-wrinkled forehead when he rang the doorbell. I wondered if he thought he was abandoning me. Or was he nervous that they might not want to keep me? Or a little bit of both? I never found out what he was feeling.

We climbed up the mosaic staircase. I could smell the moist concrete all the way to the third floor. Theo put a hand on my shoulder and pushed on the round white bell button next to the green door. The ding-dong sound pierced my heart and traveled to my knees. I wanted to run back down the three flights of stairs before anyone opened the door. A click sound on the latch interrupted my thought. My new mamá, Marianthe, and her sister, Mitsa, my new aunt, opened the door wide.

"Welcome, welcome, come in." They both stretched one arm for us to enter.

Marianthe's thin red lips formed a smile which put me at ease. Mitsa was smiling also but I did not have the same reaction to her expression. Her eyes were not smiling. Her gray-black hair was slicked back into a bun. *Her nose is so pointy. If she let her hair loose with that black dress and her cane, she would look like the witches in the storybooks.*

We followed them into the living room. Mitsa and Theo towered over Marianthe and me. My new yiayia, Lisavouda, sat in a large armchair. Theo Pavlos greeted her first. I followed his example; I bowed and kissed her hand as was the custom to show respect to an old person. Her facial features were softer than those of both daughters. Her black kerchief framed her face. Her face, although wrinkled, was white as if the sun had not set its rays on it for years, unlike the weathered faces of the yiayias in the village. The all-black attire did not surprise me. All the grandmothers I knew wore black. However, her traditional Naoussa outfit was distinct and differed from the other yiayias. The top of her dress buttoned from the neckline to the fitted waist. The puffy sleeves buttoned at the wrists. From her waist countless yards of fabric formed gathers all around and flowed and pooled around her feet.

The combination living room/dining room was the length of the condominium. I slid as close to my theo as possible on the cushiony green sofa. I ran my hand over the sofa's smooth brown wooden arm. A lion's head was carved at the end of the arm where I cupped my hand.

My new mamá was not dressed in all black. Her blue shirtdress was similar in style to the pictures I had seen in the magazines hanging at the periptero. A matching belt tied into a bow in the center of her small waist helped me to overlook her age. I wondered how the waves of her short brown hair stayed in place and didn't budge when she moved her head. There was no comparison between her and the almost-mamá in Veria. I was relieved by her modern look even though she was older than the mothers of my peers.

As if Thea Mitsa wasn't scary enough, when she plopped with a thud on the armchair next to the yiayia, her left leg stretched out in front of her and almost reached across to where we were seated. I stared at the straight leg.

"I had an operation two years ago. After my recovery the knee will not bend."

My new family members focused on the benefits of the adoption. I listened to the adults while I indulged in the cherry glyko. How I will be going to America, the opportunities for a good education, and a better life in general. Theo Pavlos listened and agreed with them. I fell into the spell of my new life. I looked at the surroundings and found them inviting. The afternoon light poured through the floor-to-ceiling glass door next to the sofa. The oval dining room table at the other end of the room was surrounded by eight cushioned chairs. The more I looked around, the more I was able to accept the permanence of my separation from Theo's family. My gaze lingered on the green carpet under the table. It was dotted with roses as big as cabbages. The painting over the buffet had roses in a vase with the same pink shades as the ones on the carpet. Across from the buffet, the china cabinet was chock-full of glassware and dishes. I liked everything I saw but the twinge I felt from the time we got to the front door lingered inside me. Even though I knew I had to stay, something inside me stirred.

I kept thinking, *it's going to happen any moment.* They had already served us the glyko. When they offered the bonbons, once again I said the obligatory no thank you, but of course they insisted, and I obliged. All the adults shared a cordial served in dainty short glasses. They raised their glasses and cheered for the union of the two families. The only thing left to render the visit proper and complete was the coffee. The demitasse cups, with little red roses and gold trim on their rims, caught my attention. They matched the dishes in the china cabinet.

And then the moment came. Theo Pavlos stood. I sprang up and took his hand. With a bow he took the yiayia's hand and kissed it. The rest of us walked through the dining room to the hall. Theo and the two women shook hands goodbye. I felt a trail of tears down my cheeks and neck. I was squeezing Theo's hand and would not let go. He placed his free hand on my back as he bent over and hugged me. Between sobs I could hear his reassurances that everything would be okay. I could not stop crying. I think he was trying not to cry.

"Come now, don't cry. You will have a good life. We will see each other when you visit summers."

"Why are you crying? You are so lucky you are going to America," scary Mitsa snapped.

That made me cry more until I heard, "Leave her alone, let her cry. It's her uncle."

Although I didn't stop crying, my new mamá's statement calmed my insides. I noticed the difference between the two sisters' reactions. Marianthe's permission for me to cry brought on a new bout of tears, as if something guided her to validate and honor what I was feeling—exactly what we now consider proper in dealing with children's emotions.

Theo Pavlos let go of me. He wiped my face with his neatly folded handkerchief and handed it to me. He hugged me one last time and walked out.

Just like the courthouse scene in Veria, the hallway scene at Arrianou 40, Thessaloniki, is not only a vivid memory in my mind, but it is also seared in my heart.

I squeezed the handkerchief against my cheek and sobbed. I cried over the loss of the one person who connected me to my parents. I felt secure with him. And now he was gone too.

My new mother guided me to the bedroom I would be sharing with her. The room was grand compared to the onta I shared with Theo and his family. French doors opened to a balcony. Not even the luxury of the wall-to-wall closet could cheer me up.

Instead, I had other things to consider. *How will I manage with new parents, a new school, new relatives, new friends, new country? How long will I stay in this apartment before I leave for America?* I did not think it would be bad, I just wondered how it would be. I watched Marianthe unpack my few belongings.

"We will shop tomorrow, and we will fill the closet with all new clothes."

As nice as that sounded, I could not get excited. I twirled the handkerchief around my index finger in silence. She placed a porcelain doll and a pink stuffed poodle next to me. Both were a novelty for me. My friends and I had only fantasized about those kinds of toys. But instead of grabbing them, I stared down at the white and blue plaid handkerchief.

Two aftereffects from the separation that took place in the hallway stayed with me for decades. First, the handkerchief became a treasure in my mind, a relic I held on to. It moved with me wherever I went. Second, I acquired an emotional response to seeing my theo. I cried every time I saw him on my later visits back to Greece.

I experienced an automatic crying response whenever I visited him. Moments before I reached his house or the appointed meeting place, my heart beat faster, my entire being welled up with a mixture of physical sensations. All came at once; palpitations, a lump in my throat, sweaty hands, and tears, lots and lots of tears. The same occurred when we parted. Whenever I hear or read Dr. Jo Dispenza or others who remind us that the mind doesn't know the difference between what's real and what isn't, I think of my crying response at the sight of my theo. Did my mind go to the little girl who didn't want to be separated from her beloved theo? The little girl who had lost her parents and her sister? The little girl Theo Pavlos had handed a handkerchief to dry her tears when he left her at Arrianou Street in Thessaloniki? Whatever triggered that response, it lasted for decades. It dissipated when I reached my late forties and little by little it ended. At almost fifty years old, I noticed I was in front of my theo's door and had not felt any of the sensations nor did I cry when we greeted each other with a hug.

It took all those years for me to see the man as he was, not to see him as the man I had made him to be in my heart. He was not the man I had created in my mind during my need to deal with the loss of my parents and my sister. He was a man who found safe places for his nieces, places where they would be better off than if he had kept them. He was a man who raised a family of his own with the knowledge and abilities he had.

"Another mouth to feed" was a prevalent saying in Theo's culture. I believe that saying motivated him and Thea Kitsa more than the idea that his nieces would have a better life elsewhere. Of course, that was a true statement but perhaps not the main reason he did it. I have heard stories about impoverished Greek families that have taken care of orphaned or neglected children. If our yiayia had been alive, we would have been raised in the village for sure.

When Theo Pavlos left me clutching his handkerchief, my eleven-year-old world had collapsed. As much as I thought I had accepted that I must be situated, my heart was shredded. I tried to comfort myself with thinking about a better life that loomed ahead. I even rationalized that it would resemble the life my biological parents had planned for me and my sister in Thessaloniki. I reminded myself that I was back on familiar ground, not too far from my old neighborhood. But I was still apprehensive.

13

In My Hometown, All New Faces

I woke up to the early spring sunshine flickering through the sheer curtains. I peered across the room to see the other bed in the room where my mother-to-be had slept. The bed was made. I lay under the covers, not knowing what to do. I wanted to use the bathroom, which was down the hall, but what if I ran into one of the women? *Should I get dressed first and then go to the bathroom?*

And just like magic my mother-to-be walked in and smiled.

"Good morning, did you sleep well?"

I nodded.

"Go ahead, wash up and come to the kitchen. I have fresh bread slices with butter and honey for you."

The indoor bathroom was a luxury I had heard about. In addition to the toilet, it had a sink and a bathtub, hot and cold running water. No more boiling water and baths in a portable aluminum tub in the backyard or in the living room. Looking at the tub while I sat on the toilet, I thought of how embarrassed I would be when Marianthe or Mitsa gave me a bath. It was common knowledge that even eleven-year-old children did not bathe themselves. I dreaded the thought of their seeing me naked. So many new things to get used to.

Eating breakfast with the yiayia and the two sisters was a pleasant experience. Calling the grandmother Yiayia and the aunt Thea was easy. I was used to calling non-relatives by their respective titles. It was second nature to us kids in the village. But to address Marianthe as Mamá? That word stuck in my throat. It wouldn't come out until later in the day. It felt fake. It did not feel natural. I felt as though I was telling a lie to myself, but I said it.

"Mamá, where is my sweater?" I asked from the adjacent room. I felt uneasy to say it in front of her. Kind of embarrassed because I knew she wasn't my mother. But the delight shown on her face when she breezed into the room with a big smile reassured me that I had done something good.

"Come, I'll show you where I put everything."

I didn't even need a sweater. It was an excuse to test my ability to call her Mamá.

The rest of the day was a whirlwind of relatives who stopped by to meet Marianthe's daughter.

After breakfast I met their cousins and according to the custom, I called them Thea and Theo without a problem. They showered me with gifts: a gold cross, gold pendant, rings, an ID bracelet, all of which were engraved with my name. I recalled how I had admired the ID bracelets of my former neighbor friends Dimitra and Fotini from Veria.

In the afternoon I met Rena and Maro. Rena was my age and I learned we would be going to school together and be in the same grade. Maro was four years older and became our teenage role model. I felt comfortable with my new neighbor friends. I ended up spending a great deal of time with them in the penthouse of our building and in the nearby park.

The flurry of activity, gifts, and the making of new friends in the same building helped to ease the awkwardness I felt in my new home. But I agonized over going to a new school, a new teacher, and new kids. *Will the teachers and students be as friendly and accepting as everyone I had met today?*

After a few days I adjusted to my new surroundings as if I was in a pretend play. I had accepted the separation from my theo. It became easier to recall and reflect on the emotional scene in the hallway, where we said our final goodbye. I still cried but every time it was for a shorter period. During the crying sessions I reminded myself of the villagers saying, "the older one has to get situated." Somehow, the saying that had aroused anger and apprehension in me back in the village now calmed me in my new home with my new family. It helped me to accept that this was my life now and to embrace its permanence. I tried to feel more comfortable when I called Marianthe "Mamá." The hesitation and nervousness of saying it gradually waned. I tried to remember how I behaved and felt with my biological mother. I wanted my new family to feel real. I wanted things to work out.

When thoughts of Theo Pavlos floated in my head, I pushed them away. I kept reminding myself, *I'm situated, and it will be good for me for the rest of my life. Theo Pavlos did this for my own good. Look at all the nice new relatives and friends I have. And I've only been here a few days.*

I find it peculiar that my theo popped in and out of my thoughts, but I don't recall thinking about my parents. Were the events during the past year severe enough to have pushed their loss to the recesses of my mind? Was I suffering from a childhood trauma syndrome? Even though I remembered my parents, I did not feel the distress I had felt on the days of their funerals and during the dreary days that followed. It was as though they had not existed. How could I not yearn for my mother's warm embrace? Or my father's winking at me and patting me on the back just before he mounted his motorcycle? What about playing with my sister? It must have been my way of coping with my losses, to put them out of my mind. Again, childhood amnesia comes to mind.

Many years later I revisited those tender memories of my mother, father, and sister. I recalled and sensed my parents' tenderness and love. My sister's attachment to me and the shared fun and even the squabbling times we shared became alive. The responsibility and care I felt for her back then became a glue for us later in life. But all those feelings and memories were obscured during the years I was adjusting to finding my new place in life. Once I had accepted that I needed to be situated somewhere, I focused on making my new life a success.

Even though I knew I would be leaving Thessaloniki, I was eager to like the new school. My desire to feel settled into a new life had increased in the few days I had spent with the new family members. My new friend, Rena, gave me encouragement.

"You'll see all the kids, especially my friends, will welcome you."

She assured me that by my first day of school she would have paved the way for a smooth transition. My new friend's kindness lifted my spirits. I looked forward to attending school.

Even though I looked forward to attending a city school again, I found myself feeling nervous. An older student escorted me to my classroom. He skedaddled before I could muster the courage to knock on the door. Relief replaced my apprehension when I spotted Rena in the classroom and an empty space next to her on the two-seater desk. Her chestnut-brown braid hung halfway down the back of her seat, thick and long. Its color and thickness reminded me of how anxious I was for mine to grow back to the length it had before my almost-mamá in Veria chopped it off. *Ugh, that woman was awful, thank God I said no to that adoption.*

The teacher's wide smile and pleasant greeting removed the unease I felt. Her crisp white blouse was a striking contrast to the ruby lips that formed her welcoming smile. When she stretched out her arm pointing to the room and instructed me to take any empty seat, I liked her. I made a beeline toward Rena's desk and slid into the seat next to her. At recess a group of girls surrounded me and Rena. Their curious glances were replaced with smiles as soon as someone suggested we all play hopscotch.

It felt natural and good to walk home with my new best friend. I was excited to go home to tell Mamá about my day at school and to do my homework. Rena and I made a good team working on school projects. Both of us were good students, focused, and were sponges for knowledge. I brought home my final report card with a ten, the highest grade possible. Just like when I did when my parents were alive and in the fourth grade in Veria. Mamá, Thea Mitsa and Yiayia praised me and showed off my report card to visitors. *They must be happy they adopted a good student.* Why did I even think that?

The end of fifth grade meant I was getting closer to my departure for America. I would be leaving my new friend behind. An entire new world awaited me. I was looking forward to getting on with it. I was curious, I wondered what this America was like. I chose to believe and accept that I was lucky to be going. At the same time, I was afraid. What would it be like so far away from Theo Pavlos, my sister, and all the people I knew? Even though I had not seen any of them since my arrival in Thessaloniki, I still felt my connection to them. I kept thinking we would soon see each other again now that school was over.

A combination of relief and apprehension came over me when my new mother informed me that she had to return to America without me. At first, I thought, *Great, I don't have to leave Greece, I can stay near the people I know.* But then I wondered if I was really going to live with my new parents. *What if I am left with Thea Mitsa forever? Marianthe is the nice sister and my mamá.*

"Who will take me to America?"

"Thea Mitsa and the lawyer will make the arrangements. You don't have to worry about anything. By the end of summer everything will be in order."

I did not want to show my concern about being left behind nor my happiness of staying in Greece. I didn't know what I was expected to say. I felt conflicted. *Will I be able to see my sister? Will I visit the village to spend time with Theo Pavlos and all the people I know? Who will take me there to see them?* I didn't dare to ask. I didn't know if I was allowed to talk about the people from my past. When I had asked about seeing my theo, Mamá said, "You can write to him when we get to America." After that I was afraid to ask. Since I was staying in Greece for the summer, I got it in my head that I would get to see him.

I fluctuated between a sense of insecurity and satisfaction. Rena and I said a tearful goodbye with a promise to write to each other and to send pictures when her family left to spend the summer with her grandparents. My new parents would be far away, and Thea Mitsa would be in charge of me. None of that felt comforting. On the other hand, I would remain in familiar territory and meet more new relatives in Naoussa. Thea Mitsa's assurances about the fun I would have with my new cousins boosted my spirit. "You will go on picnics, hikes, and festivals. You'll see, it will be a fun summer for you."

14
Summer of 1959

THE MONUMENT COMMEMORATING THE WOMEN AND CHILDREN WHO THREW THEMSELVES
IN THE ARAPITSA RIVER IN 1822 TO AVOID THE TURKISH BRUTALITIES.
PHOTOGRAPH IS COURTESY OF GEORGE DOUTSIS.

In the summer of 1959, I felt I was an orphan again. Neither of my adoptive parents was with me. I was left in the care of Thea Mitsa while we waited for my adoption paperwork to be completed.

In Naoussa, Thea Mitsa would be tending to her peach orchards and the business of exporting them to Germany. She moaned and groaned about how difficult it would be now that her husband was dead, and she had to do it alone. She wished her son was not serving in the military so that he could be there to help.

Before we left for Naoussa I met her son, my new cousin Dino, short for Konstantinos. He spent a few days with us before our move to Naoussa. The twenty-one-year-old soldier made an impression on me. The khaki uniform, his short, wavy black hair and olive complexion reminded me of men I had seen on the covers of magazines. I was puzzled by his doting over his mother and grandmother. It was unusual to see a man serving a beverage or food to women. He fussed over them; he straightened the afghan over Yiayia's legs. I was surprised as I watched him place a crochet shawl over his mother's shoulders. He was gentle and affectionate. I had not seen anything like it before.

Dino also helped with the dishes and even swept the floors. Everything I had seen and heard stressed that tradition dictated the women did all the caring. The men did not get involved in house chores nor did they show the kind of sensitivity my new cousin exhibited. At eleven years old, I did not know that tradition was a form of male chauvinism. Later in my teenage years, I learned about it and abhorred the concept. But as an eleven-year-old, I found it strange for Dino, a seemingly strong and vivacious young man, to hang out with the two elderly women and me.

There was a tearful goodbye when we got in the taxi for Naoussa. Dino reassured his mother that he would write and try to get another leave during the summer.

I sat in the back seat with Yiayia. Thea Mitsa sat next to the driver so her straight leg could fit. Another taxi ride on the same roads and through the same villages as my first taxi ride. Although memories of the past entered my mind, this time my anxieties were different. I would be meeting many more relatives. When we drove through Veria, nostalgia took hold of me because I knew Kostohori was nearby. I hadn't seen Theo Pavlos for months. I wondered if he missed me. If he knew I was still in Greece. If he had talked to Nitsa. I longed to hear news of my little sister. Veria was behind us, and Thea Mitsa did not mention Kostohori or my theo.

The scenery changed when we turned off the highway and onto the dirt road toward Naoussa. The official name is the Heroic City of Naoussa. It is situated at the foothills of the Vermio mountains, the same shared by Veria and Kostohori. So close and yet so far away for me and the people I loved and had left behind.

After ninety-six kilometers of driving, we began our ascent to the city of Naoussa. Endless views of lush orchards of peaches, cherries, apples, and grapes whizzed by us. Naoussa is known for its peaches. Once you hold that velvety, juicy, aromatic fruit and bite into it, you will yearn to taste only peaches like that, always. Naoussa is also known for its grape variety which produces a dry red wine,

Xinomavro. Naoussa's vineyards and wine-making activity date back to the 16th century. Thea Mitsa kept turning her long neck from left to right and pointing out her orchards.

In addition to its ancient Greek history, Naoussa is known for a dramatic action taken during the Greek War of Independence from the Ottoman Empire. When the Turks overcame the Greek resistance and took over the city, a general massacre followed. The rebels left the city. Women and children were being taken as slaves. To avoid slavery and other acts of cruelty, some of the women, with their children in their arms, threw themselves over a cliff into the Arapitsa River.

Thea Mitsa's and my adoptive mother's house was a block from the Arapitsa River. The house, like all others, was built to the edge of the street. The dark wood double doors reached all the way to the second floor. We stepped into a cobblestone entry the size of a modern drive-way. It extended the depth of the house. In the past it had accommo-dated the horse and buggy with room to spare. The first floor offered more cobblestones for the entryway which led to the stairway. At the next landing a regular-size door opened to the old barn converted to a storage area for the wooden fruit crates that would be filled with peaches.

One floor up was the living space. The high ceilings and large rooms reminded me of the village. With one big difference: there were multiple rooms here, not just one onta. Much of the furniture was built-in and covered in traditional hand-loomed textiles. The dark reds and blues formed birds facing each other on a black back-ground. There were several seating areas with as many designs of birds and flowers covering the numerous seats and pillows. The wall benches displayed an array of colorful seating options. I would learn later about the handweavers' pride in carrying on with the tradition of making coarse and durable fabrics.

"Bring your things in there, you will be sleeping in that room." Thea Mitsa pointed to the second door off the living room.

"Yiayia and I sleep here." She walked through the first doorway.

I was surprised that the bathroom, which was on the same floor but separated by a covered porch, had a Turkish toilet and a sink out-side of it. I was familiar with the cement toilet, which consisted of a hole in the center with the shape of two feet formed on either side of it. I was challenged every time I positioned my little feet on either side of the hole.

Throughout our first evening in Naoussa, Thea Mitsa spoke incessantly about the next day's activities.

"Relatives will be coming over to welcome Yiayia back and also to meet you." It was protocol for all relatives to stop in to welcome the people returning for the cool summer weather. There was a price to pay if you dared not to follow this rule, especially when the returning person was elderly. The offended party would go as far as not to speak to the offender for a long time. Only after a viable excuse or an apology would there be sufficient reason for a reconciliation.

"You will meet many aunts, uncles, and cousins," she had said. As I pulled the night covers over my head, I tried not to be nervous about the next day. I felt like I was a spectacle to be scrutinized by the new relatives. *Come to see the orphan Marianthe adopted.* Thea Mitsa's words replayed over and over in my mind.

"They all want to meet you."

The hustle and bustle the next day was overwhelming. There was a parade of aunts, uncles, and cousins. They were all second cousins to me. Their parents were first cousins to my mamá and Thea Mitsa. My female cousins ranged from the same age as me to six years younger and to three years older. The boy cousins were older by three to six years. As encouraging as the prospect of having choices for playmates was, the flurry of activity was daunting. The adults congregated at the far side of the living room and enjoyed their coffee and sweets. The boy cousins made an appearance and took off to play outside. That left me with my female cousins. I wondered if they felt as awkward as I did. We sat across from each other, occasionally staring, but without saying much of anything.

Thea Sofia and her five daughters left first. All five wore their long, brown hair in two braids. They sprang off their seats in unison as soon as their mother gave the signal to get up. Thea Maria, Thea Sofia's sister, continued in a quiet conversation with Yiayia. Her older daughter, Litsa, had left, leaving her twin daughters, Katina and Antonia. They whispered to each other and then to my surprise I heard, "Can we take Stella out to meet our friends at the park?"

My spirits lifted at the prospect of being accepted enough for them to spend time with me without being told by an adult to do so. I had a feeling they came to meet me because they were told they must. I was certain they were curious to see the orphan their aunt adopted. In my mind, their asking me to go out meant they liked me. Permission was granted and the seed of friendship was planted. Antonia and Katina were six months older than me. On the way to the park the shyness we had exhibited in the living room vanished.

"What is Thessaloniki like?" Katina asked.

"We've only been there once to Thea Mitsa's apartment," Antonia added.

"It's really big. I used to live near Vardari Square, where the bus station is. Arrianou Street near Kamara is not too far from there. There are movie theaters, tall buildings, and in the center, there are department stores."

After a walk in the park, back at the house, I asked, "Will you come over tomorrow?"

"We will pick you up after breakfast," Katina said.

I walked through the big wood doors feeling lighthearted. All my apprehension about my time in Naoussa melted away. I skipped all the way to the stairs. *I will have a good summer until it's time to leave for America.*

Friendships with my other cousins sprouted. Veta, the oldest of the five sisters, became the unofficial guardian of us. She was instructed to always keep an eye on us. Next in line, Athena was my age. Dina and Anastasia were two and three years younger, followed by the baby of their family, Soty. At five years old, Soty was not considered part of our group. It would be decades later when she and I, the unlikely playmates, became close friends and koumbares.

I began to feel at ease in my new environment. Being the object of curiosity did not bother me as much. My acceptance by the relatives as one of them enabled me to endure the quizzical glances from the other locals. The news of an adoption is big in a small city where everyone knows everyone. People looked at me as if I was an oddity. That is how I saw it. I felt embarrassed. It resurrected the feelings I had back at the village when those black-clad creatures looked at me with pity.

There were picnics and outings with the relatives. Whether at the peach or cherry orchards or the farm, it was always a fun time for us kids while the adults worked the orchards. I realized the games we played were universal: hopscotch, hide-and-go-seek, koumbares, jump rope, and climbing trees.

As I waited for the summer of 1959 to come to an end and for my paperwork to be finalized so that I could be on my way to America, I was not aware nor did it affect me in any way that Alaska and Hawaii had officially become US states. However, the same year I arrived in America was also the year Mattel's Barbie doll arrived in toy stores. Barbie never made it into my doll collection, but I find the idea that we both debuted in the US at the same time a childhood point of interest.

Meanwhile, in anticipation of my big trip, I became impatient. My cousins went back to school, and we were not spending much time together. Thea Mitsa kept reassuring me that the paperwork was almost complete, and I would soon be leaving to unite with my parents.

15

America on TWA

MY PASSPORT PICTURE AND ITEMS FOR ONBOARD ENTERTAINMENT.

At last, my adoption papers and visa were finalized. This meant I would soon be leaving my homeland and the familiarity of its customs. I would also be leaving the life I knew growing up in the village, and my two stints living in Thessaloniki, with my biological parents and sister and later with my adoptive mother. The glorious summer I experienced in Naoussa was coming to an end. I would be separated from all my relatives and friends. I was experiencing anxiety reflecting on what I was leaving behind. But I also felt eager to begin my life in America with my adoptive parents. By the end of the summer, I felt resolute in accepting the adoption.

Excitement prevailed as we prepared for my departure. The festive atmosphere was quite a contrast when compared to my initial arrival in Naoussa. When I had arrived in Naoussa I was nervous and apprehensive as to what awaited me. But after a summer full of fun activities and new relationships, I felt like a welcomed member of my extended adoptive family.

The evening before my departure, the traditional goodbye parade lasted for hours. The visitors expressed wishes appropriate for travelers in general and a few specific to me.

Safe trip, give our regards to your parents, be careful, send us pictures so we can see what it's like in America. The most repeated one was remember to write. Antonia and Katina were the last ones to leave.

We didn't cry, we just hugged, a big and long bear hug.

"Remember to write," Antonia said.

"And send pictures," added Katina.

Thea Mitsa tended to Yiayia's needs and put her to bed. Then we finished the last-minute packing.

Yiayia would be looked after by the aunts while Thea Mitsa and I travelled to Athens for my flight to Boston, Massachusetts. It was a customary practice for other family members to care for the elderly relatives when the caregiver was away. From what I remember, no one complained—or at least not outwardly—about having the responsibility added to their busy family lives.

It took me a while to fall asleep that night. The anticipation of the next day's trip brought a stream of thoughts that kept me awake for a long time. The next morning, I was startled when I heard, "What did you do? You went back to sleep?" Thea Mitsa pulled the sheet off my face.

I sprung up. "I will get ready fast."

"Breakfast is ready. Thea Sofia and Theo Christos are here."

I put on my clothes as fast as my nerves allowed. I was upset with myself. *How could I have gone back to sleep?* I hurried to the bathroom and washed my face before I went into the kitchen. We had been taught, "You never say good morning to anyone without first washing your face."

"Here, eat a piece of *tiropita*," Thea Sofia urged me.

"I am bringing the suitcases downstairs. Don't be long," Theo Christos said.

Thea Sofia and I kissed on both cheeks. I kissed Yiayia's hand.

I bolted down the stairs, eager to start the beginning of my journey. Behind me Thea Mitsa and the clunk-clunk-clunk of her cane followed.

We walked to the bus station. Theo Christos carried the two suitcases, and I carried the carpetbag. Workers passed us as they hustled to their jobs. The aroma of fresh-baked bread that spilled out onto the street was inviting. There were *koulouria* displayed in a huge basket in the window. There was no way one could walk by on an empty stomach and not go into the bakery. Good thing I had eaten the tiropita before we left.

As expected, Theo Christos had covered the three blocks to the bus station before us. By the time we arrived he had loaded our suitcases on the bus. Theo Christos ensured the first row was reserved for us. Being in the first row gave Thea Mitsa the space she needed for her straight leg. He wished us a safe trip before leaving to join his friends for coffee.

Our overnight in Thessaloniki was long enough to pick up my airline ticket, for friends and relatives to say goodbye, and to take a train to Athens. After the travel agent handed the ticket to Thea, the young woman passed a package to me containing a bucket bag. The polite agent did not look old enough to have what I considered such an important job. Her chestnut-brown hair brushed across her shoulders every time she reached for a piece of paper and a pen. I admired the bangs that covered her forehead all the way to the top of her eyebrows. Right then and there I made up my mind to have bangs when I got to America. *Surely my new mother will say yes.*

"Thank you, Mrs. Mitsa." The agent and Thea Mitsa shook hands.

To me, she said. "Have a good trip."

Thea Mitsa and I stepped out onto Aristotelous Square, the main square of Thessaloniki. The wide square was bordered by neoclassical buildings, cafes, restaurants, shops, and offices, all interspersed with beautiful gardens of flowers and greenery.

While my thea was putting on her sunglasses and adjusting her purse on her arm, I held the Olympic Airways bucket bag against my chest. And then I held it away from me to take a closer look at the words "Olympic Airways" in blue ink, and the five interlocked Olympic rings in blue, yellow, black, green, and red.

I looked around at the line of old buildings and down past the Thessaloniki promenade, across to the bustling harbor. At the time I did not appreciate the grandeur of the architecture or the view of the Thermaic Gulf. Instead, I was engrossed in my bucket travel bag and my airplane ticket to America.

My big trip finally started when we boarded the train at the station in Thessaloniki destined for Athens, where I would take my flight. The train station was next to the bus depot at the Vardari Square neighborhood. I recognized the bus depot, Agia Paraskevi Cemetery, and the familiar hustle and bustle of the area.

My mind took a detour and traveled along the cemetery wall up to Mrs. Azat's house. I saw my mother and father sitting in the back yard. My little sister was on my mother's lap. My father had pulled a wooden crate next to his chair and patted it for me to sit next to him. He ran his hand over my head smoothing my hair.

"I have news for you girls." He drew me closer until my head rested on the side of his lap. Nitsa stopped playing with my mother's cross and turned to face him.

"I am getting a sidecar for my motorcycle. All four of us can go places together. To the beach, to the fairs and to visit friends."

I sat up and hugged him. After he kissed the top of my head, he sat me on his lap. Nitsa sprung up off our mother's lap and landed on our father's. She laced her arms around him.

The sound of screeching brakes and loud horns blowing brought me back to the reality of Vardari Square and the train station.

The train ride was another first for me. Up until then my modes of transportation had been on foot, on a horse, in a farm wagon, in a taxi, and on a bus. I found the seats on the train to be like the seats on a bus except there was more legroom. The train ride revealed exceptional scenery which I noticed at the time, but did not give the appreciation it deserved. There were glimpses of beaches, an abundance of mountain views, including Mount Olympus. I saw panoramic vistas consisting of endless green farm fields and flowing rivers. We passed through mountain gorges and through little villages. In the background I kept hearing the clickity-clack of the train and was eventually lulled to sleep.

The train ride took over five hours.

The screeching sound of the brakes as the train approached the Athens station woke me. It was the end of the line.

"You stay with the suitcases while I find a porter to help us."

After our overnight with relatives, Thea Mitsa and I took the Olympic Airways bus from Syntagma Square in Athens to Ellinikon International Airport in Glyfada. Excitement and apprehension were my new companions. I had never flown before and I was to make this trip by myself. No one had told me how long the flight would be. "Before you know it you will be in America" was what I had heard in the days prior to the flight. My friend Rena helped me practice the two words I would need, yes and no. That was the extent of my English.

"Don't worry, the airlines have people to translate for you," Thea Mitsa reassured me.

She accompanied me as far as the final checkpoint at the gate. When the officer started to open my bucket bag, I thought I would die. I could feel my cheeks on fire and my eyes brimming with tears. In my prized bucket bag was a box of sanitary napkins. I had got my period two days prior to my flight. I was mortified. I assumed no one was supposed to know when I was menstruating.

I was scared and embarrassed the first time I got it. It happened a week after Theo Pavlos dropped me off at Mamá's condominium. No one had ever explained menstruation to me. At first, I thought I would ignore it and not say anything. But there was blood on the toilet paper, and it scared me. The three women were at the kitchen table.

"I have blood."

"Oh, don't worry. It's normal. It's your period, you will get it once a month. Come with me. I will give you a cloth and show you what to do."

Yiayia said, "You are now a woman."

Thea Mitsa added, "I will make a special meal to celebrate."

In the village I had seen Thea Kitsa washing the square cloths with blood on them. I never knew what they were, but I had assumed they were for women, not for kids. My mamá showed me how to fold and pin the cloth to my underwear to hold it in place. The sanitary napkins Thea Mitsa bought for me were for my trip; up until then I had used facecloths.

When the officer took the box out to get a better look inside the bag, I closed my eyes to keep the tears from flowing. Of course, that did not work. Once he tightened the string on my bag, I regained my composure. I looked up and waved goodbye to Thea, who by then was on the other side of the gate. A kind woman dressed in a pressed blue uniform approached me. She held papers in one hand and took my hand with the other, leading me to the airplane.

The rhythmic click-click of her heels hitting the marble floor made her important in my mind. She smiled and told me she would escort me to my seat and then the nice ladies on the airplane would take care of me. No one had told me that she would be the last person to speak to me in Greek. She escorted me to the first row of three seats. I sat next to the window. She put my bucket bag on the seat next to me. Her cherry red lips parted in a smile as she wished me a good trip.

Apprehension returned as the two beautiful women in light blue uniforms with smart pillbox-type hats knelt next to me. They were smiling and I was certain they were saying something pleasant, but I had no clue. My blank stare was all I could give them for an answer. I noticed their lapel pins with the letters TWA. I found out later those were their wings and the name of the airline.

I was on board a Trans World Airlines flight on my way to the USA. I left Athens on September 29 and arrived in New York on September 30. Nowadays we consider an eleven-hour flight long. Today's eleven-hour flight took sixteen hours in 1959. I must have slept most of the flight. No matter how hard I have tried throughout my life to recall details of the long ride, only two images have stayed in my mind and heart. Two sweet, friendly young ladies in light blue suits kneeling or sitting next to me. To me they were stylish girls like the models I had seen in magazines. I couldn't think of them as women.

One memory is of the time they offered me food. I used my English and said no. The food looked different than what I was used to, and I didn't know if I had to pay. No one had prepared me for what to expect or what to do on the airplane. Another memory is the toys, including wings, they gave me. I wasn't familiar with those either. The blond flight attendant, whose complexion reminded me of the porcelain-faced doll my friend Rena had, sat in the seat next to me. She peeled strips off one side of the board and created images on the other side on the smooth black surface of the *magic board*. The other flight attendant stopped by and offered me a beverage which I refused. It would be years before I found out TWA called their flight attendants hostesses. I can't imagine that I didn't use the bathroom, especially since I was menstruating. It's likely one of them led me to the lavatory and showed me how to use it. And did I not drink nor eat anything? All those hours? Why did I block most everything out? It was a major event in my life and yet the details have remained dormant somewhere on the hard drive of my brain. I have savored the memory of two kind, sweet girls who showed genuine concern for my wellbeing. They made several attempts to make my flight pleasant and comfortable.

Before we landed they placed the toys and wings in my carry-on bag. I kept that bag a long time. But after years of being packed away and surviving several moves, the bucket bag with the Olympic rings logo deteriorated. With a pang in my heart, I held it against my chest, brought it to my lips and placed it in the wastebasket under the kitchen sink in Brighton. But the toys and the wings have been packed and unpacked with every move I have made and still reside in a drawer in my home. A reminder of my journey to my new country.

16

Arrival, Pick-up, and Delivery

Early in the morning on September 30, 1959, after two stops and almost twenty-four hours since leaving Athens, our TWA flight landed at Idlewild Airport in New York City in the United States. I had landed in America. Today, that airport is known as JFK. It was renamed John F. Kennedy International Airport, following the 1963 assassination of the thirty-fifth president of the United States.

I had no idea what to expect. I had watched the flight attendant place the toys into my bag. I thought she just wanted to tidy up. My real focus was watching the water and buildings on the ground. They became larger and more distinct as the plane got closer to them. Suddenly, I was forced to look away from the window. My stomach started to churn, the same as when I was at the bus stations traveling in Greece. There was no diesel smell, just the churning sensation in my stomach. The noise from outside got louder and louder and sounded like a rushing wind mixed with running machinery. And then with a loud bang the plane hit the ground. The people burst into applause. I looked around to see why. *Everything must be okay if people are clapping. No one looks scared or upset.* They were smiling and patted each other on their shoulders. As the plane continued to move ahead, I felt as though we were speeding over bumps and at the same time, I was trying to talk my stomach out of feeling sick. *I cannot throw up. It's almost over.* Finally, the airplane came to an abrupt stop. I watched passengers get up from their seats and pick up bags from the floor, sweaters, and packages from a shelf above their seats. I didn't move. I did not know what to expect once the plane landed. The flight attendant had probably explained it, but I didn't speak English.

I was relieved to see her smiling face as she approached me. The pillbox hat with the TWA logo on its side complemented her blond hair. She unbuckled my seat belt and took my hand. She gently guided me off my seat, picked up my treasured bucket bag and led me out the door and down the metal staircase. Everywhere I looked I saw

TWA letters displayed. On the stairs, on the concrete buildings across from where we were standing, on the white bus next to the airplane. *This is America. I am here.*

At the bottom of the stairs another model-like young lady met us. The two of them conversed in a language I did not understand. They signed some papers, and I was turned over to the new person as the flight attendant waved goodbye. I felt so small walking next to that beautiful stranger as we walked through the terminal. We were in a huge area of the building with people milling around. I stood close to her, and I trusted everything was going the way it was supposed to go. I just wanted to make sure I didn't get lost. She retrieved my suitcase. We walked through two areas where she showed my passport and the man in a dark blue uniform looked at the passport and then at me. He stamped something on it. I thought that made it official I was in America. At the next stop, another uniformed man wearing glasses checked something on my suitcase and waved us on.

At last, I thought I would see my parents. The TWA representative and I walked down a long corridor. I was wondering how long it would be before I could talk to someone in Greek so I could ask for my parents. Finally, she opened a door where two men waited. *One of them is my father. Of course, not the one behind the desk. But the other one is too old to be my father.*

More papers were signed. The representative patted me on my shoulder and said something. Perhaps, welcome to the United States, good luck? I'll never know.

Ah, what a relief when I heard in my own language, "Welcome, your parents sent me."

More relief. *He is not my father*

He put his glasses on before signing some papers. Then he stood, buttoned his plaid suit jacket, and shook hands with the man in the blue uniform behind the desk.

"Come, I will drive you to Boston where your parents are waiting for you."

Mr. Kutrubes was the travel agent my parents used for all their travel needs. Because of the distance and the paperwork required for my entry into the US, they engaged him for his services. *Why didn't they come with him?*

"Your parents don't have a car. And their English is not good enough to deal with the paperwork and the authorities."

I accepted his explanation. What other choice did I have?

I'm almost there. He said it will be a four-hour drive. Two hundred and fifty miles, whatever that means. When will I see my parents? Are they really in Boston waiting for me? This man seems nice enough; he's like a grandfather.

He asked me about my trip. I shared what I remembered. He assured me I would be happy with my life in the United States. I had my doubts about that. I already realized how difficult it is not being able to communicate. I decided to sleep and not think about any of it.

Sleep was my way of avoiding the thoughts and questions swirling in my mind. I had expected to be met by my parents. I thought I was going to Boston. Instead, I found myself in New York. I wished one of my parents had come with the travel agent to meet me. But in my usual style, I settled down and accepted the situation. Accepting situations is what I had been doing the past year and a half. I wish I had not outgrown that character trait as I entered adulthood. I could have used that simple wisdom in my thirties and forties when I had difficulty accepting life's challenges. That ability I had at ten and eleven would have come in handy. To meet those challenges without resistance. It took me some years to work my way back to the resilience I had at that age and through my adolescence.

I don't remember Mr. Kutrubes waking me up. Next thing I knew we were sitting in his office in downtown Boston. After the vastness of the airport, I thought his office was small and cluttered. My parents, Steve and Marianthe Pardalis, arrived to claim their prize. They must have felt as awkward as I did. I did not feel the excitement I had felt when my father Nikos came home after work. I did not feel the warmth I remembered of my mother Sofia when she hugged me. I did not feel the security I felt when I was with my parents or with Theo Pavlos. We kissed on both cheeks.

"Welcome, how was your flight?"

They shook hands with the travel agent. Outside they informed me, "You will spend the night with our friends. The apartment we rented is not ready yet. And we are staying in a one-room studio."

"But I don't know your friends. Do they speak Greek?"

"Yes, they do, don't worry. They are very nice ladies," my new mother reassured me.

Meanwhile I was processing my first impression of my new father and their welcome. *He is too old to be my father. He is the age of Mr. Kutrubes. Why didn't they have the apartment ready before my arrival? Were they happy to have me? If they were, why didn't one of them come to New York to meet me? How can they have me stay with strangers my first night in the new country? Why did they adopt me?* I wanted to believe it was a case of being practical. I didn't want to think they did it to have someone to take care of them.

"You have a good night's rest, and I will see you tomorrow," my new babá said to me and then turned down Tremont Street to their studio apartment. A few blocks from the travel agency my mamá and I arrived at the friends' apartment. We climbed the wooden staircase to the second floor of the brick building. Three sisters in bright print shirt dresses greeted us.

In their kitchen, all three sisters tended to serving coffee, koulourakia, and lemon cake. The white crochet cloth on the table made me feel at home. I could finally relax. I had not felt at ease since I had boarded the airplane in Athens. It seemed so long ago. I felt reassured, being surrounded by friendly women who spoke my language and served familiar delicacies. The oldest one, wearing her glasses at the tip of her nose, looked at me from above the black frames and in soft melodious voice offered me a piece of cake. I accepted it without hesitation.

"We will have lamb and potatoes in two hours. Do you like meat?" asked the sister in the dress with yellow roses.

I felt the comfort I had expected and did not feel at the travel agent's office when my parents had walked in. Perhaps I felt comfortable with the three sisters because I was inclined to accept them without reservation, since they weren't going to be family. After the coffee Mamá walked me to the bedroom. She had taken a dress out of the suitcase and handed it to me to change before dinner.

"You don't have to wait for me to change." I shouldn't have been embarrassed to change in front of her. I had done it in Thessaloniki.

"If you are sure. I will leave you now. Babá and I will come over tomorrow night after work."

"And then will we go to our apartment?"

"Unfortunately, we have to wait one more day before we can move in."

I was spending the first night in the USA with strangers, not with the adoptive parents. *This must be what adoption is in America.*

Two days later we arrived at our apartment on Lorraine Terrace, Brighton, Massachusetts. Many Greek immigrants who had settled in this northwestern neighborhood of Boston were originally from Naoussa. It was common and practical for immigrants to gravitate to the same neighborhoods as their own countrymen. The seasoned ones helped the newcomers find jobs and housing. They helped them acclimate to the new world. My parents' friends found the apartment for us, across the street from theirs. The Papazlis family had been living there since their arrival from Naoussa, a year earlier. Their oldest son, Dimitris, was already working as a barber. Teddy, the diminutive for the name Lefteris, was in high school. The baby in the family, Evelyn, the American version of Evaggelia, was two months older than I.

My parents spoke in animated tones as they described our new neighbors. It was the way adults talked to children when they wanted to convince them of something. It was their way of removing the unease I expressed about being in my new country. I did view the prospect of a Greek girlfriend as a lucky thing. But it didn't take away the sting of being far away from the familiarity and comfort of Greece. *How will I learn American?* I thought of Rena back in Thessaloniki. She was so helpful with my adjustment to school in a new community. I wondered if Evelyn would be the same.

17
Rocky Start

Four days after my arrival I mustered all the confidence I could for my first day of school in America. My father and I walked to the Thomas Edison School. From Lorraine Terrace, we turned left onto Kelton Street to the corner and waited to cross Commonwealth Avenue (Comm Ave). The green streetcars or trolleys dominated the center of the wide two-way street. The volume of traffic overwhelmed me. The screeching sounds from the green streetcars traveling both ways in the center between the roadways created a confusion in my head. It brought memories of Vardari Square in Thessaloniki on a busy day.

We waited at the traffic light, in front of Harry's Bar. Every time the clerk opened the door to dump trash into a barrel by the front door, the stench that came out was unfamiliar to me. I would learn later it was the beer and liquor odor normal for a bar. The previous evening when Mamá walked me to the corner to show me the trolley stop, I had peered into the bar. A metal planter with orange chrysanthemums was holding the door open. There was a sign on the door. At the time I did not understand it but when I learned to read English, I read "Ladies Are Welcome." I saw men and women sitting in the darkened barroom. The foul smell of liquor, cigars, and cigarettes had assaulted my nostrils.

"Look there." My father pointed to a pole ahead of us. "See the red light? That means we cannot cross. When we see a red and yellow light together then we can go."

We crossed Comm Ave onto Warren Street.

"We are almost there, and you'll see everything will be fine," he said.

I didn't believe him. The tingling inside my body intensified. We were silent for the remainder of our fifteen-minute walk. The school year had begun a month before my arrival in the United States, but this was a familiar scenario for me. I had spent the last two grades jumping in and out of schools in mid-session. My apprehension increased as I thought about the unfairness of starting school late, again. I felt at least if I had been there from the beginning, I would have felt more comfortable. At the time I hadn't considered that most of the students would have known each other from the previous grades.

As we approached the school, I noticed clusters of kids scattered throughout the schoolyard. The scene resembled that of the school-yards in Thessaloniki and Veria. However, the scene's familiarity did nothing to ease the churning in my stomach. I wasn't sure if my stomach churned because we were steps away from the entrance or because I had not yet come to terms with my father's age in relation to me and wondered what my classmates would think. The few days we had been together had not been enough to get the age thing out of my head. I was eleven years old. I didn't want my father to look like he should be my grandfather. I quickened our pace to get inside the school before the students could see us.

The secretary and my father spoke, he signed some papers and then said, "You will be placed in the sixth grade."

I was relieved I would not repeat the fifth grade. When it was all quiet in the corridor, the woman placed her glasses on the desk and walked out of the office. She returned with a student to whom she handed a piece of paper.

"He is going to walk you to your classroom. I will see you tonight when I get home from work," my father translated.

That was it. I was left alone with the student. My English vocabulary had grown to include thank you, how are you, good morning, good night.

The familiar light-headedness, as if thousands of ants were crawling in my head, intensified with every step I took next to my escort. The student with red hair and freckles handed me the note he had been given, knocked on the door and bolted down the hall. When the door opened to reveal what felt like a million eyes staring at me, I thought I would cry. The teacher's smile and gentle manner took my attention away from the curious eyes. She pointed to an empty desk with a stack of books, a notebook, and a pencil on it. I lifted my eyes long enough to spot Evelyn's round face at the other end of the room. Her black ponytail and short bangs looked stark, next to a girl with blond hair who shared the desk with her. I wished I were sitting next to my new friend and neighbor who spoke Greek.

No sooner had I taken my seat, and everyone stood up. I noticed Evelyn stood so I did too. She and I were the same height, but I noticed her dress did not narrow at her waist like mine did. Her shape was squarish compared to my spindly frame. To me she looked more like the other girls in the class than I did. As the students rose, they placed their right hand over their chest, including Evelyn. I kept my arms by my side while they recited what I assumed was a prayer. I couldn't believe my friend participated in it. *We are Greek Orthodox; why is she praying American?* I had no idea they were reciting the Pledge of Allegiance to the American flag and the country. Later at home I relayed my surprise to my mother.

"Evelyn prayed American in school."

"I will ask her about it later. You may have to learn it too."

She didn't appear as concerned about it as I was.

My first day of school was one continuous awkward string of experiences. I opened whatever book everyone else opened. I stared at the strange writing and listened to the teacher without understanding a word. My limited English vocabulary did not help. Whenever students looked at the chalkboard and wrote in their notebooks, I did the same. I had not learned the alphabet but managed to copy the letters.

Evelyn and I walked home in silence. I did not get the security and encouragement I had expected from my new friend. She did not offer to introduce me to her friends as Rena had done in Thessaloniki. I got the feeling she was embarrassed to be seen with me. She had been in the States long enough to have acclimated to the American way of life. Perhaps she felt about me the same way I felt about my father's age.

At home, not knowing what to do with my books, I sat on my bed and cried. By the time my parents came home from work I had calmed down but started crying again as I relayed my first day at school.

"I don't want to stay here; I want to go back to Greece."

"Tomorrow will be better."

My father added, "Maybe Evelyn can help you."

They both went about preparing dinner.

My first week in school was an exercise in futility. I went, I came home, I cried, we had dinner, I cried, went to bed. On the last day of the week my father came to school with me.

After a short conversation with the principal, my father said, "You are going to a new school next Monday."

"Is it near here? Will they talk to me in Greek?"

"No, you will have to take the streetcar to downtown Boston."

The thought of taking the trolley by myself sent me into a crying frenzy.

"It will only take thirty minutes. Tomorrow I will ask Teddy to ride the trolley with you so you will know how to get there."

That was another dreaded experience. With his dark hair slicked back in the fashion of the times, my neighbor looked like most high schoolers. Like his sister, Evelyn, he had acclimated to the American way. He was probably as embarrassed as I was to be riding the train with me.

But on Monday, in my navy-blue jumper over a white blouse, I walked the one block to Comm Ave. A few adults, some holding newspapers, were already at the streetcar stop. Once on board I stayed alert to ensure I got off at the right stop.

I was relieved to see my school two blocks down from the stop. I walked fast, I felt my heart pound with every step I took. In front of the big double doors, I stopped to make the pounding go away. I walked in and entered the first office I saw.

Upon checking my papers, a woman guided me to the second floor and to my classroom. It was a regular classroom, but the students were adults. No one had warned me about that. At least the adults did not gawk like the sixth graders had done.

After checking my paperwork, the teacher directed me to the third row, second seat. I was the only child in a classroom of adults aged from their twenties to my parents' age. The Christopher Columbus High School was the nearest school to Brighton offering English as a Second Language (ESL). Once again, I could not understand what was going on in class. The students were immigrants from various countries, but I could see they were able to follow the teacher and respond to her.

I began my learning journey by copying and doing homework

without knowing what I was doing. At least now I could go home and do work even though I didn't know what any of it meant. The teacher showed me every day what I had to do. Crying became part of my daily routine. I wanted to be back in Greece. I managed to complete my assignments on my own. My father spoke English fluently but his reading and writing skills were insufficient to help me. My mother's English got her by at work and at shopping. As far as I could tell I was doing well in school. My papers had a few red marks on them. I had figured out the fewer red marks they had the better.

After a month in school, my frustration subsided. I understood a little of what was said in class. In three months, I spoke conversational English. After six months my English was fluent. At the end of the school year the adults and I completed the course, and we could communicate in English.

At the graduation ceremony, a diverse group of ages and nationalities occupied the front rows of the enormous auditorium. On other occasions, on our way to attend Assembly, the raucous sounds of several hundred students were normal in the packed auditorium. At the ESL graduation, the class of twenty-three students and their families appeared like a drop in a lake.

My father came to the graduation on his way to work. Neither my parents nor I knew the cultural norm of attending a graduation. If we had known, I want to believe my mother would have taken the day off from work to attend. My father picked up the paperwork necessary for me to attend regular school in the fall. The end of the school year meant my mother and I would be going to Greece. They had promised that to me. It was their response every time I had cried and complained about not wanting to stay in the United States.

"We will go to Greece in the summer."

That promise of going to Greece in the summer motivated me to keep learning, do well in school, and to stop crying. The learning I was accomplishing, but the crying continued along with wanting to go back to Greece. "I don't want to live in America" had become my slogan. My parents insisted I would get used to it and be happy. I could not imagine how I could be happy. The language, the houses, the people, everything was different. There were many adjustments I needed to make.

18

Assimilation

I had walked into the ESL class like a lost lamb, but I emerged like an eagle. Placed in a room with other non-English-speaking students forced us to communicate in the language of our new country. We spent the entire school day hearing, writing, and reading English. The immersion method works, I tell everyone that will listen.

As my English improved, my crying sessions diminished. My new capabilities gave a tremendous boost to my confidence, and they hastened my adjustment to my new environment. I was able to converse in the classroom and comprehended what I was doing for homework. At the stores I spoke to the clerks instead of not saying anything or passing the clerk a note. I had watched my mother and other immigrants struggle using hand signals to augment their limited vocabulary. I was too embarrassed to do that.

My new confidence allowed me to venture out on my own.

"I played with the girls across the street today!" I exclaimed when my mother returned from work.

"Bravo, see? We knew you would adjust."

"Evelyn wasn't even there." It was the first time I had gone out to play with the neighborhood children without my trusty interpreter, Evelyn.

After three months in my new country, I had become my mother's interpreter wherever we went and speaking English was required. One adjustment I still needed to overcome was calling my parents Mamá and Babá. It did not feel natural to me to call them Mom and Dad. I felt a distance and a coldness between us. Nothing like when I called my biological parents Mamá and Babá, and I wanted that feeling.

I longed for the warmth I felt when my Mamá Sofia hugged me. I missed sitting on the edge of the bed while she carefully combed the snarls out of my hair. How she would hold my head and say, "This one is really bad; it will hurt a little."

And it did hurt. She would put the comb down for a minute and then start combing again.

I missed my Babá Nikos's wink. Whenever he planned to take me with him to his tailor shop without my little sister, he gave me our secret wink. "She is too young to go with us," he used to say.

My mother would have to distract Nitsa in the back yard or take her to visit a neighbor. I would climb on Babá's motorcycle, and we would be off. I missed the exclusiveness he channeled to me. I felt a deep connection with him as far back as I can remember.

I did call my new parents Mamá and Babá. I had an intense desire to have parents. But I wanted them to be more like mine were or at least to resemble the ages of my schoolmates' parents. I placated myself that I was okay with their ages, as long as my friends or any other kids my age didn't see me with my father. It's what my eleven-year-old heart and mind told me.

My father's quiet demeanor fit perfectly with his small body frame. His sparse gray hair accentuated his age. In my mind only grandfathers had hair like that. I liked his methodical and gentle manner. Whether it was to prepare a meal or to put away groceries, he displayed calm and confidence. As I got more secure in the relationship and dared to be argumentative, that's when he showed his disciplinary side. I didn't mind it when he raised his voice to reprimand me, which was rare. I welcomed it. I had seen and heard my friends' parents scold them. My friends had talked about arguments, scoldings, and punishments. So, when my new mamá and babá reproached me, I felt more normal, as if I were their real child. I wanted to be a normal kid with normal parents. Somehow, I knew I had to find a way to overlook their age. I sensed that they cared and provided for me as their child, but their emotional cords had not connected with mine.

They showed their pride in my progress with the English language by offering my interpreting services to their friends. Even my father felt I could do a better job than he did. They had me filling out forms for their work and for the utility companies. Six months after I started school, my command of the English language was such that my parents' friends asked for my help. Their requests were like my parents'. I filled out forms for them, I read directions to them for appliances, made medical and other appointments for them, and contacted their employers to convey messages.

Several times during the school year my father and I had a date at his work. I walked the few blocks from school to the private social club, the Somerset Club on Boston's Beacon Hill.

My father went to Boston after his arrival at Ellis Island, New York. His friend from Naoussa hired him to work in his diner. Like many of the early immigrants, he had come to achieve the American Dream. His desire for the dream motivated him to work hard. He developed the knowledge and skills to land the chef's position at the prestigious private men's club.

The first time I tiptoed on the white tile floor in the club's kitchen I was in awe. The club's kitchen was the largest I had ever seen. Ovens, stoves, and cabinets lined the length of the kitchen walls. Seeing my reflection on the metal surfaces accentuated its sterile appearance. My father looked like a miniature figure in a large dollhouse. I thought he was too small for the size of the kitchen. Nevertheless, he exuded confidence and pride in his spotless uniform. Seen through my young eyes, he looked distinguished and proud in the black-and-white checked trousers, the crisp white coat, and of course the white pleated hat.

One Friday afternoon he looked particularly excited when I arrived in his kitchen. With one swift move he pulled loose the white napkin that was tucked on his back side and patted his forehead with it.

"Wash your hands quickly and follow me."

I placed my books on a stool in the designated area for the staff.

"Why? Where are we going?

He was too absorbed to answer.

He dried the sink area after I washed up. He picked up a tray with a single sandwich on a white plate. I eyed the bacon, lettuce, and tomato (BLT) sandwich and longed to have one. It was something American and not on our menu at home.

"I'm going to introduce you to the president of the club. He is a very nice man."

I wished my father had waited to introduce me until after I had better command of the English language. At that time, because of my limited vocabulary, I was shy about communicating. What if I used the wrong word? And then with the accent, I knew I sounded different. The president appeared friendly and spoke quietly. He did all the talking. My single-word answers were soft as I kept my gaze on his shiny black shoes. He towered over my babá and me in his brown suit and striped tie.

When we returned to the kitchen, my father made me a BLT. I savored every bite and washed it down with a tall glass of chocolate milk. My sweet father, the man I didn't want my friends to see me with, sat across from me. He sipped coffee and dragged on a Lucky Strike cigarette. The president of the club was still on his mind.

"He really is a good man. He is the head of everything in here and he is very kind to me."

Even at my age I sensed his happiness and that made me feel good for my father. I did my homework while he waited for food orders. After he finished working through the dinner hour, we took the streetcar home. *I am going to tell Mamá I had a BLT sandwich and met the president. I hope she's home from work when we get there.*

Mamá and our neighbor, Mrs. Papazlis, worked at a women's dress factory in the Roxbury neighborhood of Boston. It was a treat for me and Evelyn when our mothers bought ready-made dresses for us during the factory's end-of-season sale. Ready-made apparel had become popular, but we generally wore homemade clothes. It would be decades before I would appreciate the quality of custom-made clothing. As kids, we wanted to be like our American peers and wear store-bought dresses, pants, and blouses.

"Your classmates are not as lucky as you are. They don't have a mother who can sew fancy dresses for them."

I was used to having my clothes made for me, but I resented that my mother continued to make them. I wanted to be like my peers and wear store-bought clothing. I can't believe how I acted when my mother was making a dress for me to wear to a wedding. I acted like a brat. The dress was a pale blue organza. She spread the delicate fabric with matching lining out on my bed with the Simplicity pattern next to it. Her hands barely touched the fabric as she smoothed it out for us to admire. Usually, she made her own patterns for my dresses, but this was a special occasion. During fittings I clenched my jaws. She would repeatedly demand that I stand up straight. I didn't want a handmade dress; I wanted to buy one in the store. At the final fitting, she had me turn around slowly. She placed pins in different places at the bottom of the dress.

"Take it off, I have to add these and then you will try it on for the last time."

She stitched individual crocheted white daisies with yellow centers. The hemline was dotted with the quarter-size flowers.

"Come, come, it's all finished."

I sauntered into the living room, dreading another fitting. She handled the dress as if it were a newborn baby. When she deemed it was smoothed out and puffed out enough, she nodded and turned me to face the mirror. How could I not like it? The bodice hugged my body to my waist and from there a sea of blue flared out showing off white daisies. I twirled and looked at my image from every which way I could. I am so glad I showed my pleasure with the dress. It took away a little of the shame I felt for my reaction during the fittings. How could I have been so obstinate and mean? But she endured my behavior and continued to create beautiful pieces for me. It had to be a way of expressing her love toward me.

After all my whining and complaining, I wore the dress to the wedding. Even at that age of twelve I knew my mother had created a stunning garment.

All the guests wore their special-occasion clothes. The men looked very similar in their suits and ties. The women, on the other hand, had distinguished themselves from each other. An array of satin and organza dresses filled the large ballroom. Most of the women wore small round hats that matched their dresses. All the guests clapped when the bride and groom bounced into the room with smiles wide enough to light up the entire building. Evelyn and I gazed at the bride in awe.

"She looks like a princess," I said.

"When I get married, I am going to have a long lace train too," Evelyn answered.

"Me too. And I am going to wear a veil with a lot of netting."

We enjoyed the dinner and the dancing that followed, but I was more excited thinking about my trip to Greece in two days.

I had been waiting for this trip since the day I arrived in Boston. "I am going to kiss the ground when I get off the airplane," I had told Evelyn. It is what I had heard adults say and I did think I would do that. The prospect of seeing Theo Pavlos, my new and old cousins, my friends, and relatives had elevated my mood to a happy status. A summer of reunions and fun was within my reach.

19

Foreigner in My Homeland

The promise to go to Greece in the summer was not bait to appease me during my outbursts about not wanting to live in America. We did go to Greece, and I didn't want the summer of 1960 to end. In July 1960 Mamá and I boarded a plane for our flight to Greece to spend a month in my homeland.

I had looked forward to the trip for nine months. I kept thinking about and imagining the reconnection with my cousins, aunts, and uncles—both biological and adoptive. The ongoing thought of seeing them again helped to alleviate my sadness and loneliness. A reunion with Theo Pavlos and his family was a movie I played over and over on my mind's screen. I could hardly stand still when my mother said, "We will go to Kostohori to see your Theo Pavlos during the first week."

"Does he know that?" I pushed back happy tears.

My mother and I arose at daybreak to arrive in Veria in time to catch the only bus to my theo's village. I did not complain about having the early wake-up time because I couldn't wait to see Theo Pavlos and his family, but especially him. There was standing room only on the recently added bus service from Veria to Kostohori. To my surprise it was the first time on a bus where I was not overcome by motion sickness. The dirt road had been paved but the zigzag and hairpin turns remained.

Kostohori was and still is a desirable vacation destination for the city folks. Now it has electricity, indoor plumbing, and cell service. The old dirt road with its hair-raising turns is now wider and paved. The old farmhouses have been renovated into single-family homes. Strict zoning laws are keeping the village close to its original size and scale.

My anticipation of the approach into the village sparked a flurry of activity in my stomach. I yearned for a glimpse of the fountain and plane tree defining the entrance to the village. I moved my head left and right to find an opening between the people who blocked my view. Finally, the man in front of me leaned over to speak to his companion, creating enough space for me to see out the window. And there they were ahead of us, the plane tree and fountain, just as I remembered them. My heart began to pulsate faster and faster. *I will see him in just a few minutes.* I squeezed the bar I was holding so hard my knuckles turned white. I couldn't tell if my insides were vibrating from my anticipation or from the bumpy ride on the dirt road leading to the village center. There were people in front of the Katarahias Taverna. Some were there to greet people disembarking the bus and others to pick up packages. With one quick touch my hand wiped the tears off my cheeks, and I stepped off the bus.

Mamá was already shaking hands with Theo. When I reached them, he engulfed me in his arms. The closeness I had missed for almost a year unleashed tears of sadness, and joy. I dug my nails into the small of his back. For a split second I felt embarrassed that the onlookers were seeing me cry. Then it hit me: I knew they were sizing up the woman who had adopted Sofia's older daughter. That thought occupied my attention more than my crying. Amidst the jumble of emotions I was feeling up until then, I added an overwhelming desire for the Kostohorians to approve of my new mother and to accept her. I looked around to read their faces. Their nods to each other showed approval. I was used to the indiscretion Greek adults oftentimes exhibited. They did not try to disguise their feelings; whether negative or positive, they let them show. They nodded, pointed, and stared overtly. I concluded they approved.

The three of us walked down the hill to Theo's house. I was still nervous about my mother's acceptance by the villagers. Two groups of women, their arms interlocked, followed us halfway down the hill. I stole a glance and saw them talking and watching us go into the yard where Thea Kitsa and my cousins Despina and Kostas were waiting.

"Welcome, welcome. How was your trip?" Thea's smile revealed a gold upper tooth I didn't know she had.

She and my mother kissed on both cheeks as was and still is the custom in Greece.

"The bus was full, we had to stand the whole way."

Thea Kitsa turned to me. "Stella, look at how you have grown. Welcome." She hugged and kissed me.

"Despina, say welcome to your cousin Stella." Theo Pavlos bent down and coached her.

Despina looked up at me with her big round brown eyes and said nothing. Her black curls were held off her face by a white ribbon tied into a bow. It reminded me of the bows my Mamá Sofia used to tie on my hair. I bent down and kissed my little cousin. Meanwhile Kostas had run off chasing the chickens.

We sat around a table under the fig tree. Thea Kitsa had prepared a feast for the occasion. She made *pites* which were as good as my yiayia's. She probably learned from Yiayia, who had a stellar reputation for being a good cook.

"Kitsa, the *katsikaki* (goat) looks delicious," my mother said.

"Here, this piece is nice and tender." Thea Kitsa placed a chunk of meat on my mother's plate.

She then spooned out a hefty serving of roasted potatoes from the round aluminum pan and placed them next to the meat. My eyes were on the potatoes. I could hardly wait for my plate. The golden-brown color guaranteed crispiness on the outside and softness inside. From the other round pan Thea cut and served tiropita. She remembered I liked the crust. "Here, Stella, this one has extra crust on it." Her remembering that detail about me delivered a warm wave in my chest. Thea Kitsa had fed the little ones while Theo, Mamá, and I visited and nibbled on a cucumber and tomato salad, grilled sausage, feta, and olives. The adults sipped on ouzo. While we feasted on our main meal, the little ones played with the toys we had brought.

As if on cue, no sooner had we finished our meal when neighbors trickled in. Their curiosity was laced with mournfulness. After they greeted my mother, they squeezed me and cried. "You have grown, look at you." And then they started talking in Pontian and kept wiping tears away. I couldn't understand every word, but they lamented Sofia's death.

"Oh Sofia, where are you to see your first born?"

"Look at her, she has Sofia's face."

"Poor Sofia, she went so young."

They went on and on. I remembered them. They had been in this same yard two years prior, wailing and lamenting. Thankfully they were subtle about it on my first return visit, and they did not stay very long.

I walked around the property with my little cousins while the adults had coffee. The outhouse had been upgraded. Real stucco walls replaced the metal structure, but it still had a Turkish toilet. Next to it they had added a cement sink with running water. The stone oven was as I remembered it and it stirred memories of pites and breads my yiayia used to make.

I had watched Yiayia prepare the phyllo dough for pites. She rolled the dough into a large circle so thin you could see through it. Years of experience made the task look effortless. She rolled the dough on a long dowel like a broomstick on a floured table, then flung it away from her and quickly rolled the flawless sheet of dough back on the table. She repeated the process several times.

"It has to be very thin before you place it on the baking sheet." She stressed it as if I was going to be making it the next time.

One of many possible fillings had been prepared in advance. Plain feta cheese filling, feta and spinach, feta and leeks, ground meat, or for something sweeter but not a dessert, squash filling. After she spread the filling over the phyllo-lined pan, she covered it with another phyllo sheet. I marveled at the speed with which she sealed the edges and pinched the phyllo sheets together to keep the filling from oozing out. The pinched edge formed a design that looked like a thick necklace. Next, she brushed the top with butter or oil, and she placed the pan in the oven. Whether served fresh out of the stone oven in the backyard or at room temperature, all of them beckoned to be devoured. My favorite was and is the plain feta pita (tiropita). I coveted the crispy edges. The thought of biting into it, its crackling sound, my catching bits of phyllo before they reached the floor makes my mouth water. Despina tugged at my blouse and brought me out of my memory.

The barn, the chicken coop, and everything else was familiar and at the same time everything felt impersonal. At the time I did not identify my feelings. I felt detached from all of it, as if I never belonged there. And perhaps that was a good assessment. I find it interesting that I could sever that strong unwavering attachment I had felt two years prior. Or is it because I knew I had to let it go and immerse myself in my new life?

When we saw the bus make its way from the soccer field parking lot to the Taverna, we all walked up the hill together. Despina and

Kostas engaged in a race to the top. By the time we reached the bus, the crowd had thinned. There were more gawking looks toward us. Mrs. Katarahias spotted us and came over.

"Pavlos, is this the older one? Stella?"

My theo nodded.

She came over, hugged me and started crying. Then she shook my mother's hand. "Glad to meet you." She hugged me again and walked away wiping her tears.

It was my turn for tears as I hugged Thea Kitsa. I needed someone to pry me away from my theo when I hugged him goodbye. I couldn't do it on my own. He put his hands on my shoulders.

"Come, don't cry we will see each other again," he said with tears in his eyes.

Fortunately, we had seats for our return trip. My mother and I drew more indiscreet looks and whispers from fellow passengers, and we made the trip to Veria in silence and in time to connect to the bus for Naoussa.

I was relieved to see the lights of Naoussa as the bus made its final ascent. It had been a long and emotional day.

My visit to Kostohori with my theo's family was the highlight of my summer. The only thing that could have perfected the highlight would have been a visit with my sister. *Where is she?*

During the rest of our vacation, my mother and I spent time in Naoussa and Thessaloniki. In the close community of Naoussa my cousins and I were safe to come and go as we pleased. There was always someone about to monitor our moves. It could be a relative, a neighbor, a storekeeper. Any of those people had the authority to correct us and/or reprimand us. Like the time Antonia and I were walking back from Thea Sofia's house during the quiet (siesta) time, which is generally from 2 p.m. to 5 p.m. Mr. Marneris was in front of his bookstore.

"What are you two doing out at this hour? Go home right now," he scolded us.

"That's what we are doing. We just left our aunt's house."

We rushed away towards home, humiliated.

Our days consisted of visiting relatives, sharing long-lasting meals, or going on picnics at our relatives' farms. We spent most evenings playing at the city's park and walking the promenade.

In Thessaloniki my mother and I spent time with her best friend Vera's family in Perea Beach, seventeen kilometers to the south of Thessaloniki. Thea Vera's daughter Dimitra and I had developed our relationship during my visits to Greece and with our letter writing. Our stay at their camp site as always was a joyous time whether we were frolicking in the turquoise water or just sat in front of their enormous tent and watched the water slosh over our sunbathed bodies.

Upon our return to Thessaloniki Mamá and I finished our gift shopping at the souvenir shops in the White Tower neighborhood. I didn't want to think about the trip's end, but I knew it was imminent.

We spent our last week in Naoussa where another tearful departure from the familiar places and people concluded our month of fun and adventure.

I did not want to return to the US. I did not want to continue to adjust to all the changes. Looking back, I see the irony of enjoying being called Americana (American). I took it as a compliment, a privilege of which to be proud. A feeling of being special which should have made me want to go back and be the Americana. As exclusive as that made me feel while I was in Greece, it's not what I felt when I was in the US. Although I had accepted that my life belonged in the States with my new parents, I didn't feel the connection. Suddenly it felt as though I was a foreigner in both countries.

On my return I would be faced with adjusting to a new school. Meeting new teachers and new students presented a new challenge. I would be the foreigner. My concern that my accent would be noticeable, and the kids would make fun of me, distressed me.

20

Duty vs. Education

MY PARENTS AND ME

Back in Brighton we prepared for my return to school. The certificate I received from my ESL class indicated I could advance to the seventh grade. I was relieved I did not have to stay back.

It was a fifteen- to twenty-minute walk from my house to William Taft Junior High School on the corner of Cambridge and Warren Streets in Brighton. The biggest challenge to overcome on my way to school would be to wait in front of Harry's Bar to cross Comm Ave.

The three-story brick building was smaller than the Christopher Columbus High School where I attended the ESL program the previous year. I was thrilled to start this school year on the same day as my classmates.

I delved into the books with a determination to do well and to get good grades. My progress in school surprised and pleased me. My teachers praised me and encouraged me to do extra work. Mrs. Parker, our Latin teacher made me feel special. She called on me to read more often than the other students.

"Your pronunciation is excellent!" she exclaimed.

Most of the students had to work hard with pronunciation. I was lucky because Greek is a phonetic language which came in handy with Latin. My English teacher had a similar reaction to my work in his class.

"Excellent work," he said whenever he handed me my test papers.

I excelled in English. I received Magna Cum Laude awards in Latin. My report card reflected my success, achieving honor roll grades. At the end of seventh grade my report card was a source of pride for my parents.

The summer after seventh grade, we spent another month in Greece. When we returned, I was excited for my second year of junior high school.

During the eighth grade, I thrived both academically and socially. Evelyn had become my best friend. The encouragement from our families was to stay connected to our Greek culture. In addition to speaking Greek at home, we rode a yellow school bus that picked up Greek kids from the surrounding areas and deposited us at the Greek Orthodox Cathedral on Parker Street in Boston, where we attended Sunday school classes and church services. The obligatory participation in poem recitals, religious-based plays, and learning folk dancing was a source of pride not only to our immigrant parents, but also to first-generation parents of the parish. As much as our parents wanted us to assimilate and be faithful Americans, they were also adamant about our upholding the Greek cultural traditions.

Of course, at school my friends' last names were Smith, O'Neil, Hogan, Morrison, Chin, Wong, Walker, Paolini, Krauss, and Glickman. Some of us were immigrants. Others were first- or second-generation Americans. We were curious and compared the traditions and rules we had to follow at home as well as the foods we ate. I was amazed at my comfort level and achievement in the two years I had been living in the United States. I was enjoying my life.

At the beginning of the eighth grade, the letters from Thea Mitsa became weighty. It was my job to read and answer letters for my parents. Yiayia's old age had caught up with her and she was bedridden most of the time. Thea Mitsa complained and griped in all the letters.

By the new year, the letters were angry and demanding help. In February 1962, Mitsa wrote, "Marianthe, you have to come back home. Our mother's health requires more care than I can provide. You are away and you don't realize what I must do to take care of her and keep up with the silk production Dino and I have started in Naoussa."

My mother reached for the package of Kent cigarettes and in a slow motion she extracted one. She stared at it before placing it between her lips and drew in her breath when she held a match to the end of it. I continued to read.

"When Vasilis was alive, it was different."

She went on and on about why my mother had to go back to Greece. I finished reading the letter and went to my room. Halfway through my homework, my mother summoned me to the kitchen.

"Stella, I can't leave work to go to Greece. You will go to help Thea Mitsa with whatever she needs."

"What about school?" My lips trembled.

"You are an outstanding student. Your teachers like you. Your father and I believe a few months will not make a difference. Don't worry, when you come back you will still advance to high school."

"How long will I stay?"

She lit another Kent.

"The rest of the school year. I will come to Naoussa in July, and we will fly back together."

It took me a while to fall asleep. I lay in bed tossing and turning. *How can they do that to me? I like school. They are sending me back to Greece to take care of a sick Yiayia. That's not fair.* My emotions were all over the place. I tried to talk myself into being excited to be going in February during Carnavali (Mardi Gras), but it did not work. Sort of happy that I would miss school. Fearful that I would have to repeat the 8th grade.

"Remember to tell your teacher you will be leaving school," my mother instructed me the next morning.

Miss Moscatelli, my homeroom teacher and mentor, was appalled. She had taken a personal interest in my development and assimilation. I waited until all the students were out of the classroom before I approached her desk. She took off her cat's-eye glasses, placed them on her desk and looked me in the eyes. On the first day of school, she had encouraged us to see her after class whenever we needed extra help or had questions about anything. She always had time for her students. When we were in seventh grade, we had heard stories of how strict she was and to be careful if we got her in the eighth grade. Five months into the eighth grade, I found her to be fair, kind, and devoted to her students.

I bit my lower lip and looked down for a moment. Looking at her kind eyes I got the courage to blurt out: "I must leave school. My parents are sending me to Greece to help care for my grandmother."

Her statuesque figure towered over me when she placed her hands on the desk and sprang up in defiance. "You cannot leave school. You are a child, and your place is in school."

"But I must do what my parents tell me. They said my grades are good enough that when I come back for the new school year, I will be promoted to the ninth grade."

She was adamant. "Listen to me. You are an excellent student but there is still a lot of material to cover. You will have to repeat the year. You are a student, and you need to be in school. Your parents should not be taking you out of school."

She handed me a tissue from her desk drawer.

"My grandmother is sick and needs help."

"That is the job for adults. I will speak to the principal. This cannot happen." The horizontal lines on her forehead relaxed. She pursed her lips, rearranged some papers on her desk, met my eyes and held me by the shoulders. "Stella, you must stay in school."

I loved that woman. She was my mother's age and had dedicated her life to teaching and to her students.

A few days after my conversation with Miss Moscatelli, I arrived in Naoussa, Greece.

As unfair as it was to yank me out of school, arriving in Naoussa during Carnavali was special. I had experienced Naoussa's famous celebration of Carnavali before, with my godparents.

When I was seven years old, my parents, Mrs. Azat, Mrs. Ismini, Mary, my sister, and I were in the living room discussing possible costumes for Carnavali. Nitsa and I ran to the window when we heard click-clack on the front steps. Our mother answered the three soft taps on the door.

"Oh, welcome to the koumbarous. Stella, look, Nonós and Noná are here."

My sister and I ran over to get a closer look at the garment my noná was carrying. We both knew it had to be for me. After all, they were my godparents. While the adults exchanged pleasantries, we gushed over the red satin gown.

"Stella, I had this poppy costume made especially for you." Noná held it up for everyone to see. "Come on, let's see how it fits. We are taking you to Naoussa."

At the time, I had not heard of Naoussa's Carnavali. Nor did I know my godparents were coming to take me there. My mother did not know it either. But that was how things were done back then within the families of godparents and their godchildren's parents. As a matter of fact, that's also how things were done between relatives and friends.

The costume reached to the floor. The puffy sleeves fit just right. I stepped into a skirt-hoop which stretched the shiny fabric into a circle. Red satin ribbons hung from my waistline which was adorned with red bows and ribbons. Large fabric poppy flowers fastened at my shoulders and along the hemline completed the costume. I wanted to twirl for all to see but there wasn't enough room, so I moved slowly in a circle. They all gave approving looks.

"How beautiful you look," said Mrs. Azat.

Mary added, "You look just like a poppy."

Everyone showed enthusiasm except my little sister, who went into a crying fit because she wanted a beautiful costume for herself.

Everyone but my mother and Nitsa came out to see us off. I ignored my little sister's crying. They had to smush the dress to fit in the car. I felt like a princess not like a poppy, enfolded in the sheen of the gorgeous red fabric. I was mesmerized by the costumes I saw and the fanfare we experienced.

Seven years earlier I had arrived in Naoussa as a visitor to indulge in the city's famous celebration. Now, at fourteen years old I arrived as the Americana, who was sent to care for her ailing yiayia. *How exactly will I be caring for her? Would I take care of her personal needs and hygiene? Surely, they don't expect a fourteen-year-old to do that.* I comforted myself that my work would be limited to house chores. I anticipated there would be free time to spend with my cousins.

21

Carnavali and an Unwanted Suitor

The unexpected trip to Greece in February 1962 exposed me to two distinct and opposite experiences. One was all about fun and not having to go to school and the other was the discovery of cultural differences pertaining to teenage moral standards. At age fourteen, the fun aspect of my sudden relocation exceeded my expectations. It softened the resentment I felt for being forced to leave Boston to help care for Yiayia. Reconnecting with the extended family I had met three years earlier strengthened the bonds we had cultivated during my summer visits. My cousins and I, all of us in various stages of adolescence, engaged in the typical teenage behaviors. The male cousins, in addition to exploring adolescent romance, were charged with ensuring their female cousins did not take part in such forbidden acts. However, it was Carnavali season, and we were teenagers. The ten-day celebration with all its revelry offered the opportunity for us to go out at night unchaperoned.

On Carnavali's opening night, my twin cousins Antonia and Katina arranged our evening out. We linked our arms as we walked down the street. That was how we walked most of the time, but in preparation of our big night out there was much silliness among us. When one slowed down the other tugged and dragged us forward and we laughed in merriment.

"Come on, let's go faster or we'll miss the beginning of the parade."

"Why Antonia, is there someone special you want to see?"

We felt grown up to be out on our own. We were mesmerized as we walked alongside the high schoolers. They were only three to four years older than us but at that age it made a big difference. We teased and nudged each other as we pointed at boys.

"Oh, so you like him?" Antonia pointed to the dance leader.

"Be quiet, do you like him?" I answered.

Spending the night at their home after all the teasing, I confessed my instant crush on the tall senior boy. The next day Katina and I made it our mission to run into Nikos. The name alone was enough to win my heart (as it was my biological father's name).

"So, you are the Amerikanaki (diminutive of American)."

I squeezed Katina's arm at the sound of his voice as my heart pounded extra beats. *He knows of me.*

"We have to go before someone sees us talking." Katina urged.

I wasn't used to the idea that we could not be seen talking to boys. In the Unites States I had become accustomed to talking, walking, and hanging around with boys. I considered the rule not only archaic but also absurd. In Greece, girls who were observed talking to boys were labeled as loose and parents demanded their children not befriend them.

Missing five months of eighth grade gave me a different kind of education. I saw the two cultures shaping a new version of me. Rejecting unfair practices and adopting practices I considered fair, progressive, and good.

I seized on the way a person's age was calculated in Greece. You are considered the age you will become at your next birthday any time within that calendar year leading up to it. So, by this calculation I was fifteen, not fourteen. That closed the age difference between me and Nikos, who was nineteen. I embraced the extended family connections and relationships of dinners together, casually stopping by and being invited to stay for the meal. The downside was that the culture allowed the extended family members to intervene in personal matters. Sometimes that could be helpful. The security of having people caring for you was worth it.

Arranged marriages, something I had not heard about in the US, were still prevalent in Greece. I could just hear my friends back in the States: What? The parents tell you whom to marry? On rare occasions a couple chose each other but convincing the parents to agree was an arduous job.

Ten days of masquerade parades, gallivanting around town, out at night unchaperoned, getting a glimpse of Nikos from afar, and fantasizing about my first romance came to an end as we entered the Lenten period.

My cousins spent more time with their schoolwork, and I got more serious with the work I was sent to do: spending more time doing housework for Thea Mitsa.

The novelty of not having to go to school wore off. I wondered why I had to be removed from school to care for my adoptive grandmother. My contribution of dusting, washing floors, ironing, and whatever other menial chores Thea demanded could have been handled by a hired person. Other households had help with housekeeping.

"Why doesn't Dino come to help you with the silk production?" I dared to ask.

"Silly girl, he has a job in Thessaloniki. You expect him to quit his job?"

"I had to quit school and was sent to help you." I got nervous after I blurted that out.

"That was your mother's choice. I asked her to come. Besides, Dino helps when he comes on weekends."

I can't believe I had that sort of conversation with my aunt. At the time I felt I was being defiant and disrespectful, and I see it that way now. I behaved in opposition to what I had been taught by my parents Sofia and Nikos. I was boiling inside once the fun of Carnavali was in the past and my cousins were back in school.

During the week I endured the stern demands and complaints of Thea Mitsa. "What would people say of your American-looking attire?" She didn't approve of my wearing pants, which had not yet become acceptable apparel for the girls in Naoussa.

On weekends the cousins and I went out and met with boys. Funny thing is, the girls (and sometimes with the help of liberal male cousins) had devised a system of covering up for each other. We would all start out together as a group and the older ones who had boyfriends split from us younger ones who were in the curious stage of romance. We were eager and happy to assist the ones who had found a secret someone. Our biggest fear was not getting caught by our male cousins, but by the worst possible person to uncover our secret, our Theo Christos. He was the strictest of the strictest. He kept a tight rein on his five daughters. But in the culture of the time, his authority expanded to the children who were his relatives and friends. His youngest daughter, Soty, who at nine years old did not grasp the importance of secrecy, would in her naïveté tattle on our escapades whenever she had something to disclose. All of us were on the look-out for little Soty.

In addition to our fear of relatives witnessing our transgressions, anyone who knew our relatives was also someone to avoid. Such was the culture of the times, everyone felt obligated to meddle in the business of protecting each other's children. In three years in the US, I had not heard of such protection and intervention except in ethnic families.

One spring day an agitated Thea Mitsa met us in the downstairs hallway. Katina, Antonia, and I had returned from a walk in the park. My cousins took one look at Thea, then turned and bolted to escape her wrath.

"Rumors have reached Dino's ears that you are involved with Nikos," said my aunt.

I stared up at her, not knowing if I should lie or what. After all, my involvement with Nikos was only in my head.

"I don't believe it's true, but it has angered and upset Dino. You know he has been waiting until you are old enough to marry you."

I couldn't believe what I was hearing. Dino was ten years older than me. I didn't want to marry him. I wasn't even aware that was the plan.

"What? I don't want to marry him. I'm still very young. Does my mother know this?"

"She agrees as long as you say yes."

"I say no, I am just a kid."

"You are not going to marry now. But he needs to know you will wait for him. Perhaps you can wear a ring as your commitment to marry him."

"Oh, you mean wear the ring, but it really won't mean I am going to marry him?"

I thought she would clobber me with her cane.

"WHAT? You want to deceive my son?"

I thought the ceiling beams would crash down.

"You want to lie to my son? Shame on you. I want you to wear a ring and wait for him."

"No, I am not going to do that."

I ran up the stairs. My cheeks were burning. My body was shaking. I could not believe what had happened. I was embarrassed that they knew about Nikos. I thought my head would explode. I held back my screams. How could they all think that I would marry Dino? A few years later I heard all the details about the plan.

Since Dino and I were not blood relatives, we could be married. Thea Mitsa and the late Theo Vassilis had adopted Dino when he was five years old. If Dino and I married each other, the two sisters did not have to be concerned with how to split the family properties.

After the argument there was no more talk about the marriage. Whenever Dino came home he was cold and distant with me, but that did not bother me.

I view this as the second pivotal moment in my life. In both cases, first saying no to the adoption in the courthouse in Veria at age ten, and then at fourteen saying no to a marriage in Naoussa.

Without knowing, I had applied the principle of "love yourself." Louise Hay, the motivational author and founder of Hay House Publishing, would have been proud of me on several occasions throughout my life. Even at a young age I was fortunate to have found the ability to follow a guiding system, my intuition, my gut feeling, my inner voice, whatever we want to call it. I realize I accepted certain undesirable circumstances without their tearing me apart. I summoned the strength to drudge and sometimes muddle through whatever shattered my security. I can assign principles to specific challenges I learned to overcome from reading numerous Hay House authors. Once I discovered Louise Hay, Wayne Dyer, Marianne Williamson, and others, I attributed my overcoming setbacks to an inner knowing.

My mother arrived in July to spend a month in Greece and to take me back to the US. She signed over her inheritance to her sister except for the co-owned condominium in Thessaloniki. I assumed that made Thea happy and I did not hear nor observe any friction between the sisters.

Having my mother in Naoussa gave me a sense of security I had not felt since the outrage over the marriage plan. She was eager to hear details I had not written in my letters. To my surprise she was happy I had refused to marry Dino, but she wanted us to keep the sentiment to ourselves.

My mother's visit seemed to have moved time faster. Before I knew it, people were wishing us a safe trip back. I was feeling the pangs of separation from my cousins. During my long and unexpected visit, we had developed a close relationship and I knew I would miss them. At the same time, I was anxious to return home, hoping to enter high school in the fall.

22

Success and Responsibility

My hopes of starting high school were not fulfilled. Just as Mrs. Moscatelli informed me before I was forced to leave school in the middle of eighth grade, I had to repeat the eighth grade. My new classmates became my new friends. I overcame the fact that I was one year older than they were. Eighth grade the second time around was easy for me since I had gone through half of the material the previous year.

After I graduated from the William H. Taft Junior High School, my mother and I made our annual trip to Greece. Another month of reconnecting with the cousins in Naoussa, with Dimitra in Thessaloniki, and Theo Pavlos in Veria, where he and his family had moved. On that trip I did something I hadn't done before. I wrote to my junior high school friends. I had finally made American friends and I would be going to high school with them. Toward the end of the month the conversation with the cousins and friends turned toward school. Antonia and Katina were going to beauty school to become hairdressers, Dimitra, like me, was going to high school.

Upon my return I connected with my junior high school friends. We shopped for our school supplies and our clothes for back to school.

We were familiar with Brighton High School, the colossal gray stone building across from our junior high school. The massive structure on the hill emanated power and the promise to create the foundation for our adult futures.

Between changing classrooms, and meeting multiple new teachers and new students, we had to plan to see our old friends. I had to tell my made-up story to the new people in my life. I had decided when I first arrived in the States what I wanted was to fit in and be accepted by my classmates. In my mind that meant being normal, being a kid with parents. Except to my parents' friends, to everyone else I was an only child. I held a belief that there was something derogatory about being adopted. As a result of what I had heard in Kostohori, after my parents' deaths, I believed it wasn't normal or a nice thing to be adopted. I felt being adopted stigmatized me. The question came up often.

"Do you have any brothers and sisters"

"No."

If I had said I had a sister, the obvious next questions would have been, "Where is she? Why is she in Greece?" Then I would have to go through the story of our parents' deaths and all the aftermath. It was easier to be an only child.

I avoided talking about my family. During high school my trusted four friends became privy to my secret. We called ourselves The Group—Donna, Laura, MaryEllen, Sue, and me. Our friendship has endured the test of time. Decades later we are still in touch, regularly by phone and social media, and periodically in person. There are geographical distances between us, we are scattered along the East Coast of the US, but when we get together, we pick up where we left off and still cry and laugh together.

High school became a haven for me. New activities occupied my time after school. And if I wasn't at a school activity I was at a friend's house. I felt free and independent.

"In high school you will have the opportunity to join several clubs," Miss Moscatelli had informed me.

"What kind of clubs?"

"There will be a club for almost all your classes. I suggest you join and become involved."

I took her word literally. Although I was shy around people and did not talk much, I joined every club my schedule allowed. Math, English, Art, Spanish, and the school magazine. I had to wait until I was a junior to try out for the cheerleading squad. As a first-year student I watched the squad practice on the school's front lawn. I had never seen anything like it. I was intrigued. The cute little short orange jumpers, the white knit sweater with the orange and black B centered on the chest. They were all smiling and using deep voices as they spelled out Brighton, and football players' names. Two of the girls wore black jumpers and they were leading the squad. I made up my mind I would be one of them as soon as I could. In my junior year I took advantage of the opportunity to try out for the squad. During my junior and senior years, I cheered for our teams. In my senior year I wore one of the black jumpers.

I embraced everything the school offered. My limited exposure to a non-Greek environment spurred an immense interest to partake in my new environment's smorgasbord of activities. My mind and eyes soaked up the conduct, the demeanor, the jargon, and the attire of fellow students. I absorbed the information I gathered to customize my likes and values, and to broaden my cultural viewpoint. Conversations with classmates revealed different lifestyles and philosophies. Unlike me, they were aware of what to expect in high school.

The social, sports, and academic activities available in high school impressed me. I knew my counterparts in Greece were all about academics. Anything beyond that they had to find outside the school environment. They spent more time studying than we did and those whose parents could afford it went to private tutoring classes. Good students attended these classes to excel in a specific course, others to improve, but the focus was always to study hard. My friend Dimitra, an excellent student, wrote in her letters to me, "By the time I do my homework and attend tutoring classes, I have no time for fun. If I'm lucky on Sundays, I get to do something with friends."

Away from school my world consisted of interacting with my parents and other fellow expats. I paid close attention to the different and new norms and traditions to which I was exposed. I picked and chose to create the American version of me. Some students worked after school. Most girls wore makeup. Not only was I not allowed to date but I was told that when I was old enough to marry, I would have to marry a Greek. Wearing makeup and sheer stockings was out of the question.

"No, you cannot get a job while you are in school. Your job is to be a student."

Students in Greece did not work unless it was necessary to help with the family's financial needs. In my sophomore year, my parents acquiesced and allowed me to work in a bakery on Saturdays. Despite the stringent rules at home, I was immersed in the social and academic scene of high school. Victory parties after the football games, gatherings of the various clubs, and of course spending time with The Group doing homework or going shopping. I even managed to attend the senior prom when I was a sophomore.

Ricky, the quarterback on our football team, and I met after the first game of the season. We got to know each other over the course of the school year. In the spring he asked me to the prom. I could not wait to tell The Group.

"Guess what? You won't believe this. Ricky asked me to the prom." Donna was the first to hear it.

"Are you going?"

We were standing on the front lawn of the school by the steps leading to the street. The other three joined us.

"What are you guys so happy about?" asked Laura

"Ricky asked Stella to the senior prom," Donna answered.

Maryellen and Sue's eyes almost popped out of their sockets. They all knew Ricky and they had teased me about his liking me, but I hadn't given it much attention. I had been enjoying my friendships with the boys without having any attachments.

My popularity in school and my successes and fun at school compensated for my life at home. My mother had recovered from leg surgery. During her convalescence, I had become her caregiver. To my parents' credit, they allowed me to keep up with my school activities as long as I could take care of my chores when I got home. We thought she was fully recovered but she still hadn't gone back to work two months after her surgery.

"Moving to a house with a yard will do me good," she said.

"We'll ask around," I heard my father reply and that is all the conversation I heard about a move.

Before my sophomore year we moved to our third location since my arrival in the US. Moving to Brock Street in Brighton meant I would still attend Brighton High School and keep the same friends. As a sophomore in high school I anticipated good grades, and a busy social calendar. What could possibly go wrong with a teenager's solid plan?

23

Another Hurdle

Boxwood bushes, holly bushes, and hydrangeas grew inside the white picket fences of the triple-decker homes on Brock Street, which were distinguished only by their paint colors. Otherwise, the row of houses looked exactly alike. Triple-deckers lined up like soldiers along the left side of the street. The opposite side presented an array of single- and two-story houses sprinkled with a three-decker here and there. We made our home on the second floor at number 50, painted light blue. Our landlady, Mrs. Paris, a widow, lived above us on the third floor. She was a first-generation Greek. The next two houses were owned by two sisters, also first-generation Greek. The mother of the two sisters, who had emigrated from Greece, owned and lived in the last triple-decker on the street.

As far as I was concerned, everything was wonderful. We settled into our new neighborhood. Our home had a back yard, my mother had Greek neighbors with whom she could visit, and her other friends remained close by. My schedule stayed the same. My father's commute to Boston was a little longer but he didn't complain.

We continued our regular visits with the Papazlis family. Friday nights were card game nights for the adults. Evelyn and I saw each other at family gatherings. We each had acquired our own non-Greek friends. However, we did participate in church events together, although we no longer went to the cathedral in Boston. We attended the Saints Constantine and Helen Greek Orthodox Church in Cambridge. The summer Greek festivals which at the time were referred to as picnics, sponsored by each of the area Greek churches, were popular and fun.

People throughout metropolitan Boston flocked to the Sunday events. The festivals or pikiniki, the Greek immigrant version of picnic, enabled us to indulge in the culture of the homeland and provided time to see friends, to eat and dance, and for singles to meet other singles.

At the Cathedral's picnic, in the summer of 1964, Mrs. George asked me for a favor.

"A father from Greece brought his seventeen-year-old son to Boston for a medical treatment that is not available in Greece."

I listened to her and wondered what that had to do with me.

"Because you speak Greek and English, I thought you could visit at the hospital to translate for them. The hospital is near your high school."

"Sure, I can do that. Call my mother and tell her the details."

I had experience with hospital visits. I spent numerous days visiting my mother at the New England Baptist Hospital in Boston when she had her surgery. *At least I won't have to take two streetcars to visit this boy. I'll walk there from school.*

And so began my volunteer career. Up until that time I had been helping adults with their bills, appointments, and correspondence. I felt confident I could help the father and son. After all I had translated for my mother when she was in the hospital.

I am glad I helped Mr. Pappas and his son, Yiannis. On my first visit, the sadness etched on the man's face when he squeezed my hand and mouthed thank you, travelled to my heart. After two months of stopping in to visit even when they did not need my interpreting, Mrs. George called. I sensed from her trembling voice why she called. "Stella, you don't have to go to the funeral, you are just a kid."

Going to Yiannis's funeral brought back all the feelings of loss I had experienced: my parents, my almost-adopted father, and my separation from my sister, from my theo, and from my country. Mrs. George, Mr. Pappas and I were the only ones there. Just three of us and the priest in the huge Greek Orthodox Cathedral along with the casket holding Yiannis's body. I could not believe that this father, full of hope, had brought his teenage son for treatment and he ended up burying him in a foreign country, almost five thousand miles away from home. He left the United States without his son. He didn't have to tell us how sad he was. His stooped shoulders, red eyes, and unshaven face told it all. I wanted to hug him and make him feel better.

Meanwhile on Brock Street, our own drama was unfolding. My mother did not achieve the results she expected from living in a house with a yard. We made frequent visits to the doctor. She spent days at a time in bed. After countless visits and tests, she was diagnosed with lung cancer. I had no idea of its severity. I didn't think it was a good thing, but I kept waiting for her to get better. Instead, she remained bedridden for weeks. The doctor began to make house visits. Every time the doctor visited, I believed he would tell us she was getting better. Instead, at the end of November she was again admitted to the New England Baptist Hospital for cancer treatments.

In December 1964, Martin Luther King Jr. received the Nobel Peace Prize for his contribution to the American civil rights movement. The Beatles released *Beatles for Sale*. Also, in December 1964, at age sixteen, I visited my mother in the hospital every day after school.

I liked it when the other bed in my mother's room was vacant. I could spread my books out on the extra bed and do my homework. However, when she had a roommate, I felt embarrassed to be talking in Greek. Most of the time my mother was well groomed. She applied her Coty face powder and lipstick.

"Did you do your hair yourself?"

"Yes, I used the rollers you brought me. And I will need more hair spray soon."

"I can bring some tomorrow. It's good you are wearing the red lipstick. It looks good on you."

A few times I had seen my mother without powder and lipstick. On those occasions I avoided looking at her directly. Her skin had turned ashen, her sunken cheeks looked like they had been punched in. The blue-black circles under her eyes gave her a bewildered look. *She looks so sick. She might not get better. She may never come home.* I encouraged her to use her powder and lipstick so that I could evade those thoughts. I wanted to believe that she would get better and come home.

The letters from my uncle to me had been clear about my responsibility as a daughter. "You are their daughter, if you don't take care of them who will?" I wanted to write back, "But I'm only a kid." Instead, I did what I believed my culture dictated I should do. My friends from Greece were writing, "You are a student and a kid. You shouldn't have to take care of your mother." My American friends did not comment. Our neighbors praised me. I did what I believed a good daughter should do.

On those days, at the hospital with my books spread out on the adjacent bed, I thought a lot about my sister. As far as I knew, her parents were healthy. I wondered if she was having a normal childhood. Was she thinking and wondering about me? What were her favorite foods, what kind of music did she like? Did she have a lot of friends? I spent weeks of daydreaming and doing homework in my mother's hospital room. I had not detected her deterioration and my father had not shared anything he may have known.

For some reason the telephone's ring was different on Tuesday, December 22, 1964. It pierced through my insides. I stumbled into the kitchen as I was pulling my red jumper over my head. I had been hurrying to get ready for school. Babá placed the telephone in its wall cradle and slumped on the chair. In his blue and gray striped flannel pajamas, he appeared smaller than usual. The tears ran in tracks formed by the wrinkles on his face. He crossed his arms on the Formica table, looked at me with two red-rimmed eyes and said, "She died last night."

I sat in the chair next to him and I took my turn at crying. We sat there immobilized. Our thoughts about our loss rested safely in our hearts and minds. After he drained his cup of coffee and stubbed out his Lucky Strike my father regained his composure.

"Call school and tell them your mother died and you will be absent. I will call my work. Then we will go to the funeral home to make the arrangements."

Among the names on the list for me to call, he included my cousins, Litsa and Veta. They had moved from Naoussa to Brighton after their marriages to men from the United States. They and their parents made the sacrifice of being apart in pursuit of the American dream. They were the older female cousins with whom I had bonded during my eighth-grade stint in Naoussa. The sound of their sobs burst through the receiver upon hearing the news. That triggered a new bout of crying for me and that's how it went with each of the calls I made. The person on the other end cried and I joined in. Litsa and Veta agreed to come over to help with the preparations. I knew both were deeply saddened. To their families and to them, our family was the only relatives they had in the United States.

"I am not wearing all black. I don't believe in that."

"Stella, listen, you must. She is your mother. It is our custom," Litsa, the older one, said first.

Then Veta, "You have to do it. We will find some black clothes for you. What will people say if you don't wear black?"

"I don't care what people say. I'm willing to wear gray or brown. Those are dark colors. I am not wearing black."

Perhaps it's the image from six years earlier. The ladies in all black at the village wailing and screeching at my mother's funeral and again for days following my father's funeral.

At the Hasiotis Funeral Home in Brighton, I wore a gray wool straight skirt with a gray wool knit sweater. I was relieved there were not wailers and screamers present. A small group of respectable mourners attended the then-customary two-day wake. For two days I endured throughout the afternoon and evening visiting hours. At sixteen years old I wasn't certain how to mourn for a mother I had only had for five years. I soaked my cotton hankie wiping the bout of tears every time someone new expressed sympathy, after having paused at my mother's coffin. Their attempts to comfort me with expressions such as "She left us too soon," "You are too young to be orphaned," and "You and your father must take care of each other" brought on the tears. It was an automatic reaction, sympathy crying because others were crying. My father's red eyes accentuated the circles underneath. Aside from his distressed face, he looked impeccable in a black suit and black tie. Litsa and Veta temporarily lost their youth in their all-black attire. They resembled untimely widows rather than the two attractive young mothers they were.

Mrs. Paris and our next-door neighbors Lucky and Helen arranged for the mercy meal at our house. I lost the battle of wanting to bypass the traditional Lenten meal consisting of fish, rice, feta, and olives. I wanted to include meats. Tradition prevailed. Fish is a symbol of Christ's resurrection; the side dishes are plain and not celebratory or modern. Except for biscotti, which is associated with the mercy meal, no sweets are served. I don't know why I had it in my head I did not want a morbid atmosphere, I wanted a lighthearted one and thought roast lamb or pastitsio or moussaka would accomplish that. I was relieved when everyone left and I didn't have to listen to mournful conversation. It was just my father and me at the house alone, as it had been for almost two months.

24

Two of Us

MY FATHER AND ME.

Christmas school vacation afforded my father and me the opportunity to establish a routine for the two of us. My father and I had been on our own for almost two months while Mamá was in the hospital. Before that, although she was at home, Babá and I had managed all the household chores because she was too weak. We were happy for the days she could sit outside on the porch and visit with the neighbors. They drank coffee, smoked, and caught up on everyone's business. Thus, taking care of Babá after Mamá's death did not seem like an onerous responsibility for me. Two years prior I had been sent to help take care of Yiayia. Helping people felt natural to me. The words of the visiting mourners drifted in and out of my mind. "You and your father must take care of each other now."

That directive did not seem as daunting as "Take care of your sister." That had been a standard instruction from our parents back in Thessaloniki. As the older sister I enjoyed caring for and protecting Lena. But when my friends and I got to be eight and nine years old, her presence annoyed my friends. I had the freedom to go all the way down to the end of street to play with Eli and the rest of the kids.

We felt older and did not want anyone's little siblings to tag along. Our mother's promises and tricks to dissuade from her whining and crying when she was told not to follow me proved useless. Lena invariably cried herself into one of her tantrums. It was a victory for me whenever I bolted out of sight before she recovered from her tantrum. When my escape failed, I reluctantly held her hand as we shuffled down the dirt street leaving a trail of dust behind us.

One time, giving in to her demand did not serve her well. On the last day of school, after receiving our final report cards we met in front of the school as usual.

"What did you get?"

"Ten," I said. Ten was the highest grade.

"Give it to me and you take mine," she demanded

Her grade of six was just enough to get her promoted to second grade but she wanted a ten. I handed it to her without hesitation. In my naïveté I thought she just wanted to hold it and feel good about holding a "ten" report card until we got home.

The sound of the motorcycle announced our father's arrival home from work. Lena quit her turn at hopscotch and dashed into the house. She returned holding our report cards. She handed me one of them and pranced over to our father and presented what was allegedly hers.

In the early evening light, her face shone like the sun. As poised as a first grader can be, she tilted her head back and fixed her eyes on Babá in anticipation of his praise.

"I got a ten."

"Is this your report card?" he asked.

Her poise melted away as she nodded and kept her gaze to the ground. He grabbed her by the shoulders.

"Look at me. Where is your report card? This is Stella's."

I handed him the report card I was holding.

BAM came the slap on her cheek.

"And you? Why did you give her your report card?"

I was relieved he didn't sound angry with me. "I didn't know she was going to say it was hers."

My poor little sister was not aware the report cards had our names on them. I wished I had not given it to her. Had I known what she was planning to do I would have refused. But I was accustomed to appeasing her, protecting her, and taking care of her.

So, at the age of sixteen, taking care of my father was not a problem.

Babá went back to work the day after the funeral. We agreed we would have dinner together on weeknights. No more need to meet at the hospital and come home late. On Saturdays I would clean house and do laundry while he visited with his friends at the Naoussa Men's Club.

A group of men originally from Naoussa had rented an apartment in the South End of Boston. They converted the one-bedroom, living room, kitchen unit into a meeting place. On any given day they could count on finding at least one or two of their countrymen at the club. I had experienced their camaraderie whenever I met my father there the year I attended Christopher Columbus School. The wooden stairs creaked as I mounted them to the second floor. The disrepair of the staircase and the walls leading to the apartment were a contrast to the club's interior. Inside, the place was spotless. The glass cabinets above the sink displayed the demitasse cups lined up and ready for a Greek coffee. A variety of glasses were arranged according to their size and purpose. First the beer, water, and highball glasses, as they were the same size, next the stemless wine glasses, and the smallest of all for ouzo or Metaxa brandy. The aluminum percolator with the small glass bulb on its cover was on the stove next to the briki, which is for making Greek coffee.

On every occasion when I arrived, the men were in various stages of their visits. Some occupied a table and were absorbed in their card game. There were nickels, dimes, and quarters on the table. Others sat engrossed with a newspaper. The men seated at the table closest to the kitchen shared a beverage or a meal one of them had prepared. The men, in their sixties, seventies and eighties, all had emigrated from Naoussa. This oasis gave them the opportunity to share news from back home, to seek and find help for their needs, and to give direction and aid to newcomers. While my father was at the club, I knew I could carry out my chores and still have time to meet up with friends on Saturdays. I also knew there would be Saturday night parties and pajama parties and I would have to get permission for those outings.

We decided Sundays we would spend either with Litsa's, Veta's, or friends' families. We also planned to spend a month in Greece during the summer. Before I returned to school, we had a week in which to implement the plan and all indications pointed to its success. I felt compassion for the sweet, mild-mannered man who had become my father. The embarrassment I felt for his age aside, I sensed and appreciated his complete devotion to do a good job as a single father. He was strict but trusting, and I felt badly whenever I took advantage of that trust by not disclosing that I was going out on dates. He was caring. He ensured I had what I needed to flourish as a teenager.

"Do you have enough money for lunch?" On the days I wasn't buying my lunch he had a brown bag all ready with a ham sandwich on white bread, or peanut butter and jelly, an apple or Oreo cookies.

The day before I returned to school, he took out a blue Maxwell House coffee tin from the pantry shelf and ceremoniously placed it on the kitchen table.

"This is where I keep some cash. I don't want you to ever be out and not have money to come home. If you forget to ask me for money and you need it, take it from here. Just tell me when you take money, so I'll know how much to put back." How could I not care for and love the man?

During the Christmas break, Gale and JoJo, Lucky's daughters, surprised me with their frequent invitations to join them next door. I was sandwiched between them in age by one year. The traffic in their house was as busy as the intersection at Brighton Center. At our apartment, aside from us and an occasional visitor, quietness prevailed.

Gale was old enough to have her boyfriend visit and sometimes his friends joined them. JoJo had girlfriends stopping in and out. Their two brothers who were in elementary school had friends visiting. I took pleasure in watching Lucky having coffee either with her sister Helen or another neighbor. They sat at the green Formica table dragging on cigarettes—drinking endless cups of coffee. I fantasized about what it would be like to be part of a family like theirs.

I felt awkward on my first day back to school after my mother's death. I wondered if my classmates would want to know what happened. Would they look at me in a strange way? The way those villagers looked at me when I lived with Theo Pavlos? My friends knew what had happened but the students with whom I associated only in school might make inquiries. I created all sorts of scenarios for nothing. I discovered my classmates were experiencing awkward moments in my presence. They avoided direct eye contact. A typical response from the boys after saying "hi" was to look down and sweep away something that wasn't there with their shoe. The girls commented on my outfit or homework. I realized we were all experiencing normal adolescent behavior, which lasted a few days.

The teachers took a direct approach. They pretty much expressed it the same way: "I am sorry about your mother's death. If you and your father need assistance, let the school know."

Babá and I managed fine on our own. Babá gave me cash for food shopping, school supplies, and clothes. For personal spending I just had to ask or go to the coffee tin. During that period, thoughts of my sister surfaced more frequently. *She probably doesn't know I lost another mother. How is she doing as a fourteen-year-old?* According to Theo Pavlos, who occasionally corresponded with her father, she was doing well. However, her parents continued to refuse my communicating with her. They feared that if I corresponded with her, her threats of the past would resurface: "I know I have a sister. If I find out where she is I am going to her." I did find comfort in receiving information about her well-being but my relationship with my sister had been stymied. For six years we had not heard each other's voices. We had not hugged or held each other's hand like we used to do when we walked down the street. As teenagers we hadn't shared our escapades, our successes, our fears. Does she have many friends? What do they do when they get together? Does she like boys? When did she get her period? Does she miss me? Do her friends know I exist?

Our neighbors, our Greek community, The Group, and our relatives knew that I was adopted and had a sister. My pretending to be an only child to the rest of the world became an inner struggle. In the privacy of my mind, I kept Lena alive as much as I could. However, I sensed the birth of an emotional distance. In my mind she remained the little sister I had been instructed to take care of—the one who constantly wanted to be with me. I thought of the times she threw a tantrum when my friends and I didn't want her to play with us. I saw her almond-shaped green eyes filled with excitement, playing in the school yard at the village. I saw scattered images of the almost eight-year-old in Kostohori after our parents' burials. The happy-go-lucky little girl relishing yellow American cheese at the one-room schoolhouse in the village. And then poof, one day she disappeared. That was as far as our relationship had developed. My closeness to Donna, Laura, MaryEllen, and Sue—The Group—filled the void of my sister's absence.

The five of us shared our yearnings, complaints, ambitions, opinions, our adolescent insecurities, and curiosities. I felt these were the threads that weaved relationships. I believed by not sharing these feelings with my sister someone pressed the pause button on our relationship.

In preparation for my annual summer month in Greece, I asked for help and had eager participants from The Group. We made several shopping trips to downtown Boston. Two or three of us at a time scoured the floors of Filene's and Jordan Marsh department stores. All five of us tried to meet up for Wednesday's dollar day at Jordan Marsh. Both stores occupied an entire block and were across the street from each other. I felt privileged to have been allowed to shop at these stores. They were popular with our peers who were of middle class means. On the other hand, Newbury Street shopping, in the Back Bay neighborhood with its elegant shops, was not even in our vocabulary. I didn't even know anyone who shopped on Newbury Street. It would be years before my wallet held credit cards from Bonwit Teller and Tiffany & Co.

"Be careful where you keep the money," my father instructed as he handed me one hundred dollars. "First, buy all the presents and next week I will give you money to buy for yourself."

I appreciated his generosity in gift buying, which included my Theo Pavlos's family. From the beginning of my adoption, they allowed my theo's family to be part of ours. My mother and I had shipped packages to him a few times a year

As sophomores, our social life had become an integral part of school. Apart from joining various clubs in school, we were mindful of after-school socializing. Who got invited to which weekend party. A lot depended on which boys we liked or which boys were interested in us. On any given Saturday, all or some of us ended up invited to the party of the boyfriend du jour. The events had to be local or accessible with public transportation. Sixteen was the magic year for dating. Although I had turned seventeen and was a year older than the others in The Group, I was still not allowed to date. Of course, that did not stop me. I took advantage of my father's trust in me. Since he hadn't asked about it, I didn't volunteer that I was going out with Ricky, a senior at school. When I had told her about my going to the prom with Ricky, Donna had asked, "Are you going to tell your father?"

"I can't do that. I am just going to tell him I am going to a school dance, and I need to buy a gown."

Being from an immigrant family herself, Donna understood the ramifications of seeing someone outside your ethnic background. I had spent a great deal of time at the Chin household and knew the Chinese shared similar beliefs to the Greeks as far as holding on to the cultural norms.

The five of us espoused similar ethical views that our parents had embedded into us. So, when we came up with ideas to violate the rules, we gave it a lot of thought and discussion and mostly rationalized.

"They are old fashioned, they don't understand, things have changed."

Or, "It's not like we are sleeping around."

There was a fine line we did not cross. We stayed away from alcohol, drugs, and sex. Maintaining our virginity, holding off until marriage to have sex, had been the utmost, all-important virtue for us girls to keep. The unfairness of this rule had us discussing it past our bedtimes. It was the same every time.

"It's not fair. Why are the boys not bound by the same rule?" one of us would say.

"Why the double standard?" from another.

"How about when men brag about their sons scoring? Or asking them if they have?"

"Right, whose daughter or sister are they scoring with?"

That one got to me the most. And then there was this: "It's really not fair how they talk about the girls when they say she is easy. And then any boy thinks he can go after her."

We rehashed the issue over and over.

Although we were in the midst of the women's rights movement, we were not aware of its importance. It wasn't anything my father would have discussed with me at home. I don't even know if he was aware of it. Did the Greek newspaper he read publish the US news?

The Group finished sophomore year with good grades and a full schedule of social events. Once we put our books away, we were all about shopping for summer clothes in preparation for the beaches and swimming pools. I had the added pleasure of gift shopping for Greece. After multiple trips to Downtown Crossing, the sunroom in our house resembled a miniature store. White, blue, yellow, and green dresses were spread out on the daybed. The blue and white striped two-piece bathing suit met my father's approval after I convinced him that's what all the girls in Greece would be wearing.

For the flight I wore a straight white knee-length dress. I felt at seventeen I was old enough to wear a straight skirt. To my surprise my father agreed to a ride from Ricky's father. I had introduced Ricky to my father before my mother had gone to the hospital.

"He is not my boyfriend. He is my friend."

"I told you I don't want you going with boys. And he is not Greek."

"I met his parents and his sister; they are good people."

Yes, I lied. He was my boyfriend. The demand to uphold the custom of staying within one's ethnic group for dating and marriage was prevalent among my immigrant peers. As much as our parents had become loyal Americans and wanted us to do the same, they held on to a strong belief in continuing their ethnic lineage. For most of us teenage expats, it was a difficult order. We viewed dating as a novelty, something that was not allowed at all. We saw it as an opportunity to participate in our new culture. At that age we were not thinking of marriage and carrying on our ethnicity. We resorted to covering up our courting.

And that's how I was able to arrange for Ricky and his parents to drive us to Logan International Airport.

25

A Wish Almost Fulfilled

LEFKÓS PÝRGOS (WHITE TOWER), THESSALONIKI.

Greece, the summer of 1965, my first visit after my mother's recent death. I agonized about seeing Thea Mitsa and all the relatives. I didn't want it to be a morbid summer. Luckily two days after our arrival in Thessaloniki, my friend Dimitra stopped by to invite me to the family's summer camp at the shores of the Aegean. I fell into the rhythm of summer immediately, swimming, socializing with friends, and engaging with what I had missed of my homeland.

Dimitra's family still had the same spot for their humongous tent which sheltered anywhere from three to six of their family members. Not that everyone slept under the tent, especially on hot nights. It was normal to sleep outside the tent under the starry sky. Exhausted from the day's activities and the evening's rambling, we found the light show reflected on the Thermaic Gulf soothing.

After a few days of toasting in the sun I returned to Thessaloniki so that my father and I could go to Naoussa together. I was relieved the discussions of my mother's death did not stir up the drama I had expected when the relatives filed in to welcome us. They thanked us profusely for the gifts we had brought. My cousins and I picked up with our shenanigans where we had left off the previous summer. One of my first priorities was to figure out how to connect with Nikos. Through my secret correspondence with him I knew he was serving in the Air Force and was planning a leave at the same time I would be in Greece.

The girls had the information for me and on my second day in Naoussa my dream meeting with the tall young man with the piercing brown eyes became a reality. There was an extra surge of electrified energy going through me as I hustled down the dark street looking around to make sure no one I knew saw me. The streetlights were a blessing and a menace. They provided light for both me and any gossipmonger to see me and report my clandestine activities to a relative. Those surreptitious rendezvous woke every nerve in my body. The anticipation of seeing him after a year was unbearable.

"Come here, Amerikanaki." He reached for my hand, pulled me close and planted his lips on mine. We walked hand in hand in the safety of the soccer field until we reached the street and blended into the group of Nikos's friends at the cafe.

Those were the romantic encounters of my summers in Greece. So simple and naïve yet they carried a ton of emotion. I had a feeling I was a pleasant intrusion in Nikos's life. After all, he was four years older, tall, handsome, and charismatic. Our relationship consisted of writing letters and seeing each other during my annual trips to Greece. As far as I was concerned, he was my boyfriend in Greece, and my intrusion in the States was Ricky.

Another emotion tugged at my heart on this vacation. A state of optimism and excitement hovered over me whenever I thought of it. Two months before we were to leave for our trip to Greece, I had come home after school and read the most exciting letter from my theo Pavlos. I couldn't believe what I was reading.

"Lena's parents invited us to visit her this summer." I reread it to be certain I had read it correctly. It was incredible. Finally, they said okay. In the past seven years when Theo corresponded with Mr. Apostolos, Theo had asked to go see her.

The answer had been, "It's not time. She is still restless, and we are concerned that any contact with you and her sister will make things worse."

I could not wait to tell my father and The Group. The prospect of seeing my sister on this trip stirred up my yearning to see her again and the excitement it created within me increased with each day.

I spent the night before our excursion at my theo's in Veria. We arrived at the bus station early as we had done in our previous attempts to see Lena.

Theo Pavlos purchased our bus tickets as he had done for the earlier two trips to Katerini. Both of those trips ended in disappointment. Lena's parents had not allowed us to see her.

The only cafe open was across from the bus station. We chose a table facing the rising sun and the bus depot. It was a déjà vu moment. *I hope this time they let us see her. They can't say the same thing again.* "We fear that seeing you will exacerbate her restlessness."

I stared at the empty table and fidgeted before I blurted out, "Do you think they will let us see her this time?"

Neither one of us had seen my little sister since her adoption.

"That's what I am hoping. Stella, they are good people. From the beginning she had threatened them to run away if she found you. That's why they haven't allowed us to see her."

Theo gave our order to the waiter. Even though I was seventeen, I ordered what I as a child had considered a special breakfast treat. I spread the butter with such precision as to cover the entire surface of the thick slices of bread. I drizzled the honey slowly, forming a design of amber-colored rivers crisscrossing on the slices, causing my stomach to send signals of what lay ahead. It happened to me every time. The breakfast triggered the memory of other bus rides and their effects on me.

Pedestrians passed by our table. The city was waking up. Across the street people lined up to purchase tickets. My stomach churned in earnest, and I dreaded the near future.

"It's time, the bus just pulled up."

As much as it was possible, I tried to push away the nauseated feeling. I wanted to savor the treat I had just finished. The distasteful odor of diesel fumes hit my nostrils and landed in my stomach. I knew the combination of the bus's bumpy ride and the pungent odor would make me vomit. The more I tried to ignore the thought, the worst my stomach felt. Before the bus reached the city limits sign, the bread, honey, and milk found their way into the bag we had brought. It was difficult to ignore the putrid sour stench and bitter taste. Theo's hand on my shoulder eased my embarrassment but it did not stop the tears—but falling asleep did

"Wake up, we are here."

I wondered how my uncle, the man who towered over most other men, could have such a gentle touch. I looked up and saw concern in his crystal-blue eyes.

By the time we walked the two blocks to Mr. Apostolos' office my stomach was better, but I was experiencing a different kind of sick. Just as we were about to ring the doorbell, I asked, "Will he really allow us to see her?"

"I don't know. We will see." The uncertainty in his voice rang louder than the bell.

Mr. Apostolos greeted us graciously and offered to order refreshments. His office was like what I would expect a lawyer's office to be— dark wood furnishings, a giant desk, and shelves filled with books.

I sipped my lemonade while Theo Pavlos and Mr. Apostolos waited for their coffees to cool off. I followed the clouds of steam rising above the white demitasse cups.

"She is a good student," Mr. Apostolos told us. "This summer she joined a swim team and will also take up horseback riding." The Katerini beaches on the Thermaic Gulf of the Aegean Sea offer easy access to a variety of water sports.

"I know I told you to come so you can see Lena," he continued. "However, this morning my wife became nervous about it, and she decided it was not the right time to see her. She feels that now that Lena is a teenager, seeing you may unsettle her."

My heart plummeted to my feet.

"Mr. Apostolos, it's been seven years," my uncle said.

His voice had a calming effect. "Pavlos, I know this is difficult for you both and I apologize. My wife is afraid that Lena will be stirred up if she sees you and will become more difficult to deal with."

Suddenly drinking lemonade didn't feel so special. *Another trip in vain.*

Mr. Apostolos touched his gold tie pin, and slowly traced his tie down to its tip. The diagonal stripes in shades of brown complemented his dark brown suit. He leaned forward with a sneaky look.

"I have thought of something in order for your trip to not be a total waste. You will go to the house under the pretense that Stella will be a teacher in Katerini this coming school year. You will say you are in search of a room to rent, and you heard there is a room for rent at the house."

"If you think that will work with Mrs. Nitsa, we will do it. Right, Stella?"

What was I to think? My heart and head were in motion again. *How can I be a teacher? I'm seventeen years old. I know that I think I look mature for my age, but a teacher?*

I nodded in agreement.

"That's what we will do. You go now and I will call to inform my wife how she is to handle it."

We shook hands. Mr. Apostolos walked us out to the street and gave us directions to the house.

"Theo, how am I going to pretend I'm a teacher?"

"I don't know but we will do as her father suggested. We will finally see her."

I could see the pink bougainvillea blossoms that peeked above the brick wall. The entrance was around the corner. Theo Pavlos pressed the rectangular button. My feet froze in place and then we heard the click that released the metal gate. Dread and excitement penetrated every cell of my body.

"Who is it?" We heard the voice of a woman.

I followed my theo. *Look tall and mature like a teacher,* I instructed myself. A girl, in white, appeared next to the stout woman with curly gray hair who wore a pale blue flowered dress. As mother and daughter moved forward, I fixed my eyes as discreetly as possible on the gorgeous teenager. *That is my sister. She is not the little girl I remember. So grown up, almost as tall as her mother. I would not have recognized her if I had seen her on the street.*

"Good morning, we were told you have a room for rent. My niece here will be teaching in Katerini this coming year."

"You're mistaken; we don't have a room for rent but come upstairs."

Of course, it was weird that she would invite strangers in, but that was the plan Mr. Apostolos devised.

I felt my sister's eyes on me with every step I took. *My sister.* It was a strange feeling. The flutter in my stomach intensified by the time I reached the landing. They stepped aside to let us in and closed the door.

"Come in, come in. I don't know why they gave you that information." I sensed Mrs. Nitsa was as nervous as we were. "Lena, why don't you make us coffee and bring a glyko."

Once the kitchen door closed, the proud mom repeated the same accolades Mr. Apostolos had shared regarding their daughter's schooling. She added, "For the most part she is good. But she is defiant and difficult with the rules of the house."

Like a perfect hostess, Lena took the coffees and the glyko off the silver tray and placed them on the coffee table. She did not hide her gaze on me. For a few seconds I glanced at her beautiful almond-shaped green eyes. The white dress hugged her perfectly symmetrical figure. *She is gorgeous, my little sister.* I had a chance to sneak enough glances at her before she left the room. According to the culture at the time, a fifteen-year-old would have to be invited to visit with the adults.

Mrs. Nitsa picked up where she left off.

"You see, because of her rebellious state, I don't feel a reunion with her sister and other relatives will be a good thing. I think it will add to her disobedience and defiance. Let's give her a little more time."

"We appreciate your inviting us in to at least see her. She looks wonderful and I know you are taking good care of her. Both Stella and I have been waiting for this moment."

I don't remember if I contributed to the conversation other than the appropriate pleasantries.

We left without saying goodbye to Lena.

"Theo, she has grown so much. She is beautiful. Do you think she recognized us? Do you think she believed the teacher story?"

We would have to wait to find out the answers. It was absurd to pass me off as a teacher.

I survived another typical Stella bus ride of motion sickness back to Veria. I did not allow the nausea and all its aspects to take away from the triumphant feeling of seeing my sweet sister. I basked in the visions I held of her at the top of the stairs, her setting down the coffees without spilling one drop while she gazed at me. Reliving the day's events lulled me into sleep. I woke just before the bus arrived at the station.

Theo Pavlos waited until we heard the boarding call for Naoussa. Our usual emotional embrace ended with promises to write to each other when I returned to America. I had been through enough embarrassing moments that day to not be concerned about the tears streaming down my face and the need to blow my nose. He looked blurry but I could see him, wiping his eyes. I waited until he faded in the background and wiped my face for the last time that day.

To my relief I did not get sick on the ride to Naoussa. By the time I finished relating my day to my father and Thea Mitsa, the cousins arrived, all geared up for a fun evening. I wanted to freshen up and change clothes, but Antonia and Katina were too eager to meet the rest of the gang.

"You go ahead, I will meet you at the park."

"Don't take too long. They won't wait forever."

I was still processing my visit or non-visit with my sister. I took my time getting ready. But once I stepped onto the street, I was in my vacation mode. I cut through the main square instead of going straight down my street. I wanted to pass by the cafe where Nikos and his friends hung out in hopes of catching a glimpse of him. *Maybe they are at the park.* At the park I caught site of Katina's arm frantically waving. The small table was overcrowded with cold beverages. Our favorite *zaharoplastio* (patisserie), on the edge of the park, offered a clear view of the street. Between sips of Coca-Cola, we could comment and gossip about the people who were out for an evening stroll.

"Nikos left today for Thessaloniki. He gave me a note for you." Antonia handed me the note folded into a small square. In two days, I would be leaving for Boston, and I would not be seeing him until my next visit to Greece.

At the end of the evening, I said goodbye to everyone except my cousins. They wished me a safe trip back home and we agreed we would write to each other regularly.

The last two days were a whirlwind of meals with relatives, good-byes, presents, packing and tears. The atmosphere in the Olympic Airways bus station felt heavy. Most of the passengers were wiping tears off their faces and blowing their noses. Some waved frantically at their loved ones who were walking next to the bus until it pulled away from Aristotelous Square in Thessaloniki.

The cafes along the street were already packed with the morning crowd enjoying the view of the Thermaic Gulf directly across from them. Motorcycles and Vespas whizzed by us or weaved through the other vehicles on the one-way waterfront avenue. Their noise was enough to wake anyone who thought they would take a little snooze. I made sure I was awake to see the famous White Tower on the water side of the street.

Lefkós Pýrgos, the White Tower, was an old Byzantine fortification which was reconstructed into a fort by the Ottoman Empire. Sultan Murad II captured Thessaloniki in 1430. It was a prison and the site of mass executions during the Ottoman rule. In 1912 Thessaloniki regained its freedom. The tower was remodeled and has become the city's symbol. Tourists and locals alike have their photograph taken there to pay homage—tantamount to having your picture taken at the Acropolis in Athens. On every visit I made sure I saw the famous landmark when I arrived and again on my way back to the airport for my return home.

On board another TWA flight, I watched the flight attendants giving the safety demonstration, but I wasn't fully listening. My mind was flying its own flight pattern. Thoughts of seeing Nikos and the fun with my cousins and friends flew by fast. I was in a holding pattern with thoughts of the highlight of my summer vacation, seeing my sister. After a seven-year separation I saw her. *Did she know it was me? Did she have the urge to cry out, I know you are Stella, and run over to hug me?*

I know I had wanted to spring off my chair and not pretend to be a teacher. I wanted to say, "Finally, here you are. I missed you. Look at us, we have grown. You are gorgeous. We must get to know each other." Ideally, we would have spent time alone together to fill in the seven-year gap. Instead, we had to be satisfied with the stolen glances at each other and our own thoughts. The tears burned my eyes open;

I watched Thessaloniki disappear under the clouds. It was time to change gears and think about the other side of the Atlantic, with all the promises of another school year.

26

Abundance of Good

THE GROUP: DONNA, LAURA, ME, SUE, MARYELLEN. HIGH SCHOOL GRADUATION.

There was a lot I wanted to catch up with back home. Although the month in Greece went by fast, it was a long time. The day after our arrival I unpacked and sorted out our laundry as fast as I could, so I could go next door. I couldn't wait to hear about Gale and her boyfriend. She had been out of high school for two years. Their Aunt Helen from next door came in and we spent the morning comparing our summer vacations. I liked the idea that we spoke openly about boys in front of their mother and aunt. A huge contrast from the culture I had just left behind.

Gale was all excited. "Frank and I are serious. We are getting engaged."

"That is fantastic. You are the first friend to be engaged," I said.

As Jo Jo shared about her dates, I was still thinking how my Greek friends and cousins and I could never have those discussions with our mothers and aunts.

After lunching with my neighbors, I walked the half mile to Donna's house where she filled me in on The Group's summer. We arranged to meet with the others for a total catch-up visit and for our school shopping. I felt exhilarated and dreamed of my junior year to be the best.

I joined the staff of the school magazine, and all the clubs my schedule allowed. I became active and popular with both the students and the teachers. The art teachers trusted me to help them with special art projects. We set up exhibits of students' works. Mr. Wilson and Miss Cavanagh were two of the younger teachers in the school. I surmise it was their first job after college. Their enthusiasm about art and the way they talked to us as if we were their peers differentiated them from the seasoned teachers. I think of them on the rare occasion when I'm up in our attic and take a moment to look at the hooked rug I designed and made in their class. Why do I still have it? As Lisa Norton writes in her book *Shimmering Images*, it's "my stuff." The stuff we take with us with every move we make and may not look at for years. It is a reminder of my formative years in Americanism. By junior year I had outgrown the shyness and insecurity I had relating to my accent and my being an immigrant.

I continued to aim for excellence in grades and in my attendance in school. I signed up for the first available date for the Scholastic Aptitude Test (SAT). That way I would have another chance in the spring if improvement was necessary. I did not need to retake it. I scored high and admission to a college was certain.

"I am applying to a junior college. I don't need a bachelor's degree. I only need an associate degree to become a stewardess," I announced to my father.

"You are not going to become a stewardess. You will become a teacher."

"But that's not what I want. You must understand I've been wanting this for years."

My father did not want to hear what I wanted. He went on. "Having a teacher's degree is your security to earn a living. You need something that is dependable and respectable."

"But I am telling you I don't want to be a teacher."

"You will become a teacher. There will always be a job for you."

It seemed most parents in our culture believed becoming a teacher was a secure job for a woman. In the 1960s, popular career choices for women were limited to teachers, nurses, and secretaries. Fashion models and stewardesses were the popular fantasy careers for girls. Although women were allowed to go to college to become doctors, lawyers, and scientists, and some did, it was difficult for them to find jobs.

A product of my culture, I could not ignore my father's directive. He was adamant about my becoming a teacher. I applied to Boston State College. From 1952 to 1960 it was known as the State Teacher's College at Boston. In 1982 the college merged with University of Massachusetts. I tried to talk myself into liking the idea of being a teacher, but it did not feel right.

In the back of my mind, I held on to the desire that my father would give in and allow me to go for an associate degree. In order to have that option I also applied at the nearby Massachusetts Bay Community College (Mass Bay). Founded in 1961, its first campus was in the Back Bay section of Boston. In 1966 it relocated to Watertown, a suburb of Boston, close to Brighton. I could not get out of my head that all I needed was two years of college to become a stewardess. And not just a stewardess, a TWA hostess. That was my plan. In my head I figured even if I couldn't convince my father to let me go to Mass Bay, after two years at Boston State I would forgo getting a degree and quit. Every Sunday the TWA ad listed in the *Boston Globe* specified as one of the requirements "either two years of working experience after high school or two years of college."

I was accepted to both colleges. I had a year to decide.

A decision I did have to make in my junior year was about a pivotal event in my Americanization.

"Stella, I found out that if you don't become a US citizen before your eighteenth birthday you will have to wait until you are twenty-one," Babá said.

I didn't hesitate. After school the next day I skipped hanging out with the kids and caught the streetcar to downtown Boston. My sense of pride in my new country awakened from the moment the agent wearing a white shirt and tie handed me the forms. The authority I perceived in his demeanor opened the gates of intimidation. It's the same feeling I have felt going through customs even though I had nothing to hide. I respectfully thanked him, secured the scarf around my neck and bolted out. I held tightly on the envelope all the way home.

I spread the forms on the kitchen table and pored over them. My father was reading his paper and puffing on his cigarette. *What? Does this mean what I think it means?* I read it again. *I can't believe it. I can choose any name I want.* Whatever name I fill in the blank would become my name henceforth. Any name I wanted. From the day I had noticed my American friends had middle names I was intrigued. We didn't have that in Greece and of course I wanted a middle name. Choosing one was easy.

"Babá, listen to this."

He misinterpreted my enthusiasm. He pushed his glasses to the tip of his nose and asked. "What's wrong? What happened?"

"Nothing happened. It says here I can choose a new name. I want Paula for my middle name."

He did not object. I wondered if his feelings would have been hurt if he knew the reason I chose it. He hadn't asked. Paul is the translation for Pavlos. By taking the feminine version of Paul (Paula), I would be honoring my uncle. It would be as if I was naming a child after him. His name would become part of mine. My beloved Theo Pavlos was etched in my heart and now his name would be written next to mine. I hadn't given thought to how the two names would flow, Stella Paula. It reminds me of stories I have heard of people who got tattoos and later in their lives they reassess their choice and decide they would have made a different decision.

Before my eighteenth birthday, in my junior year of high school, I was sworn in as a United States citizen. I accepted, with pride, the compliments the US agent showered upon me. A feeling of satisfaction surged over me.

"Congratulations, you did an excellent job. You answered all the questions correctly."

I thought the swell of pride would burst through my chest. I felt I proved my love and loyalty to my new country by becoming a US citizen.

I wanted to tell my big news to the strangers on the trolley but refrained. Would they have cared? Would they have been proud of me? Instead, I opened my purse several times and with reverence I looked at and touched the soft red-white-and-blue cloth, the American flag, the agent had given me.

I placed the flag in the center of the table during our evening meal.

After that it stayed on my desk. However, I was perplexed by what was going on, at the time, regarding natural American citizens. As a foreigner I wasn't aware of the tensions between blacks and whites. I did not know the yellow school bus that brought students from Roxbury, a predominantly African American section of Boston, to Brighton High School was a result of the Civil Rights Act of 1964. I heard about the riots, and they just didn't make sense to me. *Why were people mean and abusive to other people because of their different races?* I empathized with the African Americans who were targeted in acts of violence. My ethnicity and culture were a minority in my school, but I felt accepted by most students. I did not experience overt discrimination.

Compassion led me to form strong friendships with some of the bused-in students. But even so, there was an unspoken understanding that a romantic relationship was out of the question. Hanging out with the girls from Roxbury or in a mixed group was not a problem. But to be alone with a Roxbury boy was a different story. Interracial couples remained clandestine. In 1967 a US Supreme Court decision gave the freedom for interracial marriages. Whenever we heard of such a marriage it was big news.

So, in my junior year when Bruce, an African American from Roxbury, and I acknowledged our attraction for each other, we used the universal and popular system of high school communication to keep our secret. We left notes for each other in our lockers. When we dared to walk down the hall together, we rationalized that as a football player and a cheerleader, we had earned that right. Bruce's close teammates and my group were privy to our secret love story. There was that unspoken line we had crossed and both of us knew according to society's norm we should not be dating and must keep it a secret.

Along with my winter coat I shed my boyfriend, Ricky. I'm not sure who shed whom. We realized his being in college and my being in high school was not working. I didn't mind. Bruce was in my life. I was caught up in the high school life and loving it. As much as I liked dating boys, I was not looking for a relationship that would tie me down.

After the close of grades, I was self-assured that mine would meet, if not surpass, my expectations and those of my teachers. With that knowledge I loaded up my free time with social engagements.

At the end of the school year, The Group and I engaged in our summer thing: beach, parties, and sleeping over each other's houses and the annual shopping for my trip to Greece. It had become a tradition. Gifts for friends and relatives and a new wardrobe for me. We agonized over the purchase of a gift for one person in particular for my 1966 visit.

After one of our shopping sprees, I arrived home to find a letter that had me frozen in place. I held the airmail envelope with its white and Mediterranean Sea blue trim all around the edges. I dropped the shopping bags and held it with both hands; I blinked a few times to ensure I was reading the return address correctly. I dashed up to the second floor, mounting the stairs two at a time. It took a few attempts to line up the key before I could unlock the door. I could hear my heart beating. It had to be the result of climbing the stairs and the anticipation of the letter's contents. I closed the door and fastened the security brass chain on the door. We always chained the door when we were inside the house. This way when someone knocked, we opened the door as far as the chain allowed, about four to five inches. We felt safer talking to a stranger through the small opening.

I didn't bother going to my room. I threw my books on the sofa in the living room and plopped down next to them. I stared at the return address one more time. I inserted the tip of my pen in the tiny space of the flap that was not sealed and ran it across the length of the envelope. As I pulled out the tissue-thin white stationery with its blue lines matching the envelope's blue, I could hear the thump thump in my chest.

His letter had the standard greeting. I had written the same greeting a zillion times in letters I sent to my friends and relatives. They began, "Dear so and so. We are well and wish the same for you."

After the standard greeting Mr. Apostolos, my sister's father, continued: "Your sister is in good health. She is a conscientious student, and her grades are very good." I couldn't believe I was reading a letter from my sister's father.

It was weird then and it is weird now when I am talking about my sister and refer to her father, her mother, her aunt, her uncle, or her cousin. It raises eyebrows, and questions. It confuses people and it demands an explanation. That is why for years it had been easier to avoid talking about my past.

I am holding a letter from my little sister's father. I leaned back on the cushy pillow I had embroidered. It had taken an entire year and thousands of cross-stitches to complete the two cherubs on it. Feeling the serenity that was portrayed on the pillow, exciting and good-feeling thoughts raced in my head. *He finally wrote to me. Is he going to let me see her next time I'm in Greece? Will she come to visit me in the States? Should I allow the happiness I am feeling? What else will I read?*

"As I had told you and your uncle when you visited last summer, she is involved in school and outside activities." Mr. Apostolos went on and on about her accomplishments, her school trips, and her social life. It all sounded perfect to me. And then.

"Unfortunately, we are having a difficult time with her at home. Her behavior is unacceptable. She doesn't listen to us. She is defiant and rebellious."

Oh no, here it comes. Something bad. I didn't know what to think.

Did they want to send her to me? I used both hands to steady the piece of paper.

"Please write a letter to her and advise her to start listening to us, to be well behaved, to be a good girl."

Whew! He's asking for help. But I'm only eighteen—I'm supposed to advise her to behave?

I continued to read with an uneasy feeling in the pit of my stomach.

"Up until now we thought it was best she didn't communicate with you but now her mother and I think it's time for you to correspond."

He concluded with the standard closing.

"Give our regards to your father. With fatherly love, Mr. Apostolos."

I sat there to digest what I had read. I didn't like that her parents were having a difficult time with disciplining her. I wondered if they thought of her as a bad girl. I hoped not. That was my little sister and I wanted them to think of her in the most positive and loving way. I knew in my heart she was in good hands. My theo had been passing on to me news he had from his own correspondence with Mr. Apostolos. In his letters Theo Pavlos reassured me Lena's parents were good people and were taking good care of her.

I sprang off the couch and fluffed up the pillow so that the cherubs' cheeks bounced into fullness. The need to put space between the unexpected letter and my response prompted me to make a quick change from my school clothes and run into the kitchen for a snack. The chocolate-covered ice cream, in spite of the fall temperatures, was just what I needed. I took small, calculated bites. I could feel the cold melt away, gliding down my throat all the way to my stomach, soothing my nerves. My mind went back and forth from enjoying my treat to formulating sentences for the task I was about to undertake.

I'm writing to my sister. I have never written a letter to my little sister. Like a tsunami, thoughts of our life prior to our parents' accident deluged my mind. Our father taking us to the beach on the back of his motorcycle. Our mother indulging us with a treat of cherry glyko. Lena crying to play with me and my friends. Even her tantrums were a welcome memory. Thoughts of her leaving the village without warning and her staying with Mr. Filipas until she was picked up by her adoptive parents made me feel sad.

Mr. Apostolos's letter spread out in front of me became blurry. I went to the bathroom for a tissue. My tears were a combination of joy and loss. All that reflection sent a surge of optimism which I felt from the depths of my stomach all the way up to my throat. It awakened the emotions that had been under covers for the past eight years. Sitting at my desk, ready to write my first letter to my sister, I felt weird, thrilled, grown up, and hopeful about the beginning of resuming the relationship that had been on pause. I was apprehensive about how she would receive my first communication. It was one of reprimand. One that would be telling her how to behave, to change her ways. *That should not be what your sister writes in a first letter. Not after an eight-year separation. It should be a letter of excitement filled with promises of future meetings and fun. I should not have been put in this position. But I will do it. I will be the big sister.*

I had the letter in front of me so I could refer to it. When I had started to write letters on behalf of my adoptive parents, it was one of the first things they taught me about letter writing, along with the opening greeting and the closing salutation.

"Always look at the letter you received. This way you will answer all the questions that are asked in the letter."

It began with the greeting I was taught to use.

"My dear sister, I am well and wish the same for you. I received a letter from your father. He asked me to write to you. I want to tell you that last summer I saw you. Remember last summer, the day a man and his niece came to your house looking for a room to rent? That was our theo Pavlos and me. We were very excited to see you. You have grown and are a beautiful girl. It was difficult to look at you and not be able to tell you who I was and to hug you after all these years."

I wrote about my coming to the United States and my difficulties in the beginning. I assured her I was happy in my new country. I told her my mother had died the year before and that my father and I were getting along fine. I filled her in on my schooling. I knew her parents would be reading the letter so I did not go into the teenage boy crushes or anything that might be misconstrued as bad behavior and a bad influence on her.

"Your parents are very nice people and love you very much. They care for you and want the very best for you. Your father wrote that you are not listening to them, and you misbehave. Please listen to your parents. Do what they tell you. I think if you behave, we will be able to see each other this summer."

It was the best I could do for sisterly advice.

"Write back and send me a picture of you. My regards to your parents. I have missed you and love you. Your sister, Stella."

Writing the letter opened the channels of all sorts of emotions that had been closed for eight years. It made me review my feelings. I realized as I was writing the letter, it was the seventeen-year-old me, responding to a request. For years I had been waiting for the opportunity to communicate with her. And now that I had written the letter, it did not feel the way I had imagined it. I expected to feel the connection, the joy of being a sister, the playfulness, and that part in my heart that ached when she used to have a severe tantrum. The way I felt about her when we were with our biological parents in Thessaloniki. All those feelings must have been put on hold after she was taken away.

My waiting back in Kostohori, to see what Theo was going to do with me, must have consumed my attention and pushed thoughts of my separation from my sister into the recesses of my confused mind. The deaths of my parents, the failed adoption in Veria, my going back to the village, three different schools in less than two years, and the final move to the United States must have kept me from experiencing the full trauma of losing my sister. After she left, I was consumed with "what will happen to me?"

I folded the letter carefully and slid it in the envelope. I put on a light jacket and headed for the post office. *Will those dormant feelings surface in my heart now that we will be corresponding? Will I feel them when I see her in the summer? I just know her parents will allow it this time.* I had a strong hunch I would see my little sister in the summer of 1966. After all, the girls and I had chosen the white sailor dress, trimmed with navy blue ribbon around the edges of the collar and short sleeves, for her. The prospect of seeing my sister intensified my excitement. My trip to Greece in the summer of 1966 was slated to be like no other since my separation from my sister.

27

Reunited

ME AND LENA IN KATERINI.

In addition to souvenirs from Greece for friends and relatives, when I returned to Boston after that summer trip in 1966, I brought back a part of me I had been missing for eight years. Although I did not bring my sister back physically, her memory, photographs, and the stories I shared were as alive as they could be. I described Lena and our meeting to everyone who knew of her. July 1966 in Greece was different than any other year since my adoption. The excitement had begun to percolate throughout my body from the moment I read in my sister's letter that her parents would welcome a visit from me. Once Mr. Apostolos had opened the door to our communication, the letters between my sister and me became the thread for mending the now eight-year-old tear.

The thought of our meeting conjured up memories of our taxi ride to the village with our mother's coffin in the trunk. Thoughts of my little sister's insistence to tag along with my friends in the old neighborhood in Thessaloniki. My theo and I traveling to Katerini the previous year hoping to see her.

I replaced those thoughts with thoughts of seeing her, embracing

her, hearing her. Not like the time we pretended I was a teacher looking for a room to rent. We would not have to sneak glances at each
other.

Even the bus ride from Veria to Katerini felt different that year.
Theo Pavlos and I met at the bus depot. We did not go to our cafe as
in years past. Although the bus fumes and bouncing were the same as
in the past, the embarrassment of getting motion sickness felt irrele-
vant. For the first time I wasn't concerned with people's reactions to
it. I was too happy to let it bother me.

I knew the dizziness I felt would be gone by the time we got to
their house. We walked in silence the two blocks from the bus station. I wondered if Theo Pavlos's pensive expression was the result of
revisiting memories that led to this point. My thoughts lingered on
feeling better and of how it would be when my little sister and I saw
each other.

As we rounded the corner, the bougainvillea peeked above the
wrought iron fence, its raspberry-color blossoms hugged the fence's
posts. The gate opened almost instantly after Theo rang the bell. By
the time we reached the bottom of the stairs all three of them were
on the top landing.

There she is. I couldn't hold back; I ran up the last few steps. She
met me at the top one and we threw our arms around each other. I
could feel her fingertips on my back as I pressed mine on hers. With
our heads resting on each other's shoulders, we rocked back and forth,
not caring about the tears landing on our dresses. The adults shook
hands, Lena and I held on tight, perhaps a little bit too long.

"Come on, girls, you will have plenty of time for hugs. Give your
theo a chance," Mr. Apostolos suggested.

I couldn't dry my cheeks fast enough when Theo Pavlos placed
both hands on Lena's shoulders, took a long look at her before he
drew her head into his chest, and they fused together. I had dreamed
of how that moment would be and when it happened it was as emotional as my imagination.

Mrs. Nitsa held the door open and gestured for us to enter. "Come
right in, please."

Entering the living room was a déjà vu moment. The previous
year's visit flashed in my mind. I saw a vivid image of Lena's sneaking

glances when she had brought our refreshments. I felt the nervousness of pretending to be a teacher. But instead I was experiencing a glorious day. We could look at each other openly. We could talk to each other.

"Let's sit in the dining room, everything is ready."

The table was set for the midday meal. A white tablecloth with blue crochet edging. Gold goblets filled with water and smaller matching wine glasses were next to them. The meal was plated as was the custom at the time.

Lena floated in and out of the dining room bringing in our meals. The pungent aroma of garlic and oregano promised a delicious lamb dinner. Mr. Apostolos beamed with pride.

"She does a good job when she wants to," he whispered when Lena walked away.

They used the good china and crystal for the momentous occasion. The goblets complemented the gold trim on the plate's edge. Golden roasted potatoes cut in perfect wedges gave off a citrus and oregano aroma. I wasn't sure I could eat; my stomach was full of happiness. Even though the meal included my favorite green beans in the tomato sauce, fasolakia ladera always summoned the memory of my almost-mother in Veria, who had refused to give me a second helping. But on that day in Katerini sitting down for a meal with my sister, that memory did not disturb me.

The return bus to Veria was three hours later. Plenty of time for Theo to get his fill of his two nieces. He would be making the return trip alone, leaving me to spend a few days with my sister and her parents.

Seeing him off on that day in Katerini, I did cry. The four of us stood on the landing and watched Theo go down the stairs. Both Mr. and Mrs. Papaefthemiou called down to him, "Bye, Pavlos, thank you for coming and for bringing Stella." We waved goodbye to Theo Pavlos as he closed the wrought iron gate.

The midday meal is the main meal and is followed by the quiet hours. Retail, business offices, visits, and telephone calling came to a halt. Adults took naps and teenagers played music quietly or read. That day at the Papaefthemiou household the routine had been interrupted but no one seemed to mind it. Mr. Apostolos and Mrs. Nitsa showed their interest in knowing about my life in America.

"Tell us. Is it true people work all day long? They don't go home for the midday meal?"

"Yes, it's true. The stores and offices are open from morning until evening."

"From your letters, we gather you and your father are managing well since your mother's passing," Mr. Apostolos said

"What are you saying to the girl?" Mrs. Nitsa admonished him.

"That's okay. I don't mind. We are doing well. While my mother was sick, we got used to taking care of things. After she died, we just continued."

It was a strange feeling to talk about my parents to my sister's parents. The weird thing is we are two sisters, and I could be saying to her, your father, your mother. She may ask something along the lines of how did your mother die? Or either one of us would say, my cousins and I. It feels strange. The amazing and comfortable thing is our extended families got to know us and treat us as a unit. We are welcome to their homes and into their lives.

During the visit I masked the awkwardness I felt as best as I could. I wanted them to recognize I was a good person, and I did not present a threat to their relationship with their daughter. I had surmised from our letter correspondence during the past year they felt comfortable with me and approved of the relationship that was developing between my sister and me. But, still, I didn't want anything to jeopardize the path we were on.

In the evening we walked to the main square for ice cream at one of the many *zaharoplastia*.

"So many zaharoplastia and cafes. We don't have squares like these in Boston." They lined the entire square. Hundreds of chairs stretched across the concrete.

"We always sit at this one." Lena pointed to the rows of brown tables and chairs.

The next morning there was more awkwardness. Lena filled me in on the morning routine.

"My mamá asked what we wanted for breakfast. She has tiropita or she can boil eggs for us."

"Did I get up too late?" I didn't want them to think poorly of me.

Her father had already gone to the office.

"No, don't worry. My bábá leaves before I get up."

There it was again; "my bábá." It sounded strange that she is my sister but that's *her* bábá—not mine.

"After breakfast we can go to the center. I can show you around and you can meet some of my friends and cousins."

Again, her cousins. Not our cousins.

The cafes presented a different atmosphere in the daytime. The nonchalant relaxed ambiance was replaced with hustle and bustle. We weaved in and out and in between tables and chairs avoiding bumping elbows with pedestrians who were in a hurry. They moved with purpose. They had to accomplish their chores and business affairs before the quiet hour.

For the midday meal Lena, her parents, and I went to the Katerini Yacht Club.

"You will like it, since it is right on the beach," my sister assured me.

I had no doubt I would. Everything was a new experience for me. "For sure I will like it. I want to experience as much of your life as I can in the next few days."

Sitting on the deck of the Yacht Club gave me a glimpse of my sister's summer. A gentle breeze caressed our bodies. The waves swished up to the sand only to retreat, leaving an uneven dark caramel pattern.

"Next time you visit we can come early enough to have a swim before our meal. And we can stay after and join my friends who have a summer home on the beach, right, Mamá?" Mrs. Nitsa nodded.

It was like a dream. My sister and I would be hanging around together. Her parents had agreed for her to visit me in Thessaloniki the following weekend and their invitation for me to come back to Katerini sealed the bond between us.

Her bábá went to the kitchen to select the fish.

While we waited for his selection to be grilled, we nibbled on roasted eggplant topped with garlic and feta, *horiatiki* salad, and fried calamari.

When it was done, the waiter—crisp, white towel neatly folded over his lower arm—placed the platter in front of Mr. Apostolos. The whole sea bass, head to tail, was surrounded by parsley and lemon wedges. The black edges on its tail and on the fins signified that it was grilled to perfection. I was used to the presentation, unlike my friends back home, who would have rolled their eyes at the sight of the whole fish. Mr. Apostolos carved the fish and served us. The constant soft fluttering of the umbrella over our table, the fresh scent of the sea, the glistening sand meters away, and a scrumptious meal in the company of my sister and her parents—two fine people—mesmerized me.

"So happy for you" was the response following my animated recounting of the meeting. I was happy to have had such a wonderful reunion with my sister at last.

28
The Telegram

My momentous sister news aside, the 1966-67 school year ush-ered in another significant event: my graduation from high school. The festivities leading to the culmination of four years of studying and preparing for the next phase in life for the Brighton High School class of 1967 had arrived.

Our homeroom teachers handed out the instructions and admis-sion tickets for our graduation. A four-by-six-inch manila envelope had tickets with the instructions typewritten on the back of it.

"Girls wear: white knee-length dress, wrist-length white gloves, white shoes, plain nylon hosiery, quiet (no fun) jewelry.

Boys wear: white shirt, necktie, suit or sport jacket, haircut, shoes shined.

Report to War Memorial Auditorium, Room 200, before 8:30 a.m. 6/6/67. Before entering Room 200 leave coats, pocketbooks, etc. with parents, or friends in the audience. Form lines according to the number given you on Monday, 6/5/67. No smoking or gum chewing."

On Tuesday, June 6, at 8:30 a.m., 380 eager teenagers converged on Room 200 for the 9 a.m. graduation. Like a field of white daisies, the girls filled the room. The boys sprouted above them, breaking up the white landscape at the War Memorial Auditorium in Boston.

In 1988 the auditorium was replaced by the John B. Hynes Vet-eran Convention Center. Architects Kallmann, McKinnell & Wood designed it to fit in with the style of the Back Bay neighborhood. Named after former Boston mayor John B. Hynes, it is now known as the Hynes Convention Center.

As if unleashed from restraints, the graduates poured out of the auditorium. Drivers were leaning on their horns as they drove down Boylston Street. Boys and girls, parents and friends, hugged and posed for pictures. There were last-minute invitations to parties. Slowly the crowd dissipated. Rather than attend a party The Group, along with our families, enjoyed a meal together.

The fun time would have to wait until Saturday night at my

house. Adding to the graduation excitement was the one guest I invited who was not a Brighton High School graduate. During high school my friends and I had ordered our prom and dance flowers from Minihane's Flowers on Washington Street in Brighton where Paul worked. The tall, handsome, and friendly boy attended Saint Columbkille High School, which put him out of reach for those of us who attended public schools. However, his part-time job gave us the opportunity to meet him and to get to know him casually. The flower shop was on our school route, so sometimes we stopped in to say hi. I found the courage to invite him to the graduation party at my house. My original intention was to fix him up with someone else but on the day of the party, I decided to give myself a chance with him. After spending most of the evening together as teenagers do, we went our separate ways until the following year, when I invited him to a dinner dance.

The graduation party went off without a hitch. I had convinced my father that I was mature enough and all the guests would be well behaved. His naïveté about teenage parties was such that he agreed to spend the night at my cousin Litsa's house. The fact that I was having an unchaperoned party with my father's knowledge not only raised my status with my peers but also made me deserving of the responsibility. I informed everyone, that is, the boys, since they were the ones who always brought beer and wine, that any alcohol consumption would be outside the house. My guardian angels protected me, and there was no alcohol in the house.

At the time, our house was practically void of furniture. That was because my father had decided we would move back to Greece. At first, when he brought it up during the winter, I had thought I could talk him out of it. I stared out the window. Mr. Norling across the street was shoveling a snowbank that had buried half of his car tires. I held my tears back, and turned to face my father.

"We can't move to Greece permanently. This is my home."

"You knew that from the time we brought you here. That after we had enough money we would move back."

My cheeks were on fire, but I was still not crying.

"But you haven't talked about it for years, so I assumed we were staying here. Even after Mamá died you didn't say anything about it."

"You know that's why we bought the condominium with Thea Mitsa. We are all going to live in Thessaloniki."

"It's not fair, I'm an American and I want to stay here."

A deluge erupted. I tasted the saltiness as I screamed for my rights and the unfairness of the move. "What am I going to do there? I thought you wanted me to become a teacher."

"You won't have to work. Soon you will get married and have a family."

I was certain that Mrs. Paris upstairs could hear me, but I didn't care.

"You are mean, taking me away after I got used to this lifestyle. I like going to Greece every summer—that's all—not to live there forever."

He must have had enough. With fists clenched, he lowered his voice. "We are moving to Greece."

I didn't want to look at him anymore. I slammed my bedroom door and called Donna. Through my sobbing and sniffling she got the message. Of course, she was shocked, but being from an immigrant family herself she understood that we must do what our parents demand of us. I wondered what my sister's reaction would be to the news. She and I had established a routine of exchanging letters and photographs. We replied to each other's letters as soon as we received them. A slow and steady sharing of our lives was shaping our relationship. We assumed without expressing it in the letters that her parents (again *her* parents, still weird) monitored them. We did not reference our lives before the adoptions nor share anything about boys. We knew those would be conversations in person.

Meanwhile I could not accept the move to Greece. A few days later I approached the subject with my father and persuaded him to let me stay one last summer in the United States. I wanted to have as much time as possible with my friends. I also wanted to do some extensive shopping for personal and household items to take back to Greece, since I would be filling a trunk. We had come to an agreement. I would stay for the summer and return to Greece on a ship.

"I made my reservation for Greece. I will leave after you graduate. I asked Mr. Kutrubes to find a companion for you with whom you can sail. He has a woman client who is planning a trip by ship in the fall. When she decides on a date, he will let you know to book a ticket with her. I don't want you to travel alone."

I found the statement ludicrous. I flew all by myself when I was eleven years old and now at nineteen, he wanted me to have a companion. Obviously, I felt mature enough and secure in my abilities to take care of myself. I did not need a travel companion, but I did not make a fuss about that.

I had come to terms with my moving back. I knew enough of the culture in which I was brought up. It was a good daughter's obligation to take care of her parents. I made up my mind to enjoy my last summer with my American friends.

I pondered over my change of heart from eight years earlier. Then, I had cried and prayed in silence to return to Greece. I could not stand being away from everything familiar. I couldn't stand the language barrier. It took me almost the entire school year to somewhat acclimate to my new country. Once I survived that excruciating period, I melded into the new culture to the point of no return. But there I was answering the call of another culture, to fulfill the family obligation.

My father flew back to the old country, and I moved in with my cousin Veta and her family in Allston.

Although Veta was only three years older than me, she had two adorable little girls. Even after two pregnancies her medium height was proportionately complemented by the slender figure she maintained. I admired her neat appearance and impeccable grooming. Her short brown hair was in place whether she was at the kitchen sink, over the stove, or bathing one of her toddlers. I couldn't understand her enthusiasm and display of pleasure when she prepared our meals. My mind was not anywhere close to wanting to know any of her recipes or how to cook. I was a satisfied partaker of her talents. It would be years later when she would teach me to make a pita by opening my own phyllo dough like I had seen my yiayia make, baklava, *melomakarona*, and more.

Once I digested the idea of moving back to Greece, I stopped agonizing over it. The move was another uninvited intrusion in my life and once again I accepted it.

Our Group spent time going to the beach, movies, and of course shopping. It was a team effort to fill the huge black metal trunk destined for Greece. We paid particular attention to purchasing fancy party dresses. On my previous trip to Thessaloniki a friend had shown me the party dresses she had.

"You should see the dresses they wear to go to parties and to clubs," I said to the group.

"You mean not like us? Wearing pants and nice tops?" asked Mellon, which was short for Maryellen. I had given her the nickname soon after we became friends. "MaryEllen is too long, we are calling you Mellon." I had said. And sometimes we referred to her as Mellon Balls.

Mellon swept a blonde strand of hair off her face and as if talking to herself, said, "Hah, it will be fun shopping for party dresses."

Laura wanted to know, "Do you mean all satins and organza?"

"Yes, exactly. And they get their hair done like we do for the proms," I said.

"I bet they wear nylons and high heels with those fancy dresses," Sue added.

"We should all dress up one day and have our picture taken in our usual lineup," I suggested.

Whenever we were photographed we arranged ourselves according to height; Mellon being the tallest was first. She towered four inches above us. The rest of us differentiated ourselves by stretching as tall as we could. We determined our photo lineup to be Mellon, Sue, Stella, Laura, and Donna. We split one inch among the four of us. All of us dressed our slender figures in the collegiate (preppy) style of the day.

After many trips to downtown Boston, we accomplished our shopping mission. We had packed a total of twelve party dresses, with shoes and clutches to match. By the end of the summer the trunk was full. It was weird that I had a trunkful of clothes and household items for a permanent move when a few months earlier I had been planning to go to college with my mind stuck on becoming a TWA hostess.

According to Mr. Kutrubes, I would be leaving at the end of September. "I did as your father asked. I reserved a cabin for you and my client." The information jolted me into reality. I had a month left to devour as much of America as I could.

On a quiet September day, I was on the floor with Mary, Veta's older toddler. Veta had just shut the front door behind the young man in a uniform. Mary was intently listening to my reading Little Red Riding Hood. Her legs hung over one on each side of my thigh. She ran her pudgy little fingers across the page. It didn't matter, as it wasn't as though I was reading to her word for word.

"What can it be?" Veta was standing above us with the brown envelope.

Telegrams always piqued our interest and put us on alert. Our minds went to the worst possible scenario. Either a serious illness or death. It's not as though we never received telegrams to congratulate someone or announce a birth or a wedding, but for some reason we always thought first of the negative.

"Stella, he died, he died." Veta burst into tears.

I put Mary down, gently, on the rug and stood facing Veta.

"Who died?" I took the piece of paper from her hand.

"With sorrow we inform you your father died yesterday after suffering a heart attack. We buried him today."

The telegram was from Thea Mitsa and addressed to me.

My tears rolled down my cheeks, Mary got upset watching us crying and was whimpering. She stretched her arms to her mother to be picked up. I realized I was crying because Veta was crying. A sense of confusion brought a familiar squirmy feeling in my head. I didn't feel like I thought I should be feeling. After all, my father died. *Shouldn't I be feeling distraught? Truly sad? Shouldn't I feel sorry I wasn't with him?* I did not feel the loss. I think Veta was crying because that's what we knew people did when someone died.

"I can't believe this happened." She swept Mary up off the floor. "Poor Theo Steve, he went back to his homeland to enjoy his retirement."

She smoothed Mary's hair off her face and placed her in the highchair. Thank God one-year-old Sophia didn't wake up with all this commotion. I followed them into the kitchen. The bright sun rays poking through the white sheer curtains lifted some of the darkness the telegram had delivered. I watched the child smear chocolate around her mouth and crumble the cookie, most of which was spread all over the tray in front of her.

Veta picked up the phone receiver off its wall cradle and called our cousin Litsa. Still crying she twirled the avocado green phone cord on her index finger in a way that I feared she would cut off her finger.

"Yes, I'm telling you. The telegram came a few minutes ago. The funeral was yesterday. She is fine. She is right here."

I left the kitchen to collect my thoughts. In the living room I re-read the telegram. It was at that moment it dawned on me. *I don't have to move back to Greece.* I felt a tremendous sense of relief. I tried to suppress the excitement that thought aroused in me. Not that I felt guilty, but according to my cultural beliefs I was supposed to drown in sorrow and be in deep mourning for the loss of my father. Instead, I felt unabashed freedom.

Is it possible that by the age of nineteen I had developed an under-standing of separation and death? Did I possess, at an early age, what it takes to overcome adversity without hysterics and melodrama? Or was I born with that ability? My adoptive father was the fifth parent I had lost, counting the almost-adoptive father in Veria. Although he was not a relative, I had witnessed the imminent death of Yiannis when I was a first-year high schooler. In addition to the deaths, I endured the separation from my sister, my theo and other relatives, my friends, and my country. All of which must have fortified me to withstand loss without falling apart. Was I blessed with the belief that the spirit and the soul of loved ones live on and are close by when we need them? With each challenge I faced I accepted it and moved on. I must say I lost some of that easy acceptance when I faced challenges later in my life.

Not having to move to Greece was not the only revelation to hit me. I could pursue my dream job. I thought of the irony that my parents adopted an older child to have someone to look after them in their old age. Both parents got a small taste of that benefit. I recall the adult conversations I had overheard regarding the pleasures and benefits of having children. They talked in front of me as if I wasn't present. Invariably, someone interjected, "That's why people adopt children, so they have someone to care for them in their old age." I took that to heart when I was adopted and I wasn't shocked, even though I objected, when my father demanded that I move back to Greece with him. Even if I was not committed to take care of him, I would still follow him. In our culture it was unheard of for unmarried children to live anywhere but in the same house with their parents. It was the same for males and females. In the rare occasion that an unmarried adult child moved away from the parents, it was cause for a family battle and wild gossip in the community—unless the move was for a serious career move.

My future was no longer threatened with the dreaded arranged marriage. According to tradition my future was preordained. If my father had lived, I would have arrived in Greece in the middle of October. I had imagined soon after my arrival in Thessaloniki the matchmakers would be landing at our doorstep. That thought did not disturb me once I had accepted the move. I acquiesced to the idea of settling down to a married life and starting a family. It was indoctrinated in me that the two things in my future were to marry and to take care of my father.

Eight years after my emigration from Greece, I would be returning and would need to assimilate to my birth country. Spending a month's vacation during the past summers was not the same as living in the country. As the Americana I had the unspoken approval to behave and dress differently. But to become part of the system was a whole other story. However, there was one tradition I looked forward to participating in, and that was the relationships with the extended family members and with friends.

I had experienced it during my summer visits. We could stop in at one of their homes unannounced and feel welcome. When an aunt or an uncle was present during a family discussion, no matter how important or insignificant, without being asked that relative voiced an opinion, suggested a reprimand, and gave advice. If a relative walked in on a dispute the participants continued and the relative joined in on the discussion. The idea of privacy was nonexistent. When you dropped in on a happy situation, participation was encouraged if not demanded. Many times, I had stopped by at mealtimes, and it was never a problem.

"Oh, how nice. Come sit down, join us." A welcoming directive. "Bring a chair and a place setting for Stella."

That sort of thing happened with anyone who stopped by. It's the Greek virtue of filotimo. Losing privacy with what we sometimes called the in-your-face system had the benefit of providing the security of a protective umbrella. You knew that you could count on support and protection from the extended family. I loved the idea of feeling part of the family whenever I was in their homes.

Parents could drop in on their married children, whether it was to have a cup of coffee or to drop off a pastitsio, the layered thick macaroni with meat sauce topped with rich bechamel sauce. Or who wouldn't want the straight-out-of-the-oven lemon cake which flooded the room with its freshly baked aroma? If the hostess was in the middle of a chore, the visitor jumped in and folded clothes, dried dishes or changed the baby's diaper. Although there were many traditions I couldn't wait to shed, the extended family relationship was one I espoused and added to my belief system for my future home life.

While my heart celebrated my remaining in the USA, my mind counseled that I must figure out my next steps for my immediate future.

29

The Waiting Game

STRATIS, HELEN, MARIKA, DESPINA, NINA, ME, JANE, AND ELENI.
PHOTOGRAPH IS COURTESY OF JANE ROUVAPES AWAD.

On the first Sunday after we received the telegram that changed my life, again, I began my journey for my future on my own. Veta had stressed that on Sundays we were to sleep in for as long as the little ones would let us. However, on that September morning I did not linger under the covers. Instead, I got up before anyone else.

I put on my bell-bottom jeans and a long-sleeved blue and white jersey. I tiptoed through the house so as to not wake anyone up, especially the babies. I barely heard the door lock click shut. Out on the street I rubbed my arms up and down briskly. I should have worn a sweater, but I was on a mission, focused on one thing, and didn't consider the temperature at that time of morning. I hustled to the corner of Cambridge and Harvard Streets in Allston to the convenience store. My heart settled down when I saw them. A neat pile, up to my knee, at the entrance. I picked up a thick bundle of print. The last time I bought a *Boston Sunday Globe* was in the spring for my Civics class. The assignment was to choose a news article and write a report on it. I had chosen an article about Martin Luther King Jr. The article focused on Dr. King's speech "Beyond Vietnam." He addressed three thousand people at Riverside Church in New York City.

But on that fall Sunday, I wanted the *Boston Globe* for its Want Ads section, it's what we called the Help Wanted section then. It was the go-to section of the paper for job seekers. Even though the weekday newspapers had want ads, on Sundays the section was flooded with available positions. During my research in the past year, I drooled over the TWA ads for hostesses in the newspaper. I handed my quarter to the teenage boy with long blond bangs behind the counter.

Back at the house the alluring aroma of bacon beckoned me into the kitchen. It was obvious no one had lingered in bed. I resisted the urge to follow the aroma. I plunked myself onto the couch instead. I was excited and nervous; my insides felt like they were doing a fast dance. I couldn't pull out the section fast enough. I cast the rest of the paper onto the coffee table. *Okay, here it is, that's the section. Oh yes, here it is.*

Although I had hoped for it, had expected it, I held the page against my chest. I felt it was the miracle leading me to my dream. As if TWA didn't want too many people to see it. The two-by-six-inch ad was minuscule in comparison to some of the other ads on the page. But I saw it and read it carefully.

Be a TWA hostess. Will be interviewing. The interviews will be conducted at the Hilton Hotel in Boston. Must be a high school graduate and have two years of college or two years of working experience. A minimum height of five feet two inches. Maximum weight of one hundred ten pounds.

I dashed to the kitchen where Veta was serving up French toast and bacon.

"They are having them."

"Having what?"

"The interviews. TWA. I am going Wednesday to apply. It's happening. I am going to become a stewardess." I flung out my arms in a dramatic fashion.

"So, you are going to stay in America. Okay, sit down now for breakfast."

I didn't think she believed that it would happen but that did not stop me from talking about what I would wear to the interview. De-

spite the flutter in my stomach, I sat next to baby Sophia. As I drizzled the golden honey on the piece of French toast, I envisioned myself sitting on a sidewalk cafe in Paris just like the posters I had seen.

During my senior year in high school, I had researched the quali-
fications for becoming a TWA hostess and I felt I was qualified in every way. It's what I had wanted from the moment I thought about the
answer to that question, what do you want to be when you grow up? I
never thought of myself as beautiful or good looking, but I always felt
I was attractive enough to be a flight attendant. At five feet two and
a half inches I met the minimum height requirement. I was popular
in high school and was involved in many activities. I had graduated
from high school, I held part-time jobs, at a bakery as counter help
and as cashier, a telephone operator, usherette at a theater, server for
a caterer. According to the TWA ad I needed two years of working
experience or two years of college. In my mind I had all the qualifica-
tions the airline required. Certainly, the jobs I had during high school
should be sufficient for the two years of working experience.

"Thank you for your interest in becoming a TWA hostess. If you
are accepted, you will receive a telegram within twenty-four hours."
She walked around the glistening desk. She towered over my five-
feet-two-and-a-half-inch frame. I was surprised that a middle-aged
woman with graying hair was conducting the interviews. I expected
a young, modern-looking woman, not one with hair pulled back se-
verely into a French twist. But she did exude a sense of sophistication
and confidence with her erect posture and smooth stride as she approached me to shake my hand. After a firm handshake she led the
way to the door.

The elevator door opened to reveal several applicants still occu-
pying the plush chairs and sofas in the lobby of the Hilton Hotel.
I had been one of them just an hour earlier. In an attempt to look
like flight attendants, we all looked alike in our suits. A collection of
tailored skirts and jackets in subtle tones of grays, blues, and browns.
The applications, clipboards, and pens were still on the mahogany
desk in the center of the lobby. I empathized with the anxious girls

waiting to be called by the attendant at the desk. I had gone through the anticipation and the sweaty hands, the queasy stomach and after one last glance at the lobby, I walked out the glass door.

I didn't dare leave the house. I was sure the telegram would arrive the very next day, but it didn't. Three days later, no telegram. I kept thinking there could be a delay in the delivery and waited at the house all week. By Sunday there was still no telegram so I bought the *Boston Sunday Globe* again. They were having interviews the following Tuesday.

The scene in the lobby of the Hilton Hotel matched that of the previous Wednesday. About one hundred neatly groomed woman dressed in suits displayed their smiles. The table with clipboards and pens awaited the anxious applicants.

"I was here last week, and I did not receive a telegram. I would like to know why so I can fix it in order to become a TWA hostess."

The young man in a gray suit reminded me of the younger teachers I had in high school. His brown bangs were parted on the side and were a bit shorter than the trend of the times. He hesitated a bit, leaned forward, held my application with both hands, looked at it before he fixed his eyes on mine, and with a pleasing voice he said, "Miss Morris, who interviewed you last week is one of our senior hostesses. She is experienced and well respected. We cannot tell you why you were not accepted but I can tell you what we expect." He held up my application. "Here is proof that you get along with your peers and you are popular with them. You have had some part-time jobs. We are looking beyond that. We need to see you get along with people other than your peers. We are looking for someone who has had at least two years of full-time working experience or two years of college."

That interview was much shorter. I did not linger in the lobby. I got on the trolley and planned my journey to become a TWA hostess. All I had to do was go to Mass Bay and get an associate degree.

Unbeknown to me, my father had left a will. It surprised me because in our culture, in that era it was unusual to address death, let alone make plans for after death. Talking about death and wills was looked upon as inviting death to happen. I had overheard the adults change the subject whenever the topics of death and wills were unwittingly brought up. After they silenced the audacious individual, they followed it with "ptou, ptou, may it be far from here." It's the equivalent of "God forbid." The use of ptou ptou could be applied to either ward off ill thoughts or in a case when something good happened, to ward off evil that might jinx it. Also, an appropriate usage is when doting over a baby or a beautiful person; a few ptou, ptous are required to ensure no evil eye falls on the subject. I have seen many unsuspecting souls who are unfamiliar with the custom recoil in shock at the dry spitting.

A half a condominium in Thessaloniki and an insignificant bank account. Not inheriting any other properties in Greece did not surprise me. My mother had been clear that she had signed over all her property to her sister, Mitsa. During our summer visit to Naoussa after my mother's death, my father did the same. He signed over his properties to his sister. I recall Thea Vera, Dimitra's mother, advising me to go to court to claim the properties from both parents. "They had to show a certain economic standing to adopt you. You have a right to that inheritance." I was young and not interested in going to court. It made me speculate that they did not consider me their child. Perhaps they felt they did enough by just adopting me. As I got older, I saw the adoption as a practical solution for them to have a caregiver in their old age. That could be why we never bonded emotionally.

A bigger surprise was that my father had named a guardian for me until I turned twenty-one. I had never heard of such a thing. His lawyer must have suggested it. Helen Rouvapes, his koumbara, informed me of the fact when I called about my father's demise.

I knew Helen and liked her. Her beautiful, genuine smile exploded on her entire face. I enjoyed visiting her, her husband Stratis, and their daughter Dimitra. Her progressive thinking was something I admired. Her parents had emigrated from Naoussa. She and her two brothers were first-generation Americans. When I had been taken out of the eighth grade and sent to Greece, she had voiced her disapproval to my parents. While I was there, she and I corresponded. She had written in support of my refusal of Dino's proposal. I confided in her about dating non-Greek boys. Talking to her about boys was a gift. She understood the American ways and at the same time she stayed close to her parents' traditions. But moving in with her, her husband, and their sweet eight-year-old daughter was not an ideal situation for a nineteen-year-old. Helen took the legal guardian's responsibility seriously. "According to your father and the law you have to live with me."

"But it will be difficult to go to Mass Bay from there. I can stay in Brighton. Our old neighbors, Helen and Bill Lydon, invited me to live with them. I would only need to take one trolley to school."

She let me finish without interruption, then said, "They may be very nice people, but if something happens to you, I am responsible."

"It's just the two of them. Their oldest is married and lives in California. Their middle son is in the army in Thailand. And the youngest one is in his first year of college in Florida," I pleaded.

My pleading and crying did not absolve me of the move to Malden Street, Boston. At that time the South End of Boston was not a desirable neighborhood. The brick houses on Malden Street, where I was to relocate, had deteriorated from their original grandeur. The absentee landlord had stopped their maintenance. The row of seven three-story buildings occupied by Greek immigrants was in disrepair. The neighbors helped each other with repairs. Most of them were carpenters, plumbers, painters, restaurant workers, and tailors. George the carpenter repaired the front wooden step after his mother's heel got caught between two rotting boards.

Nick, the plumber two houses down the street, did plumbing repairs. For the serious repairs, Helen was the spokesperson for the entire neighborhood, contacting the landlord.

Helen was the only first-generation resident in the neighborhood. Being the only daughter in her family, she assumed the traditional role. She stayed to care for her widowed father, who had refused to move to the suburbs where his two sons lived. Her caregiving role expanded to all the neighbors. They admired her for her acumen in all situations that required complete knowledge of the English language and the American services. Once I moved to sixteen Malden Street, I took on some of her duties.

I called the telephone company and the electric company to order services for new arrivals in the neighborhood. I translated and completed school paperwork for the parents. I am most proud of helping an older woman get her citizenship papers. I tutored Mrs. Kaliope for a month before her appointment. They allowed me to go with her to interpret. With the American flag still in her hand, she hugged me. Her face was beaming as she wiped away what I assumed were tears of joy and pride.

All the immigrants shared in the challenges of adjusting to the new country. I could relate to their loneliness, their struggle with the cultural differences, and not knowing the language. The adults had the added challenge I didn't have and that was the need for employment to support their families. I admired that they retained their filotimo and love of enjoying life. They spent time visiting with each other after work, even for a short while. They brought life to the unpainted rickety steps as they shared their day's events. The men sipped on ouzo while the women drank coffee in fancy demitasse cups. They laughed with tears as they joked about their pronunciation of English words or if one had been the brunt of a joke because of pronunciation or wrong use of a word. They had the capacity to laugh at themselves. They used the opportunities of name days and holidays to dress up to visit the celebrant's house. Invariably, after delicious food and some alcoholic beverages, someone insisted on the accordion or lyre to be produced and the singing and dancing to begin. They sang and danced their way into achieving the American dream which eventually led them out of Malden Street and into the suburbs of Boston. I kept in touch with several of them. Out of the ruins of the South End their children emerged as business owners, doctors, teachers, and professors.

As it happens in most cities, today the once-decrepit South End neighborhood is a sought-out location. It is one of Boston's most popular neighborhoods. It has become home to a thriving arts community. A diverse neighborhood featuring some of Boston's finest restaurants. It is home to the largest group of Victorian-style row houses in the United States which are still intact.

On the October day I moved out of my cousin's home, I got into Helen's white Cadillac with a heavy heart and waved goodbye to Veta and her little girls. In the past I used to feel privileged to be driven in what was considered a luxury car. But on that October day I felt a knot in my throat and disappointment. I did not want to live in Helen's house. Even with all the filotimo, love, and care she could provide, I dreaded the idea of sleeping on the living room couch which separated the couple's bedroom and the kitchen. Helen and Stratis would have to go by me to enter their bedroom. The commute to school would be twice as long. It seemed unfair, considering that I had the opportunity to have my own room with the Lydons and I feared my friends would not make the trip to visit me.

BILL AND HELEN LYDON WITH MY SON, PAUL RICHARD.

30
The Dream

TWA GRADUATION. I AM IN THE CENTER.

Meanwhile classes had started at area colleges. Donna, Mellon, Laura, and Sue had settled into their higher education routines. It took a great deal of effort to arrange a meeting for the five of us. We chose Marliave on Bosworth Street in Boston for our first get-together. That's where we had often enjoyed lunch during our shopping sprees in downtown Boston.

After listening to them comparing classes, schedules, and new experiences, I felt left out and anxious to begin my own classes.

"You sound so excited about your classes. I can't wait to begin mine," I said.

"Just think, we will be seeing each other at Mass Bay," Laura added.

"I know, I expect you to help me acclimate." I winked at her.

Sue put down her fork. "Listen, you guys, we have to come up with a plan to see each other regularly."

"Sue is right. My sister, Lilly, and her friends meet once a month at each other's houses," Donna added.

Mellon continued to wind up spaghetti into a little ball on her fork. Before she raised it to her mouth, she said, "That's a great idea. We can take turns cooking."

We set up the rotation, and our monthly dinner was our introduction to cooking and entertaining. I was relieved to know they would be coming to Malden Street when it was my turn to cook.

I was grateful for my guardian Helen's commitment to care for me until my twenty-first birthday as was stipulated in my father's will. I respected her for that, and for her kindness, generosity, and for her general knowledge. She was the most educated adult in my environment. She was an avid reader. A stack of newspapers and magazines on the square kitchen table took up one quarter of it. Sometimes there were five and six newspapers piled up. She would have to move the stack when the neighbors stopped in for coffee or drinks. On any given day there was someone stopping in. They felt secure and comfortable in her presence, not only because she cared about them, but she spoke fluent Greek.

"You are reading again?"

She would put down the magnifying glass she used in addition to her reading glasses. "I don't know why they use such small print. Sit, sit." She would place her reading glasses on top of her head and clear the table.

She showered her friends with her big smile. Her round face beamed, a sure indication of her bright disposition which had an infectious response to anyone with whom she came in contact.

Two months after my twentieth birthday and a tough commute to Mass Bay, especially on snowy days, Helen agreed to let me move in with her brother Chris and his wife Jane, who lived in Brighton. Their family of seven, with children ranging in age from eight to a newborn in their five-bedroom Victorian home, was a welcome change from Malden Street. As welcome as the change was, I was counting the months to my twenty-first birthday so I could move in with Helen and Bill Lydon.

The day after my twenty-first birthday, I moved in with the Lydons. The empty nesters were as excited as I was with the move. "We now have the daughter we always wanted." Their sincere and warm welcome allowed me to claim another set of parents. This was to be my final adoption, not legally of course, but I adopted them as my parents, calling them Mother and Father, and their sons, brothers. It seems a little strange for a twenty-one-year-old to be seeking parents and a family. My old desire of wanting to have what I considered a normal life had resurfaced. That desire must have taken a back seat the past few years. I had navigated among the various living conditions, school, and work and was managing to stay afloat without thinking about the people I had lost.

The kindness and generosity shown to me by those two people who had no obligation at all to do so is engraved in my heart. Not that I did not appreciate all the help I received from the others: My adoptive parents because they adopted me, which gave me the opportunity to prosper; my guardian Helen and her husband Stratis who honored my father's final wishes; and Jane and Chris, who opened their home to me after I asked if I could live with them until I turned twenty-one. Although they were willing participants, responsible, and generous, they were linked to the legal web of caring for me. But at twenty-one I made the choice to adopt the parents. No one was choosing them for me. Fifty-four Brock Street, Brighton, was the address from which I took the streetcar to Boston's Government Center on my way to fulfill my dream. I felt confident that after earning an associate degree I was fully qualified to become a TWA hostess.

When I interviewed for TWA two years earlier, one hundred or so young women had been gathered in the lobby of the Hilton Hotel. Now, in a startling contrast, only five of us crammed the lobby of the TWA reservations office. TWA had relocated its reservations offices and a ticket office to the newly named Government Center. Boston had revitalized and renamed the old Scollay Square in the downtown "City Hall Plaza." Courthouses and state and federal office buildings were added to the location. With its new location, TWA stopped using the Hilton Hotel for interviews.

I took the elevator to the second floor. I didn't want to be out of breath or sweaty when I arrived for my interview. If I perspired it would have been due to the anxiety and anticipation I felt. I took a deep breath before I pulled on the brass doorknob. The receptionist looked up from her typewriter and said, "Good morning. May I help you?"

"I am here for an interview. My name is Stella Pardalis."

She tucked a wayward curl behind her ear before checking my name off a list. She stood, handed me a clipboard and a pen. I read on the rectangular brass plaque on her desk, Kathy Rowan.

"Please, complete the form and bring it with you when you go in for the interview." She gestured toward the group seated at the round table in the lobby.

I thanked her and turned toward the other eager applicants. I sensed they were as nervous as I was. They held on to their leather purses on their laps like a security blanket. All of us were impeccably dressed in light wool suits in pale shades of blue, gray, and beige. I was certain their hemlines, like mine, rested just above their knees just like the ads featuring stewardesses I had seen in newspapers and posters.

Hellos and good mornings went around the table and then nothing. No conversation. *This is strange. Here we are applying for a job which requires outgoing personalities, which presumably we all have, and yet we sit in silence.* It must have been out of anxiety and nerves.

Miss Rowan called my name. I took a deep breath as I stood and smiled at her. *This is it.* I could not believe it was happening. I smoothed the back of my skirt and followed her. I carried myself as tall as I could, shoulders back, one navy pump in front of the other. One last check to ensure both collar corners of my white blouse were inside the jacket collar. I felt confident in my selection of the light blue suit for the occasion. The receptionist walked away, and I walked into the small office.

Mrs. North stood up. The screeching sound made by the chair surprised us both. Our eyes locked and with tentative smiles on our faces we shook hands.

"Nice to meet you, Stella. Have a seat."

Be confident, don't be nervous. "It is a pleasure to meet you, Mrs. North." The words came out naturally even though inside I felt nervous.

She moved her chair with care to avoid another screech and sat. The contrast between Mrs. North and the interviewers I had two years prior was dramatic. She was four or five years older than I was. We both met the minimum requirements in height and weight. I pictured myself in her yellow knit uniform. From the waist up, the green, yellow, and orange horizontal stripes across her chest were visible in the vee that the matching yellow jacket formed on her chest. The uniform fit her perfectly. After a quick scan of my application, she put forth the expected question.

"Why do you want to be a TWA hostess?"

"Before I answer the question, I want to inform you that I applied for the position two years ago." I went into the story of the back-to-back interviews, and the futile waiting for the telegram. "After the second interview I went to a two-year college and earned an associate degree in order to become a TWA hostess."

A lightness in my chest prevailed for the rest of the interview. After I answered her last question, Mrs. North leaned forward, and I observed the pear-shaped diamond ring on her left finger. It displayed additional brilliance under the light as she reached for a business card. She handed it to me without a word and watched me read it. It wasn't a business card at all. I restrained myself from jumping up and down and screaming as loud as I could, "*Finally!*". The words on the card were to the point. "Congratulations, you are on your way to becoming a TWA hostess." I wanted to hug her, but that would not be appropriate. I had read that hostesses should be calm and composed. Instead, I said, "Thank you." She had to know my heart was about to bust out of my blouse and jacket. I was certain she figured out I wanted this job so much and that I was going to be good at it.

I listened carefully to the schedule of the training classes. "I would like to take the first class. I waited this long; I don't want to wait any longer."

Before shaking hands, Mrs. North added, "When you go back in the lobby, if anyone asks how did it go? Tell them you were told to wait for a telegram."

So that's what they tell you if you are rejected.

That was a difficult lie to tell, but I did it. My heart went out to anyone who would be waiting for a telegram.

And sure enough, they asked. I answered as I was instructed.

I thanked Miss Rowan and exited the office. Little did I know that our paths would cross again in a few years and that Kathy Rowan, as well as my TWA bestie, Lark Logan, would become the two TWA friends to reside in my heart and be in my life to this day.

The sun seemed brighter when I stepped out onto Government

Center Plaza. We did not have cell phones. I walked across the plaza and found a pay phone.

"I got the job... I got the job!" I shrieked, not caring if anyone heard me.

"Congratulation, I knew you would. You were born to be a stewardess." People were used to using the term stewardess, not hostess. Mother Helen was on the other end of the phone line. She had been encouraging all along and coached me on how to conduct myself in an interview. During the interview I reminded myself of her suggestions. "Be yourself, be honest, look the interviewer in the eye." She had been instrumental in getting me little jobs for my resume while I was in high school before I had moved in with them. Her management position in the food service department at Lesley College in Cambridge made that possible. She took me along on catering events where I learned the art of serving.

My big news would take a couple of weeks to reach my sister, but I wrote to her as soon as I got home after the interview. Our relationship had begun a journey of reconnection since our first reunion. We had been corresponding and exchanging photographs across the Atlantic. We were eager to catch up with each other's lives. Our letters became the thread for mending the eight-year-old tear.

Now, three years after that visit, I couldn't wait to hear back from my sister because I knew she would be thrilled with my news. *Next time I see her, I will be a TWA hostess.*

31

Winging It

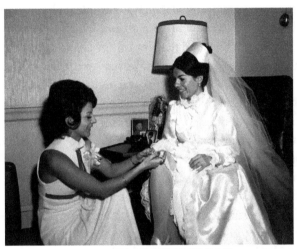

LENA AND ME SHARING MY SPECIAL DAY.

My life journey began with a taxi ride from Thessaloniki to the village of Kostohori, a move to Veria, and finally ended in America, where I found endless opportunities for a career and family. My career choice opened a gateway to travel the world.

The seed to become a TWA hostess that must have been planted in my eleven-year-old heart and mind on my first flight from Athens to New York via TWA was ready to sprout. All that seemed so long ago, as if it happened in another lifetime.

Despite the roadblocks I encountered, life offered me opportunities along the way. I went from despair about possibly not seeing my sister ever again to a heartfelt reunion which was to evolve into a slow but promising and loving sisterly relationship. Not an instant connection, but one where one link at a time we created a chain to bind us together. Our correspondence re-initiated the connection and my annual summer visits to Greece added substance and additional links to lengthen our chain. I was elated when she wrote to inform me her parents had agreed to send her to Boston to be my koumbara at my wedding. The koumbara performs the exchanging of the rings and *stefana* (wedding crowns) for the bride and groom in a Greek Orthodox Church wedding. This ceremony symbolizes the couple is crowned as the queen and king of their home.

Before Lena's arrival, I worked diligently to ensure everything, including the very last-minute detail, was completed before her arrival. I wanted to be free to show her the area in which I grew up and the places I frequented. I wanted to show off my beautiful sister, especially now that everyone in my circles was aware of her existence. Her pending arrival added to the existing excitement and hubbub with all of us as we constantly chatted and anticipated my wedding.

Donna, my maid of honor, came over for a final check on my wedding gown. She helped me step out of it after we both checked front, back, sideways and all angles possible. The reflection in the full-length mirror in Mother Helen's bedroom pleased us. As if handling a fragile child, we slid my gown onto a white satin hanger and hung it on the hook off the light fixture above the bed. We spread the luscious white satin with its long train hanging over the double bed. The headpiece, also covered with the same satin, added four inches to my height. We rested that on the crystal lamp on top of my dresser. The netting fastened on the back flowed halfway to the floor. I was impressed and pleased with the result of my efforts. Donna and I had originally shopped for a gown but after trying a few on at the store I decided to sew my own.

Windsor Button Shop in downtown Boston was renowned for its bridal fabrics and accessories. Starting with sewing patterns, instruction books, threads, bobbins, every conceivable trim, such as lace, cord, ribbons, the shop carried anything and everything necessary for sewing. With expert assistance from the saleswomen at Windsor, I crafted two unforgettable garments, my wedding gown, and Mother Helen's royal blue velvet long skirt. Its bridal department was unsurpassed; however, after a seventy-seven-year run the store was priced out of business. Downtown Crossing's high rental rates prohibited the owners from renewing their lease and Windsor closed its doors in 2013.

For one month the white satin fabric lay spread out across the bed as it was taking form. Mother and Father's bedroom became my sewing room during the day, and I sat across from the bed in front of the portable Singer sewing machine, all the yards of fabric and trimmings beckoning to be transformed. The two-inch-wide white lace for the front of the gown, the three-quarter-inch narrow white trim for finishing the sleeves and to edge the entire hemline. The Vogue pattern guided me to create the gown with the fitted bodice, a gathered waist which unleashed enough fabric to create a bell shape that reached the floor and trailed in the back. When Donna spread the circular train, it formed a one-yard half-moon behind me. Raisin-size buttons descended from the closed neckline to the bottom of the gown. I had covered the buttons with the satin fabric. My cousin Veta made exquisite bound buttonholes for me.

After our graduation from Breech Training Academy in February 1970, we were given a week off before our first flight assignment. I went home to Brighton to get my things ready for New York where I would begin my new life as a TWA hostess. One of my first stops was Minihane's Flowers, hoping that Paul still worked there. My wish was answered when I saw him behind the register. After our initial greeting he asked the obvious question: "Where have you been? It's been two years."

I filled him in on my father's death, my schooling and announced, "I am a TWA hostess. I just finished training. I'm based in New York and will be flying International from JFK."

"That's fantastic. Congratulations."

"I am glad you were working. I was hoping to see you. What have you been doing?"

"Not too much, taking classes at Boston State and working here." He stretched his arm toward the buckets filled with flowers.

"It was nice to see you." I started to the door.

He opened the door, and we stood outside in an awkward moment. Washington Street was as busy as always. Cars and buses transported passengers both ways. Customers greeted Paul as they went into the store. And just as I was about to walk down the street he asked, "Are you free this Saturday?"

I was free that Saturday and all the Saturdays that I wasn't flying.

I floated away from the flower shop and retrieved a memory of a few months earlier when Annie, a fellow trainee at Breech Training Academy had sauntered into my room and picked up the picture on my night table.

"Is this your boyfriend? You make a cute couple."

"Yes." I didn't hesitate but I felt funny. Was he really my boyfriend? We only had two dates. But after that, he was my boyfriend even though I had not seen him since that dinner dance. No one had to know the achy feeling and desire tugging at my heart.

I had purchased the only frame I found at the store nearest the training center. Relaxing in the sunken living room, we exchanged stories and one of the main topics was boyfriends. Photographs of couples in a range of poses were displayed in each girl's room. I didn't have a boyfriend but felt as though I should. I hadn't planned on displaying a picture of me and a boy, but I went through my brown leather photo album. I knew if I was going to display a picture which one it would be. In my mind, Paul was my boyfriend even though he didn't know it. I had a crush on him during the last couple of years of high school. I felt it from the time I ordered my first corsage and boutonnière from him.

Beautiful Breech Training Academy in Overland Park, Kansas opened in 1969, the same year I graduated from Mass Bay Community College. At the time, hostess positions were exclusively held by women. However, in 1972 TWA invited young men to apply and the term "hostess" was replaced by "flight attendant." It was a privilege to be in the first training class at the prestigious training academy. This state-of-the-art facility gained notoriety and other airlines periodically utilized it to train their flight attendants.

The renowned dormitories were set up in pods. Each pod was named after a region of the world. Their sunken living rooms were decorated according to the region represented. In our pod a floor-to-ceiling black-dotted orange giraffe greeted us when we entered. Floor pillows large enough for lounging covered in animal prints invited us to the safari. Fluffy zebra, faux fur tiger, shaggy lion, and plush leopard pillows kept us cozy during our evenings. One step up from the living room was a circular carpeted hallway and all ten two-person bedrooms were accessible. I lucked out and had a room to myself.

In the comfort of the sunken living room, we shared experiences about our lives while leaning against a stuffed elephant the same size as me. During these discussions I realized how sheltered my life had been. I was quite impressed to hear how most of them had connections who provided referrals and helped them get an interview with TWA. Susan said, "My mother's friend works in Reservations," Claudia had a helping hand: "My father's friend is VP of Operations." Because of a connection, Mary and Virginia, who had been overweight at the time of their initial interview, were given time to lose weight and return for a second interview. Lynn had been a flight attendant for a smaller airline. I was the only one who had not applied to another airline. They were just as surprised about my single-minded job search as I was about their connections and multiple applications.

I became aware that I had been given no adult input, no guidance on how to attain my dream job. I realized none of them had their heart set on one specific airline; their focus was to be a flight attendant. It made me realize I had limited myself by wanting to be only a TWA hostess. Once again, my gut feeling, my intuition guided me to choose and succeed.

TWA had purchased the new Boeing 747 (747) which became known as the Jumbo Jet. Positions for international flight hostesses for the 747 were announced. I applied and was accepted. A handful of my classmates joined along with more senior hostesses to train on the 747 simulator. I could not believe it was happening. I would begin my career as an international hostess and would be working the newest airplane. I felt like I could jump out of my skin from sheer happiness.

At the time I was the first hostess to qualify in Greek as my primary language. My secondary language was Spanish. I would be flying to Athens, Greece with senior flight attendants.

None of the studying, memorizing, and executing the tasks and drills required to earn my wings challenged me as much as the thought of jumping into the pool to swim to the life raft. After almost drowning at age eight, I only swam in areas where I could touch bottom.

During all safety drills, the adrenaline peaked. We admitted that to each other when we lounged in our living room. The instructors continuously impressed upon us the importance of the idea that our purpose on the flight was first and foremost for safety. Food service, comfort, and conversation were important to gain the passengers' loyalty, but safety was the main role of the in-flight crew. Nothing about the safety drills made me apprehensive. But the thought of jumping into the pool brought butterflies from my stomach to my throat. Fortunately, the camaraderie we developed during our weeks together bolstered our confidence when we needed it.

Our final test was the lifeboat drill. My sixteen angels encouraged me, reassuring me I could do it. They all volunteered to jump in ahead of me. Moments before I jumped in, thousands of ants invaded my head, making me feel woozy and then I held my body upright and swallowed those ants deep into my stomach as I pulled on the tabs and jumped into the pool. When I surfaced and began swimming to the life raft, I regained my confidence and determination prevailed. I sensed such relief I thought I would burst out of my life jacket.

For our graduation TWA offered each graduate one-round trip ticket for a parent to attend the ceremony. Father Bill flew in for my graduation. My name was called and Mrs. North, who had interviewed and hired me, pinned my wings on my uniform. We felt grown up and sophisticated accompanying our parents to a fancy restaurant in celebration of our success.

Secretly, one of the people with whom I had wanted to share the news of receiving my wings was Paul. Even though I was prepared to explore the world in my dream job and had no thoughts of marriage, I felt a desire to share my achievement with him. And that is why I had stopped by the flower shop to announce my news. And like in a novel, soon thereafter we became a couple. At that time seeing the world was my focus. However, following that stop, seeing the world with Paul added a sweet dimension to that focus. After a year and a half, our wedding day loomed ahead.

32

Together Again

ISMINI, AZAT, MARY, ME, SOFIA, AND ANNA ON MRS. AZAT'S BALCONY

Lena's presence at my wedding added a massive link to our relationship chain. Paul and I picked her up at Logan Airport. The thirty-minute ride to Brighton gave the two of them time to get acquainted. After helping with the luggage, Paul left us alone for the evening. Lena and I had the house to ourselves. Mother and Father were spending a few days in Hampton Beach, New Hampshire.

Lena unpacked toiletries and her sweats. We lay on opposite sides of the couch, each with a glass of Coca-Cola in hand and were ready for a long sisterly visit. We faced each other with our legs stretched out, which was reminiscent of our sharing a bed when we were little girls living in Thessaloniki.

"Ah, my sister, did you ever think you would be coming to America for my wedding?"

"My parents have really come around to allow me to come here by myself. Of course, it's because I proved my love and devotion to them."

In our conversations Lena always reminded me: "I idolized you. I don't remember a great deal from our early childhood together, but I do remember I wanted to be with you all the time."

"I remember that too. I also remember when my girlfriends did not want you tagging along with us. No matter how hard I tried, most of the time you ended up coming with me and my friends."

"I know, I was stubborn. I whined and cried and of course I remember using my temper tantrums to get my way. You put up with me. You were my big sister. How could I not remember you?"

"It is a shame we were kept apart after your adoption. Your parents are such wonderful people and educated. Why did they think you would not remember me?

"Perhaps if I hadn't insisted the first day they got me that I knew I had a sister and even worse I threatened to leave them if I ever found you. Maybe if I was more accepting, more like you, they would have allowed us to communicate."

We talked and talked until we decided to get some sleep. We pulled the afghan over us and stayed on the couch, a habit we continued throughout our visits.

Once we had been allowed to connect, we saw each other every time I visited Greece. After I joined TWA, the frequency of my visits increased, giving us the opportunity to strengthen our bond. Every visit, every letter, and every phone call added a link to the chain. Eventually the chain reached platinum status.

Through our constant efforts and perseverance, we found a way to merge and adapt to the different views we had acquired about life resulting from our growing up in different cultures. Although I was familiar with the Greek culture, I had not lived in it for years. Every year during my summer sojourns to Greece, I experienced it as a visitor. I had become immersed in my new American way of life. I had created my own balance between the two.

My extended adoptive family had become accustomed to my way of thinking and behaving from my annual visits in Greece. They had watched me grow into the Americanized version. Lena and I had to catch up with each other's development.

During every visit we started our conversations with early childhood memories. Our days in Thessaloniki. Our family of four living in one room.

"This is how I remember it from listening to Mamá tell Mrs. Azat and Mrs. Ismini. When our babá completed his military service in Veria, we moved to Thessaloniki." I took a sip of coffee.

"I don't remember Veria at all," Lena said.

"It makes sense, you were only three when we moved. At five years old I have memories of the military housing and Mamá's visits with friends."

"I often wondered why we moved." She took a puff of her Dunhill cigarette.

I answered, "Babá was excited for the opportunities he would find in the second-largest city in Greece. I remember the conversation when my nonó and noná visited, they encouraged Babá to move to Thessaloniki as soon as he was free from the military."

My godparents, Sofia and Vassilis Papadopoulos, had moved from Veria to Thessaloniki six years earlier and opened a successful tailor shop.

"You know he found Mrs. Azat's room for us to rent."

"I do remember that, and after a couple of struggling years our babá had saved enough money to partner with your nonó and to expand the tailor shop into a large custom-made and ready-to-wear men's clothing line," Lena added.

"Yes, and because of Babá's designing talent they went into manufacturing his version of the trench coat. Lena, do you remember that?"

She perked up, straightened her back and excitedly began praising our father.

"Because of his design and method of manufacturing the trench coat your nonó's business grew substantially. I remember overhearing people talk about the success of the coat even after he had passed. We must have inherited some of his artistic talent. That's probably why we enjoy sewing, decorating, and adding embellishments on plain articles of clothing."

"I had not realized that about the trench coat and his influence on the business. This is the first I am hearing of it."

The iconic garment got its name from its use by soldiers in the trenches during the First World War. Its origin traces back to the 19th century when it was created by English inventor Thomas Hancock and Scottish chemist Charles Macintosh. They created waterproof long jackets by coating them with rubber. In the 1850s, it was improved upon by John Emary and Thomas Burberry. They made the coats more breathable. Burberry invented the gabardine fabric, the fibers of which were waterproofed prior to constructing the coat.

In the 1950s my father reinvented the trench coat in Thessaloniki, earning him the title of master of the gabardina. Its popularity spread beyond Thessaloniki, and Babá and Nonós supplied the fashionable gabardina throughout Greece. The business specializing in men's suits and coats, both ready-made and custom-made, mushroomed following my father's arrival.

"I recall a conversation," I said to Lena. "You were there. But you were in your own world at the time. Babá had just come home from work. He was his usual jovial self. He rubbed his palms together and announced, 'Sofia, we can rent an apartment. I am making enough money now that the business is thriving.' I held my rag doll against my chest and looked up to see my mother's reaction. Remember our rag dolls? We had so much fun making them. Anyway, Mamá was sitting on their bed shortening my old Sunday dress to fit you."

"I don't remember that." Lena leaned back, eager to hear more.

"Mamá laid the dress on her lap, made the sign of the cross, closed her eyes for a moment, and placed her hands over her lips."

"Her lips. I think of her full lips almost every time I apply my lipstick," Lena recalled.

I continued with my recollection. "Mamá, this means Nitsa and I will have our own bed, right?"

"Yes, my girl. No more sharing a bed."

"And a bathroom in the house," my father added.

"Bravo, Nikos. Finally, your hard work is paying off." Our mother crossed herself.

"You know, Stella, I bet they went to the bouzoukia that night to announce their move," said Lena.

Whenever we refer to that night, or their evening at the bouzoukia, our mood turns somber, as there are so many unanswered questions.

"They were so young. They went out for an evening of rejoicing with friends and never came back to their little girls." Lena lowered her head.

"Remember how excited we were watching them get ready to go out?" My heart sank thinking about our beautiful parents who were emanating happiness that evening.

"We were happy there in our one room."

"Think about it. We thought it was normal when a family moved to the big city to share one room. What did we know at five and three years old?"

The one- and two-bedroom homes characterized our Thessaloniki neighborhood of modest means. The owners took pride and kept their homes in pristine condition. An abundance of flowers adorned every doorway. Mrs. Azat was the only neighbor who rented out a room to augment her income. Mrs. Ismini, who lived across the street with her two adult sons, was a close friend of our landlady. The two Armenian widows had become close friends and allies in their new country. Their husbands were victims of the Armenian genocide committed during the Ottoman Empire.

The Empire had systematically killed Greeks and Armenians from 1914-1923. In the 1920s, 70,000 to 80,000 Armenian survivors who were driven out of Anatolia relocated to Greece. They primarily settled in Thessaloniki, Thessaly and Thrace.

Our family of four functioned as one with Mrs. Azat, Mary, and Anna. Mrs. Azat carried the deep wound of losing her younger daughter, Anna. She was my age and died of appendicitis at eight years old. We shared with them the living room, kitchen, and the yard. Except for the few winter months, the yard was multifunctional. At the farthest point over the stream that ran behind all the houses on our side of the street was *the place*. The provincial way of saying the bathroom. As if it was crude to use the actual word or to admit one needed to use it. Our *place*, like all the others on the street, was painted white and had a tin roof. Hard to believe in the second-largest city of the country, in the 1950s outhouses still prevailed. I liken the outhouse to a slightly larger version of today's average portable restroom. However, the outhouses on the street had a Turkish toilet on a dirt floor. The stream running below the hole took care of the flushing.

Away from the outhouse there were designated areas for specific functions. From the mini garden our mothers grew an abundance of produce from which to prepare the most delicious meals, such as stuffed peppers, stuffed tomatoes, moussaka, fasolakia ladera, fried zucchini, and tomato and cucumber salads. The laundry area was next to the garden. The fire pit was used to boil water for the laundry, our baths, and for cooking.

I am certain the fun area of the yard for the hard-working neighborhood housewives was the outdoor dining table nestled under the sprawling oak tree. As they completed their chores, they stopped by the neighbor who still had work to finish, whether it was cooking or washing. At our house they sat around the square table, which was next to the kitchen entrance. The classic taverna chairs with wooden back slats forced one to sit up straight. They did not seem that comfortable, but they never complained, maybe because unlike our neighbors, Mamá had made red and blue striped cushions for the straw seats of the chairs.

They all embraced the introduction of clear plastic table covers. "What a smart invention." They took pride in using it to protect their hand-embroidered tablecloths. "We don't have to change the tablecloth as often." The demitasse cups of coffee and glasses of water were enough to keep them around the table for hours. Their mouths and hands were in continuous motion. They embroidered table scarfs, crocheted round doilies, mended clothing, or helped the hostess with the chore at hand. I often lingered nearby to eavesdrop on the adult conversation. Not that I understood everything I heard. They had a strong support system. They revealed family heartaches, complained, or praised a spouse or a child, and when they whispered, I knew it had to be serious or a secret. I wonder if at a young age I had realized how helpful their commiserating, sharing, and rejoicing together was and I embraced it as I did the extended family.

With every visit, Lena and I dredged up memories from that time in our lives, some new, many rehashing the known past. We always brought up her temper tantrums and her wanting to be with me all the time.

"You were my idol. You always took care of me. That's why I kept telling my parents, I know I have a sister. I could not get you out of my mind."

"It's amazing we both have come through all that and still with healthy minds and emotional wellbeing." She made the sign of the cross in gratitude.

We had similar conversations during all our visits throughout the years. Not only did we make up for lost time, but our bond has reached the stage where we complete each other's sentences. One of us calls or FaceTimes when the other is thinking of doing the same thing. Beyond that our hearts seem to have melded into one. The care, understanding, and the compassion we feel for each other is endless. And we wonder would we have reached this level of connection had we grown up together?

Lena seized the first opportunity to care for me following a ski accident I had. "It is my turn to be the caregiver" she had told me over the phone. Even though her husband was not able to accompany her, she used her schoolteacher's Easter vacation to assist me and my eight-year-old son during my recovery. For the previous four years, she and her husband, Christos, had supported me and comforted me after my seven-year marriage ended in divorce in 1978.

The blizzard of '78 in Boston was the storm of the century. On February 7, 1978, the storm arrived and paralyzed the entire state of Massachusetts. Schools, businesses, and roads were closed for six days. All the snow that shrouded our home in Boxford, Massachusetts didn't measure up to the numbing super-storm that had been brewing for a year inside the walls and which finally manifested itself. The roads cleared, the snow melted, the state of emergency ended and so did our marriage. The beautiful fairytale romance terminated and I was left behind—a hollowed-out version of myself. In addition to the emotional upset, I dealt with the stigma of the divorce. From everything I was taught, divorce was not an option in our culture.

For two years before my divorce, I dealt with the demons in my mind. *Don't become a statistic. Stay married. Divorce is not acceptable. I will not ever be divorced.* But I did get divorced, and it took two years and a lot of love from family and friends for me to find my balance again.

Six years later with my sister by my side, I saw a bright future for myself. In April 1984, after I had the cast off my leg following the skiing accident, we celebrated Easter in the Greek Orthodox tradition. During that visit my sister claims credit not only for assisting with my recovery but also for facilitating a match made in the Greek church of Ipswich, Massachusetts. After the midnight Resurrection service, the church council hosted the traditional Anastasi (resurrection) dinner. She invited the president of the church council to sit with us.

Charles Nahatis, who had never been married before, joined our table. Handsome, almost six feet tall, well-groomed with a trim mustache, he sat between us. He unbuttoned his blue suit jacket with ease and confidence. My eight-year-old son, Paul Richard, was excited because he was staying up past midnight. The evening ended favorably. The following Saturday Charles and I drove my sister to the airport for her return home to Greece.

I walked with her as far as I was allowed. During our tearful good-bye-hug she whispered, "I am happy I am leaving you knowing that there is someone of interest in your life. I have a good feeling about this."

With the salty taste of tears on my lips, all I could say was, "Thank you for everything, I love you and will miss you."

After her flight took off, Charles and I continued the evening with dinner and dancing at a Greek nightclub in Boston. That was our first of many dates that led to Charles's following me to Greece later that summer.

The summer of 1984 was the last trip I made to Greece as a single. Paul Richard and I spent a month together before he returned to the States to be with his dad. Since I still had connections with TWA, I escorted him to the airplane and watched his smiling, brave face turn for one last look before he disappeared into the crowd. I felt a sense of calm and ease about his traveling alone. As a flight attendant I had experience with unaccompanied children and felt very confident he would be taken care of.

Waiting for Charles's arrival felt as though every cell in my body was tingling. My sister and brother-in-law teased me relentlessly over my romantic euphoria.

The three of us picked him up at the airport. I watched him descend the flight of boarding stairs with Olympic Airways emblazoned across its length. Lena and Christos had a field day bantering with me while we waited outside customs.

On the way to Oraiokastro, Charles got an overview of the city and Lena and Christos made suggestions of what to do during his visit. I wanted to pinch myself to make sure it was real. My entire being was supercharged. I was sharing a beautiful chapter of my life with my sister in person.

When Charles and I returned from our walk, they knew we had something to announce. We had gone to have a drink at the highest point of Oraiokastro. They had recommended the cafe bar on the veranda of the Hotel Haris.

"Go to the veranda for a cocktail or coffee," Christos had suggested.

And Lena added, "On a clear day you can see Thessaloniki. And at night you will see an endless shimmer of lights."

Under the canopy of a grapevine with the view of Thessaloniki in the distance, we sipped on a frappé, like iced coffee. The city appeared mystical as the sun vanished below the horizon. It was the perfect setting for our serious conversation and for a marriage proposal from Charles.

Although I did not want another marriage, Charles the traditionalist would not have it any other way. Since I envisioned spending my life with Charles, I accepted.

33

New Beginnings

CHARLES AND ME ON OUR WEDDING DAY

Ours was a traditional, but modest Greek wedding. Charles and I agreed that since I had had the long satin gown and the wedding of my dreams thirteen years prior, we would limit the guest list to close relatives and friends. At thirty-six years old, I wore a knee-length white silk two-piece outfit. The Swarovski crystals on the three-quarter-sleeve top added enough sparkle to complement the straight fitted skirt. I created a simple sequined fascinator with a large tulle bow to complete my bridal ensemble.

My guest list, in addition to Mother and Father Lydon, included a handful of relatives and close friends.

"I can't believe we can't be there." Lena's voice was crackling through a bad phone connection.

"I am disappointed too but if you can't get away from your jobs you can't, I understand. But Charles and I look forward to your visit at Easter and we will all celebrate together then."

Charles chose most of the guests.

"Are you sure you don't want to invite more people?" he asked me before the invitations went out.

"I am positive. I told you, I've already had my big wedding."

"I just want to share our big day with as many close relatives and friends as possible." He gave me a hug.

I stayed in his embrace and told him what I was thinking. "You are lucky your four siblings and their families will be there. I really wish my sister and her husband could be with us."

Our marriage was blessed at the Assumption of the Virgin Mary Greek Orthodox Church in Ipswich, Massachusetts. I felt once again I was finding the family for which I had been longing since childhood.

Sadly, I discovered that not every family is looking to add new family members. Some families feel complete just as they are and don't have the need or the desire that I yearned for after all the losses I had experienced. I had expected that Charles's family would embrace me and welcome me as Paul's family had done. I was certain they would be pleased to have a daughter-in-law who shared their culture. I knew my being divorced was not the issue since they already had that experience in their family.

Fortunately, I got the gem of the family and am grateful for my kind, generous and caring husband. I don't tire of praising him for his expression of love, care, and generosity to me and my limited number of family members.

"You have been a terrific stepfather to Paul Richard. A pappou extraordinaire to Trey. And I love your relationship with my sister," I tell him often. I appreciate his embracing my adoptive and biological family members in the US and in Greece.

We were fortunate to have spent time with Lena and Christos twice a year between Greece and in the US. Lena and I rejoiced in the relationship that had evolved among the four of us. However, after ten years our small family suffered a tragic loss. In October of 1994, Christos had a major heart episode and died instantly.

Consoling Lena and supporting her with 4,600 miles between us was difficult. At that point, we did not have the convenience of FaceTime and our phone conversations were impeded by poor connections.

"Why don't you come and stay with us until you feel stronger?"

"Oh, I don't know, what am I going to do with the store?"

Lena had taken early retirement from teaching and had opened a thriving bridal and baptism boutique in the prestigious Tsimiski Street in Thessaloniki.

"I think Pepi will be able to handle it without you." I knew she trusted Pepi, the store manager.

"I know, I know, I will think about it."

She spent six months with us. Upon her return to Greece, she sold their home and her business. In pursuit of a new beginning, she moved to Litohoro, eighty kilometers south of Thessaloniki. Litohoro is a beautiful village at the base of Mount Olympus, the home of the gods according to Greek mythology. The mountain's foothills lead to the Thermaic Gulf with its many beaches, three kilometers below the village. On a clear day Thessaloniki and Chalkidiki come into view across the gulf. The first recorded history of the village is in an account from the sixteenth century by Saint Dionysios when he went to visit Mount Olympus.

When Lena was growing up, she and her parents had spent summers in Litohoro. Charles and I had encouraged her to move into her childhood vacation condominium before making any major moves. She agreed. "I'll stay in the condominium until I either find or build a house."

"Who knew you would be living here permanently?" we had said when construction had begun on the piece of land she purchased. We followed the progress of her reestablishing herself. Within two years of her move, she emerged a strong woman who had taken charge of her destiny.

"This is exquisite." That was our first impression of the delightful and functional villa she had built.

"Thank you both for encouraging me to move to Litohoro."

She created an oasis for herself. Charles and I make it our home base whenever we visit Greece.

Our visits to each other's countries have increased to twice and sometimes three times a year since our first reunion in 1966.

During one of Lena's visits to the US, we received a peculiar call from our Theo Pavlos. We were in the den having our late-morning coffee. It was afternoon in Greece when he called. After our how are you and all, I said, "Lena is here too."

"That's perfect because what I have to ask concerns both of you. I called you because you are older." The truth is he communicated with me more often than he did with Lena. He continued, "A man with the same last name as your biological father telephoned me and requested your phone numbers."

"That is unbelievable, after all these years a possible relative has surfaced?" Lena and I abandoned our coffees. We put our heads close together as I held the phone between us so we could both hear and speak.

"I don't know if you remember old Mrs. Yiannoula, the one with lung problems."

Theo and Thea often brought up names of villagers that they assumed we remembered from decades ago when we were seven- and ten-year-olds.

"When she went to see Dr. Spentsouras, she asked if she was related to a Nikos Spentzouras who died along with his wife in a motorcycle accident several years previous. Yiannoula pointed out that the spelling of the last name was with a z not an s. The doctor explained she was married to Georgos Spentsouras, who was Nikos Spentzouras's cousin. The spelling change happened through an error. They had heard about the fatal accident and about the two orphan girls, but it was years after the fact, and they had not been able to track them down."

Lena and I stood and paced the room with our ears pressed to the phone. We gestured with our eyes to each other's arms and the goosebumps on our skin.

"Theo, we can't believe after thirty years we will meet a relative from our father's side."

"So, it is okay with you to give him your number?"

"Give him mine, too!" Lena yelled into the phone.

It's comical how we spoke louder than normal because of the distance.

"Yes, give him our numbers. Do you have a number for him?"

Lena and I were like little schoolgirls.

"Let's call Georgos, our cousin, I can't believe it after all these years." I said. Both of us kept repeating "after all these years" until someone answered on the other end.

We were still holding the phone between our heads.

"Stella and Lena formerly Spentzouras here, calling from the United States."

A sing-song, friendly voice, its warmth reached us through the wires thousands of miles away.

"My dear cousins. I know we are cousins. We heard about the accident many years later and we could not find you." By the time he finished his sentence his voice was trembling, and we could hear his sniffling. The three of us were emotionally charged. Hearing Georgos's sniffling and choking on his words burned our eyes into tears.

We learned he and his family lived in Naoussa.

"The couple that adopted me were from Naoussa. I have relatives there. I will come to visit you when I return to Greece. We will all stay in touch." It was a short, heartfelt and emotional conversation.

Lena and I sat on the couch with our lukewarm coffees, mesmerized as we reflected on what had just happened. So many coincidences.

"The doctor, Georgia Spentsoura's office was in Veria. I bet it was due to human error their name is spelled with an s and not a z," Lena said.

"And how about me? I was adopted by a couple originally from Naoussa. All the times I visited Naoussa, Georgos has been there, and I didn't even know I had a second cousin."

Once we got to know Georgos and his family we learned a little about our father. Our new cousin was as sweet as he sounded on the telephone.

The two Spentzouras families originally emigrated to Greece in the 1930s. After the infamous Smyrna (modern Izmir, Turkey) fire of 1922 which destroyed the Greek and Armenian quarters, thousands of Greeks escaped to Greece.

Before the fire, between 1915 and 1920, some 1.5 million Armenians were killed by the members of the Ottoman Empire. Over one million Greeks and Armenians were forced to leave, and their properties were confiscated. The majority who left Asia Minor sought refuge in Greece. A minority of Greeks remained in Turkey after the fire. However, beginning in the 1930s the Turkish government instituted new laws that forced the remaining Greeks to emigrate.

In Turkey the two first cousins had lived in adjacent homes next to the grandparents' homestead in Fokia (Foca), sixty-nine kilometers from Smyrna on the Aegean Sea. The minorities who had not fled lived impoverished lives. According to Georgos's father, their living conditions and inability to envision a secure, comfortable future in Turkey forced their families to emigrate Greece.

Vangelis and Nikos ended up in the Kaminia neighborhood of Piraeus, the seaport of Athens. They had left their homes in Turkey for the makeshift open-air living conditions of Piraeus.

What they found in their new homeland was more poverty and bigotry. They were known as *prosfiges* (refugees) and were treated as second-class citizens. They found their friends and relatives living in conditions similar to what they had left behind. The promised land proved less than promising. Their settlement consisted of narrow dirt streets lined with meager one- and two-room structures constructed of discarded materials like wood, aluminum, brick, or stone, without indoor plumbing. People shared outhouses constructed of similar discarded materials or the familiar aluminum outhouses of the times. Only the refugees with decent-paying jobs had electricity. Jobs were hard to find.

Our new cousin relayed the little information Theo Vangelis had been willing to share. "My father did not want to talk about the days in Turkey nor his experiences in Kaminia. Whenever we asked him, he waved his hand and cast his eyes down, and whispered, 'poverty a lot of poverty'."

On our first visit with Georgos, he told us a little about life in Kaminia as Theo Vangelis had told it. "Families survived by providing goods and services within their own neighborhoods. The grocer, the tailor, the cobbler, and the barber set up shop anywhere they could. Some worked out of their homes, most set up their wagons or makeshift tables out of pieces of wood resting on stumps of trees or any other object sturdy enough to hold a flat surface. There, the vendors displayed and hawked their wares."

The *kafenio* (the traditional coffee shop set up for men only) was also present within the shopping area. The men gathered and commiserated on their lack of good fortune and poor fate. They sat at the kafenio for hours, going home to eat and sleep. For the men who had jobs, the kafenio was a place to rest and visit with friends. Another popular outlet for these displaced and passionate people was their music. *Rebetiko* was the music associated with the early 1920s, when the majority of the refugees arrived in Greece. Friends gathered to drink their *raki*, a clear anisette-flavored moonshine, and to play their music. The lyrics spoke of their fate, their pain, their disappointment in the Greek government that had promised them freedom and security and then left them to fend for themselves.

Although they were Greek, as refugees they were not welcome. After years of living in abject poverty in their new country, disillusioned teenagers decided to fight for a better life and took to the mountains. My father, Nikos, was one of those disillusioned teens and he found himself fighting against the government forces to bring about a better lifestyle for the refugees.

He was 17 and wanted to make a difference. He joined the resistance movement. He became an *antartis* (rebel fighter) and found himself fighting for the cause in the mountains of Northern Greece. His battalion reached Kostohori, five hundred thirteen kilometers from Piraeus.

The two cousins had lost touch with each other.

Connecting with our father's relatives provided a glimpse of his background. Unfortunately, Theo Vangelis was of the generation that did not speak of their plight.

"What can we do? We will just have to live with our questions unanswered. There is so much I wish we knew about their lives in Turkey," my sister said.

Thinking about our father's difficult past brought back a sadness we felt whenever we thought of his and our mother's early deaths. He had survived persecution in Turkey, only to find a different kind of suffering in his new country. After surviving poverty and the war, he died at the age of thirty. So sad, just when he was about to enjoy his business achievement.

34

Our Taxi Ride to the Past

LENA AND ME IN SMYRNA.

The Asia Minor Association of Smyrna in Thessaloniki maintains detailed records of the refugees whose ships landed there following the genocide and the Great Fire of Smyrna. A cold wave doused my body when I found documentation of my father's arrival in Greece. It listed Nikolaos Spentzouras and his sister, Stella Spentzouras.

"I really would love for us to do a pilgrimage to our father's hometown."

Lena's words were laced with nostalgia every time she had brought up the idea of our venturing to Fokia, Turkey. Lena was consumed with a burning desire for the trip following our reconnection with our cousin Georgos. Every telephone call included a mention of the pilgrimage. (This was before FaceTime had become our daily method of communication.) Telephone calls were how we connected when we were not visiting each other at our respective homes. Lena continued to harp on the idea of our going to Fokia to visit our father's homestead. A few years after her first utterance, the seed took root in our hearts and minds and making the pilgrimage became a priority.

"I've been looking at organized tours to Turkey but haven't found one that includes Fokia, but I'll keep looking."

"I wish Theo Vangelis was alive to give us more information."

"Georgos knows the location of their houses. They are located directly across from Agia Paraskevi Church," Lena answered.

As we gathered information, the momentum and urgency to make the pilgrimage increased. Soon, coordinating the dates for the trip became a priority. On my end, coordinating our trip was affected by previously planned events, including cruising the Caribbean with Charles in January, going to Litohoro for Carnavali in February, and golfing in North Carolina in April. Thus, May was my preference for visiting Turkey.

Lena was loud and clear, I think I would have heard her without the use of a device.

"I found it, I found it. It's a bus tour and it departs from Thessaloniki May 28 and returns June 2."

I knew it was worth sacrificing a few golf days for what the trip promised to deliver to our souls.

On May 21, 2015, I arrived at Thessaloniki's airport, Makedonia. We were always excited and animated when we saw each other at the familiar customs area. But, on that arrival the energy surrounding our hugs and kisses was intensified.

"We are finally going!" Lena exclaimed as she pushed the luggage cart.

"I can't believe it. You did it, found the ideal tour for us. In a week we will be on our father's homeland and hopefully his home is still there."

The lights of Litohoro offered a warm welcome to my return when Lena's red Fiat mini-jeep climbed the main street to our favorite taverna for *paidakia* (lamb chops).

"We are here. It feels as though we just left the airport and yet we have covered eighty-four kilometers," I said.

The distinct aroma of grilled lamb chops on a wood fire greeted us as we entered Stamatia's and Yianni's restaurant.

"You are back so soon? You were just here for Carnavali," Stamatia said as she poured homemade wine.

"I missed your paidakia."

There was no need to explain our mission to visit Fokia. Fokia, the word for "seal" was bestowed upon our father's town due to its seal population. We devoured the platter of lamb chops, smacking our lips as we left the bones bare.

Jet lag did not kick in, which meant the next phase would be to mess up the meticulously clean and neat rooms at Lena's home. That night we were pumped up more than on all my previous arrivals. In addition to the clothes and packages spilling out of suitcases, I was certain our words and laughter ricocheted off the walls. We took pleasure in laughing about the mess we created.

I was about to carry my blue Delsey suitcase to my room.

"Leave it. Sit down." Lena lit a Marlboro Light cigarette. "Can you believe in a few days we will walk on the ground our father walked on, and played on, and kicked a ball around?"

I put the suitcase down.

"We are not going to bed yet." She took a long drag on her Marlboro.

Our discussion turned to the fateful night of our parents' motorcycle accident. The young couple with what seemed like lives unfinished left the world and their two little girls.

"It is like a movie. We are now more than twice the age our parents were when they died."

And my statement turned into another night of: Can you believe? Do you remember? How happy they would have been to see our successes.

A week of preparations, unconstrained excitement, building anticipation, and visits with friends and relatives preceded our trip to Turkey. Most of the other passengers fell asleep before we were beyond the city limits. It was still dark, but in an hour or so we would need our sunglasses.

Six hundred kilometers and twelve hours later, we arrived at the Grand Hotel Temizel in the outskirts of Ayvelik, Turkey.

A walk through the hotel's manicured gardens revealed a serene beach and the beckoning blue waters of the Aegean. Nature had endowed its beauty on Turkey, but Lena and I felt the continuous ache of the harm the Ottoman empire had inflicted upon our ancestors.

"It is too sad to think about it. Why did they commit such atrocities?" Lena shook her head from side to side.

"And why does war and persecution still occur in the world today?"
I asked.

"We are not going to solve that issue for sure. But it makes me
not want to spend one euro, not one dollar, not one Turkish lira more
than necessary while we are here," Lena said with determination.

It is unfortunate we felt that way. We knew the present people
were not responsible for the actions of their ancestors. And it wasn't
fair to deprive their country of any contribution our money would
make to their economy. Intellectually we knew it, but emotionally
we felt we were standing up for our father, his family, and the Greek
people who had suffered so long ago.

Every morning the bus picked us up at the hotel for a daily tour.
Many of the sights were painful to see. They included ruins of structures the Greek people had built before the Ottoman Empire decided
to force the Greeks out. We visited one place called Acropolis with
impressive columns and statues. Other monuments were like those in
Athens, Delphi, and other ancient historical sites in Greece. My sister
and I exchanged our pained emotions.

"My heart hurts to see all this and to hear its history."

"I have a pit I want to rip out of my stomach," Lena answered.

We wished we didn't have to see any of it and that we could just
go to Fokia and Smyrna.

Finally, for us, the day on which our entire trip was based arrived.
A visit to Fokia and to Smyrna. Fokia belongs to the Izmir Prov-
ince on the Aegean coast. It was founded by ancient Greeks. After
the Greek genocide that commenced in 1914 most of the Greeks
fled. The Ottoman Empire had *muhacirs* (forced Muslim migrants)
move into the abandoned homes. Later in 1919 when many Greeks
returned, they reclaimed their homes from the muhacirs. But the
Greeks' return was short-lived after the destructive and massive fire
of Smyrna in 1922. The fires were most intense on the waterfront
streets where the homes and the thriving businesses of the Greeks
were located. That was where the nobility and entrepreneurs of the
Greek community lived and worked.

The night before our tour to Fokia, my sister and I sat on our
hotel balcony. We wrapped ourselves in our pashminas under the
bright starry sky and for the gazillionth time we immersed ourselves

in imagining how our father must have felt being forced to leave his country as a young boy. I realized even though through no choice of my own I had to migrate to another country as a young girl, it was not as harsh for me. The prospect of a better life turned out to be true for me. My father did not have the same opportunities to grow and prosper. We went to bed, our hearts filled with excitement and gratitude despite the sadness we had rehashed.

On May 30, 2015, Lena and I were the first ones at the bus pickup. In anticipation of what lay ahead in Fokia, we paced, she smoked, we poked our heads back and forth around the corner as if on a spring in search of the bus's approach. Our fellow tourists joined us. We took turns looking around the corner for the bus. Fifteen minutes past the hour I declared, "The bus is late."

"I'll check with the receptionist to see if they know anything about a delay," someone said.

Anxious eyes followed her quick steps to the hotel's front entrance. Someone else asked the security guard if he knew anything. She returned from the guard house shaking her head in disappointment.

The smokers were lighting up and puffing on their cigarettes to stay calm. Lena and I were affected most by the delay. The tour only allotted two hours for the village of Fokia.

"We came for the sole purpose of visiting our father's village," my sister and I repeated to our fellow tourists.

"The receptionist has not heard from the driver or the tour guide," came the answer.

Forty-five minutes later our group darted toward the hotel staff member who was approaching us.

In her broken English she informed us. "The bus has mechanics problem. They wait for part. They cancel trip to Foca. Bus will go to Izmir. *Tesekkur ederim* (thank you)."

Are they kidding me? This entire trip was arranged for us to visit Fokia.

Everyone voiced their disappointment but none of the others in the group felt it like Lena and me. Not visiting Fokia was not an option.

"Oh, what will you do? "I am so sorry for you." Our travelling companions commented.

"They made this trip to go to Fokia," they said to each other.

Their compassion was comforting but not a resolution to our problem.

The two taxis outside the hotel's gated area gave us a glimmer of hope. A group of us huddled to figure something out. How could we dismiss the warnings we had been given about safety and not venturing out without a guide? Lena and I decided the taxi was our only option. We conferred with the hotel security guard. He reassured us he knew and trusted the young man in the first taxi. The guard translated for us and negotiated the price. We decided to trust the driver. Although he did not speak English or Greek, he exuded calmness and understanding as the guard interpreted and explained our plight. Prior to our getting into the taxi, one of our fellow travelers made note of the driver's and taxi's information. We put our faith in a higher power and our trust in the twenty-something driver. His friendly countenance put us at ease.

We eased ourselves into the back seat of the yellow taxi. Despite the hassle, the knots in our stomachs, and the anticipation, we did take note of and admire the lush green vegetation of the mountains and the turquoise Aegean waters. We were grateful to have found a taxi willing to spend the day with us. With my sister's limited Turkish vocabulary, we found out our driver had never been to Fokia nor to the big city of Smyrna. Even so, it was a win-win situation. We would accomplish our goal and he would earn a week's pay in one day.

One block up from the main square of Fokia, we turned left. Before we turned, we saw the Aegean beach where we fantasized our father once swam and fished. The street narrowed as we proceeded away from the square. We avoided eye contact as we passed by a merchant outside his gift shop. He nodded at the two tourists, but we were not just any tourists looking to buy souvenirs and trinkets; we were on a pilgrimage. And finally, after a few twists and turns and many curious once-overs, we got to the field where the Agia Sophia Church previously stood. All churches had been either destroyed or turned into mosques. We stood there with reverence and sadness in our hearts. We hugged each other and let our tears trickle.

People gawked as they passed us by. Western women aroused their interest. When we approached the house that had belonged to our great-grandparents, a girl in a pink dress, about ten years old, bolted inside. Her chocolate brown hair hung loosely over her two skinny arms. She barely got inside the door when a rotund middle-aged woman appeared, nodded her head and approached us.

Down the street we saw a man in his thirties in a white muscle T-shirt with a little girl about age six who was pulling on his tethered pant leg, dawdle in our direction. They walked halfway to us, stopped and stared. Suddenly a single head here, then another and another further down the dirt street peered out their windows and doorways. No one spoke to us nor to each other, they just stared. The scene was unsettling. If something happened to us, would the driver know where to start looking? Their looks spoke fear but then again, I wasn't certain. My sister, who has a better understanding of their culture, reassured me that they were afraid of us.

"When they see westerners, they think they have come back to claim their property."

The large woman with the scarf covering her head got close enough and motioned for us to enter her garden. Her nervous smile revealed two spaces where two front upper teeth used to be. Through Lena's limited Turkish vocabulary, we got the feeling she understood our being there. Another hefty woman appeared and invited me to enter the home.

Lena had moved away from us. She was outside the fence, digging in the ground. The afternoon before we left on our trip she flew into the kitchen like a woman with a purpose.

"What are you up to? I thought we were going to sit for coffee."

She reached in a cabinet drawer and pulled out a gallon-size ziplock bag. She held it up triumphantly and said, "I am going prepared." She opened the silverware drawer and took out a soup spoon and waved it. "I am going to bring back soil from our father's yard." And there she was, digging into the hard gray soil. She had warned me that our presence would likely raise immense suspicion with the locals. She had told me, "Many times when people had been forced out of their homes, they hid valuables underground hoping to return and reclaim their treasures." Perhaps the curious onlookers may have thought that's what Lena was doing.

She filled the bag with enough soil for herself, me, and our cousin Georgos. Soil from our ancestor's yard. When I returned home to

America, my grandson Trey and I ceremoniously stored the soil.

"This is from your great-grandfather's yard. The yard where he, my father Nikos, played. The bottle is from *raki* we drank in Turkey."

"I'll use the funnel to pour in the soil," Trey offered.

"I will make a label for it. Let's save some soil to mix it in with the soil of an existing plant in the yard."

I felt a sense of connection with my father through this ritual. And I also connected my grandson to his ancestors. I am glad Lena had acted on her idea.

"I bet they will be doing a lot of digging after we are gone," she had said.

I came out of the house with four women and the little girl. When I had followed the two into the small dark room, I noticed the brightly colored rag rugs on benches along the wall. Two older women with kerchiefs greeted me. To say I felt awkward would be an understatement. I did not know how to interpret their stares. I wished there had been more space so I could indulge in my thinking. I wanted to visualize my father as a little boy visiting his grandfather in that very room. Sitting on his lap and listening to stories. The aura I allowed myself to feel tore at my heart. At the same time, I made an effort not to look around. There was an opening to another room, but I felt I was invading their privacy. I wish I had felt comfortable enough to ask to see the rooms. Perhaps if I knew the language or had an interpreter, the experience would have been more rewarding.

I took pictures of them alone and with me and with Lena. The women appeared as if cloned to look alike, their kerchiefs dark, and barely revealing an inch of gray hair. Their ample breasts rested just above the tie of their aprons, waist high. Other than our smiling at each other in between their suspicious looks, our conversation was nonverbal, a combination of continuous hand gestures and facial expressions. They talked to each other in Turkish while I looked on, shrugging my shoulders when they looked my way.

We waved our goodbyes to the group that stood in our great-grandfather's house and walked around the one-foot stone wall to peer into the other two houses. The next house belonged to Theo Vangelis's family and the next one to our father's family. The lush green trees and bushes shielded a slightly larger house than the one I had been in. No

one was there. "Our father played in this yard. He walked next door
to his cousin's and together they went to their yiayia and pappou's
house." Lena and I exchanged possible scenarios of how life might
have been for the two cousins before they were uprooted. It took a
lot of effort to hold my camera steady. My lips trembled and my eyes
remained misty.

We walked back in silence until we met Ahmet at the taxi area and
headed for Smyrna. To lighten our mood, Lena and I weaved a detailed scenario of what we believed the group of women were saying
and thinking about the two Greek ladies whose family lived in their
homes up until the 1930s. It's possible they were afraid the Greeks
were coming back to reclaim their properties.

We headed for Smyrna where our other ancestors had previously
lived. We imagined their prosperous lives when they were free to live
and thrive. We repeated our vow not to spend one Turkish lira. Oh,
but the scenery was spectacular, the mountainsides dense with shades
of green, the Aegean-blue sea below was breathtaking, but still yank-
ing at our insides was the vision of our father's neighborhood. The
vision of thousands of families with a few meager belongings fleeing
for their lives and leaving everything behind.

Our ooohhs and aaahs in response to nature's beauty were stifled
by the purpose of our trip. Stifled by savageries of which we were
reminded at Fokia. We left the rural landscape and entered the hustle
and bustle of the city. Horns blaring, unruly traffic on the congested
streets, and our anxiety mounted as we tried to explain to the driver
where to drop us off. He was sweet and all but not a city taxi driver
and our inability to communicate well was a problem.

We wanted to go to the waterfront to see where the fires took
place, and where women, children, and men were drowning as they
begged for the boats to take them on board to safety, after they had
jumped into the sea to avoid the intensity of the fires. Why did we
want to see that area and be reminded of all that? We have seen it in
movies several times but wanted to be on the actual spot physically. I
suppose it is the same reason we go to see war memorials and battle
sites while listening to the tour guides explain which side did what to
the other side. That was what we needed, a tour guide.

We were shocked when we realized the area of the harbor where the horror of 1922 occurred no longer exists. It is meters deep under the beautiful park the Turkish government has built as one of its now-iconic tourist attractions. The park outstretches from the famous marble clock structure to the sea.

"These gardens are magnificent," I said with half a heart. Both my sister and I admired the beauty our eyes saw but we also felt an ache because we knew what was concealed beneath all that beauty.

We strolled through beautifully manicured gardens.

"It's all filled in. No reminders of those days." Lena sighed.

We took selfies with the iconic clock in the background

After taking it all in and unable to deny its beauty, we decided we could not avoid spending some money on food.

We indulged in stuffed grape leaves, *kefte* (ground meat) like a meatball that is fried, and grilled pita bread.

"Our cuisine is so similar. They use cumin, cinnamon, and the fresh dill, mint, and parsley like we do," Lena said as she spread a yogurt dip on a stuffed grape leaf.

"There is a little twist to the flavor, though," I said. "Perhaps it's in the amounts and combination of the spices."

"Nevertheless, it makes sense, our roots go back to this land. Well, we did a good job." I pointed to the empty plates. I leaned back and patted my stomach. "Ah, I hope we didn't eat too much. We still have a trek before us to find the old Greek neighborhoods."

We inquired at three hotels in the Konak district for directions to the Greek neighborhoods.

"I can't believe they don't know anything about the Greeks having been here."

"The brochures have nothing about the Armenian or the Greek communities. But look at this, they list Jewish tourist attractions." I placed the brochure in my backpack.

"We can't blame the young receptionists. It is obvious the government would not want to include any reference to the genocides and the great fire of 1922 in their history lessons." I detected anger in my sister's voice.

"Come on, we are not giving up. We will find the neighborhoods on our own." I put my arm on her shoulder.

A stroll through the marketplace and its nearby neighborhoods revealed modern age architecture.

"I think we moved too far away from the harbor. Let's go back down to the square."

And there they were, blocks away from the iconic square, street after street of beautiful old houses.

"This has to be where our ancestors lived and worked."

"Just like in the movies. They are grand and some are preserved." I held on to my sister's trembling hand.

"It's a miracle they did not destroy them after the Great Fire. The streets were far enough from the original harbor to have survived the destruction." Lena was in tears.

I kept snapping my Nikon Coolpix to capture the magnificence before us. We feasted on what we assumed to be Greek architecture of the 1800s and before as we have seen in movies depicting Greek grandeur.

We kept our emotions under control. We stood in awe and admired the cobblestone streets and the beautiful architecture of the row houses.

"It's amazing, the streets are well maintained and yet the houses are in various stages of renovations." Lena posed in front of a stucco house.

"Their color and detailed decorations distinguish them. Stand near that one, I'll take your picture." I pointed to the bright amber-yellow one with a burnt-orange trim around the windows and front door.

Lena posed next to the door. After I snapped the picture, she looked up and waved her hand across the second floors of the row houses. "I love the box bay windows. Look at the elegant iron supports. They all have the same ornate design, yet each bay window, somehow, looks different."

The streets were quiet. Although there were cars parked, we saw little in the way of human activity. We saw signs for the Bakardi Bar, Joker Bar, and Cafe Ceylan.

"This street must be bustling at night."

"I wouldn't want to be living on the streets with the bars. We have seen similar urban renewal in Boston neighborhoods. They have become popular with the younger people. Cafes, restaurants, and bars occupy the ground floors and above them are residential and office spaces."

"I think we have seen enough, and you have taken a million pictures. I don't know about you, but my feet are protesting. What do you say we celebrate the beauty we discovered on these streets with a cup of Turkish coffee?"

I agreed. "My feet are protesting, too. We will have to leave a few more lira behind in gratitude of our find."

Over coffee we reflected on the sites we saw, the disappointment of having no tour guide, and the sad emotions which surfaced as a result of what we observed. Despite all of that, we relaxed and enjoyed the scene in front of us as we listened to the background music. The sounds of baglama, similar to the Greek bouzouki, and the def, (defi in Greek, tambourine in English). The music resonated within us.

The handwoven rugs, the man with the ornate bronze shoeshine kit, and the rich reds and blues of the wall hangings across the alley from where we sat, looked familiar and distant at the same time. We acknowledged, as we often did, that the foods, the colors, and the music of the Middle East are in our DNA, along with the resilience, strength, and determination we surmised our father must have possessed. We concluded that not only did we inherit those characteristics from our paternal side but also from our maternal ancestors, who had shown strength and resilience when they were displaced from Pontos.

Lena and I agreed our visit to Fokia was the missing piece for which we hungered to place in our father's puzzle. Our feet had stepped on the ground where he had walked and played. We compared it to the awed sensation a pilgrim feels in the Holy Land when stepping on the same ground Jesus had walked. The ache in our hearts was for the hardship our father and his family had endured. Their lives were uprooted from an intolerable situation and were transplanted to another country, where they were not welcome and lived in impoverished conditions. The conditions which had led our father to take up arms to fight for a cause he believed would create a better life.

Lena and I have discussed our being uprooted at a young age. For me it was a bit more extreme than for her. In our cases, our lives flourished, and we did not experience the hardships our father had faced. The emotions I experienced from the day's visit stirred in my mind and in my heart, beckoning for me to reflect on them. I sensed a peace and joy knowing I walked on the same ground as my father. It was a bittersweet joy. I felt grateful and fortunate that my father's resilience, strength, and determination had been passed on to me. A long, hot, and emotional day of exploration in Smyrna and Fokia came to an end, leaving much for us to absorb and process.

On the bus returning us to the hotel, I leaned back, closed my eyes, and thought how happy Ahmet, our taxi driver, must have been with his day's work. The thought warmed my heart.

Lena and I acknowledged our gratitude for the taxi ride with Ahmet. A taxi ride we chose. Unlike our first taxi ride together.

ABOVE AND RIGHT: SOFIA AND NIKOS

ME AND LENA

ABOVE: THE CORNER WITH THE THREE SPENTZOURAS HOUSES IN FOKIA
BELOW: LENA AND ME WITH SOME OF THE CURRENT RESIDENTS

ME, THEO PAVLOS, AND LENA. THE LAST TIME WE SAW HIM.

CHARLES AND THEO PAVLOS

Afterword

Being challenged in life is inevitable. Being defeated is optional.
—*Roger Crawford*

"You always get what you want," my adult son, Paul Richard, said to me after he gave in to my request. It had been a contentious discussion. Later that evening during my quiet time, I mulled over his comment. *How could he believe that? After everything I have lived through?* I took my time and revisited the major upsets I had experienced in my life. I concluded my son was right. It was a light bulb moment to see things that way. Other than the death of my biological parents, I saw all other losses and obstacles serving up what was best for me. I acknowledge with certainty that despite the obstacles thrown at me, I was able to persevere and rise up to resume my journey. I absolutely believe everything is always working out for me. Sometimes the desired result took weeks, months, and years. As I look back, in many cases, the final manifestation was even better than my original desire.

At times of need, it seemed that out of nowhere someone appeared to help me out. Synchronicities occurred whenever I needed them. I am grateful for the angels who helped me through difficult times. They were friends, extended family members from my adoptive family; they were acquaintances, they were strangers, they were Hay House authors. They filled the empty spaces left by gone-too-soon parents and the sister I had been separated from for eight years. I attribute my dedication to volunteerism to these angels. The urge to help others began in my teenage years. I derive satisfaction from knowing that the service I provide enhances someone else's life. As an adult, I knew I wanted to help children and volunteered at the Beverly School for the Deaf (Beverly, MA) and Pathways for Children (Gloucester, MA). Almost four decades ago I answered a newspaper advertisement and became a volunteer for Hospice of the North Shore (now Care Dimensions) and today I continue my relationship with this worthy organization.

As a teenager I had made two promises to myself. Decisions to which I adhered. It was a time when I thought a lot about my biological parents' deaths and the days and months that followed. All the disturbing chatter by relatives and friends in my presence had formed an impression in my young mind. I decided I would not talk in front of children about matters of which they should not be aware. And I decided I would only have one child. I felt if something happened to me and my husband, it would be easier for one child to be taken care of. The child would not have to be separated from siblings. Had I known I would live long enough to raise children into their adulthood, perhaps I would have broken that promise. But the villagers' talk carved a permanent recording on my brain's hard drive, and I kept that promise.

The reconnection with my sister turned out to be a stepping stone into the normalcy for which I yearned since our parents' deaths and my separation from her. Lena and I wonder if we would have achieved the same depth in our relationship had we grown up together in Thessaloniki with our biological parents. We look around and observe siblings who have grown up together with their biological parents and we notice not all of them share a loving relationship. We notice adults carrying wounds and blaming their parents for their state of unhappiness and misfortunes. Lena and I wonder why these disgruntled adults don't just make changes now and stop blaming their parents. But then we realize we are all evolving on our own path, and we make choices accordingly. My sister and I acknowledge our bond goes beyond the surface level; it is a bond connected and blessed by the Universe. We are soulmates. The care, understanding, and respect we have for each other is a treasure. It is the ultimate in unconditional love. We thank God often for this gift.

Acknowledgments

I am blessed with the support of many and want to recognize them.

Hay House Publishing gave me the nudge I needed to answer the call I had heard a myriad of times, "You should write a book." I accepted a seven-day writing challenge from Hay House. After seven days I never looked back. Thank you, Reid Tracy and Kelly Notaras for your lessons and encouragement.

Teddy Dimitrakopoulos, who had gifted me a journal and told me I could write. My first entry in the journal is, "Dear Teddy, if I ever write a book, it will be because of you." I appreciate the support and encouragement not only from you but also from Thanasi, James, and Christopher.

Life Writers US. Thank you, Patricia Charpentier and the members of Life Writers, for your support and encouragement. I learned a great deal about the craft of writing.

Thank you, Millie Ford and Darlene Lamb, for your feedback, your cheering, and your persuading me to come out of my comfort zone.

Carolyn V. Hamilton. You and your group, Aspiring Memoir Writers, was the first I joined following the Hay House Writing Challenge. Your willingness to share and your initial editing of my first writings gave me confidence to continue.

I cannot say a big enough thank you to my Bass Rocks Golf friends. You have been supportive from the moment you heard about my writing project. At times I thought my heart would explode from your enthusiasm, praise, and excitement. I am forever grateful. I cannot possibly name all of you, but will begin with my first fan, Joan LePage, followed by Andrea Berry, Lauren McSheffrey, Bette Hutchins, Sandy Potter, Janice Ambrose, Marlene Seltzer, Kathy Bertagna, Cathy Looney, Pat Burke, Maura Labarre, Christine McGrath, Susanne Guyer, Elaine Howell, JoAnne Fisher, Rob Berry, John Christie, Lynne and David Bianchini, Marjie and Steve Demeter, Marianne and Tom Kiley, and AnnJo and Paul Jackson.

A big shout-out to Maureen Thorpe. I appreciate your willingness to educate and guide me with the pesky business of social media and other writing content.

Thank you to an easy-to-work-with book designer. Judy Davison, thank you for making me feel comfortable in my learning the layout lingo. You anticipated my thoughts and guided me well. I am grateful for your patience, guidance, and for the fantastic final design.

What can I say to you, Kate Victory Hannisian, my editor from Blue Pencil Consulting. We clicked from our first virtual meeting, and I feel as though I have known you for a long time. You understood my intentions and desires for the book, and we proceeded accordingly. Your valuable input helped me to turn it into a jewel to be cherished. Thank you so much.

To my sister Lena. Thank you for giving me carte blanche to include in my memoir whatever of and however I remember our past. I am thankful for your insights and memories. I am grateful for you. Always in my heart, I love you.

How can I thank you, Charles? You have been there from the first page I wrote. You helped me when I became impatient with software, hardware, and my words. I appreciate your patience and sacrifice of our time together while I worked on the project. Your going through the many edits beginning with the first draft is a labor of love, I know and appreciate. Your devotion and enthusiasm about the memoir reached deeply into my heart and I am grateful for that. Thank you for standing by me every step of the way. I love you.

Names

Note: Except in formal situations, children addressed adults with the appropriate title, followed by the person's first name, as in Mrs. Azat.

Charles - author's husband

Paul Richard - author's son

Trey- author's grandson

Nitsa/Lena - author's sister

Sofia - biological mother

Nikos - biological father

Azat - landlady in Thessaloniki

Ismini - neighbor

Filipas - neighbor

Pavlos - Sofia's younger brother

Kitsa - Pavlos's wife

Marianthe - adoptive mother

Steve - adoptive father

Mitsa - Marianthe's sister

Dino - Mitsa's adopted son

Helen Rouvapes - legal guardian

Helen and Bill Lydon - author's parents at the age of 21

Mr. Apostolos and Mrs. Nitsa - Lena's adoptive parents

Greek Glossary

Babá - Dad
bouzoukia - a restaurant or nightclub that offers food, music, and dancing
filotimo – a combination of virtues, including goodness, doing good, being above reproach, hospitality and more
glyko - spoonful of preserved fruits in syrup
kilim - flat weaved rug
koliva – traditional sweetened wheat offering commemorating the dead
koulourakia - traditional cookie
koulouri - a baked sesame-encrusted dough shaped into a ring.
Koumbara – godmother at a child's baptism or a maid of honor at a wedding
Koumbares - plural of Koumbara
Koumbaros – godfather at a child's baptism or the best man at a wedding
Koumbarous – plural of koumbaros and a combination of koumbaros and koumbara
Mamá - Mom
monopati - trail, path
Noná - Godmother
Nonós - Godfather
onta - room in Pontic
pagouri – canteen
Pappou – Grandfather
periptero - kiosk
platanos – plane tree
Pontiaka - Pontic language
stipa - pickled cabbage and green tomatoes
Thea - Aunt
Theo – Uncle
Tiropita- Phyllo dough filled with feta
Tiropites –plural of tiropita
Yiayia - Grandmother

Bibliography

For further reading about the Greek and Armenian Genocides:

Books

Balakian, Peter. *The Burning Tigris: The Armenian Genocide and America's Response* (HarperCollins, 2004).

Halo, Thea. *Not Even My Name: A True Story* (Picador: 2001).

Horton, George. *The Blight of Asia* (Bobbs-Merrill Company, 1926; original reprint from Taderon Press, 2008).

Ioanidou, Theodora. *Religious Persecution of Greeks in Pontus* (2022)

Morris, Benny, Dor Ze'Evi, et al. *The Thirty-year Genocide: Turkey's Destruction of Its Christian Minorities* (Harvard University Press, 2019)

Ureneck, Lou. *Smyrna, September 1922: The American Mission to Rescue Victims of the 20th Century's First Genocide* (HarperCollins: 2016).

Websites

Britannica.com

The Hellenic Heritage Foundation: hhf.ca

Smithsonianmag.com